REPORT

OF A

GEOLOGICAL SURVEY

OF THE

UPPER MISSISSIPPI LEAD REGION,

BY

J. D. WHITNEY.

MADE BY AUTHORITY OF THE LEGISLATURE OF WISCONSIN, UNDER A CONTRACT WITH PROF. JAMES HALL, PRINCIPAL OF THE GEOLOGICAL COMMISSION OF THE STATE, IN 1859-60.

ALBANY, N. Y.
1862.

TABLE OF CONTENTS.

APPENDIX.

LIST OF PLATES AND MAPS.

Plates.

Maps.

PREFACE.

Having purchased of Prof. JAMES HALL a small number of copies of the text and illustrations of my Report on the Lead Region of the Upper Mississippi, made by authority of the Legislature of Wisconsin (under circumstances which are fully set forth upon pages 84 to 88 of the Report itself), I issue the same herewith as a separate and independent work, and with a suitable title-page, for distribution among my personal friends and those especially interested in the subject treated of in the Report.

As published by Prof. HALL, the volume which contains my Report is entitled "Report on the Geological Survey of the State of Wisconsin. Volume I:" it includes, in addition to my work, which occupies 352 pages, an introductory chapter of 72 pages, by Prof. HALL, on "The Physical Geography and general Geology of Wisconsin," and a concluding chapter, also by Prof. HALL, giving a catalogue of the palæozoic fossils of the State, and occupying 24 pages.

Since my Report is a complete work in itself, entirely independent of Prof. HALL's introduction and postscript, it is properly enough put forth as a separate volume, in which form I had also supposed that it would be issued by the State. It was delivered to Prof. HALL in October, 1860, but the printing was not begun until a year later, and was finished in January, 1862. In the meantime, however, I have had no opportunity to add to or amend it, and it is published precisely as it first left my hands, the revision of the proof-sheets having been made by my brother, Prof. W. D. WHITNEY, of Yale College: my thanks are due him for his close attention to this important, but not very attractive, portion of the labor required to bring the work to its present shape.

To my former assistant on the Survey, Dr. J. P. KIMBALL, I am under great obligations, not only for his devotion to the field and office labor prior to the completion of the work, but also for his liberal offer to Prof. HALL—of which the latter, however, did not avail himself—to put upon the Map some additional items of information, of which the notes, not ready at the time I left for California, were afterwards sent in.

To any one who may be disposed to criticise the incompleteness of my work, I would point out that, as stated upon page 87, the whole sum allowed me by the Commissioners was $4450, an amount manifestly inadequate to the satisfactory performance of a labor of such magnitude. In order that I might do the best justice in my power to the survey of the Lead Region, I postponed for six months the commencement of the Geological Survey of California, and I would have given still more time to the former had it been possible.

To my own Report are appended two brief chapters, four pages in all, by Professors WYMAN and LEIDY, containing descriptions and identifications of the mammalian remains found in the crevices and detritus of the Lead Region. The Index, it will be noticed, includes the references to Prof. HALL's introductory and concluding chapters, introduced into it by him, and which it was, of course, impossible to remove from the plates in striking off the few extra copies composing this edition.

J. D. WHITNEY.

SAN FRANCISCO, CAL., *April 10th*, 1862.

CHAPTER II.

REPORT UPON THE LEAD REGION—INTRODUCTORY AND HISTORICAL.

Geographical Position of the Western Lead Mines—Two Divisions, the Upper and the Lower Mines, or the Upper Mississippi and the Missouri Lead Regions—Early History of the Missouri Region—Of the Upper Mississippi Region—Various Geological Explorations made in the North-west—Featherstonhaugh's—Dr. D. D. Owen's—Prof. Daniels's—Dr. Percival's—Organization of the Present Survey—What has been attempted—The Maps described—Co-operation of other States interested—What remained to be done—Important Questions connected with the Region—Order followed in this Report.

The lead mines of the Mississippi valley are by far the most important deposits of this metal, so far as is yet known, upon the American continent: indeed, they are the only ones in the world where any considerable amount of lead is obtained, outside of those situated on the continent of Europe, or on the British islands. The mines in question are not only of great importance from the amount of metal they produce, which equals about one-eighth of the whole quantity obtained throughout the world, but they possess many features of interest, in the peculiar and very varying mode of occurrence of the ore, which make the region a field highly attractive to those especially interested in the phenomena of veins and the geological distribution of the metalliferous ores.

A great diversity of opinion, at least up to a recent time, has prevailed in regard to the real character of the deposits in question; namely, as to what was their relation to that class of mineral deposits which are commonly called *true veins*, and what the prospects of a future development of the mining interests of the region, and the establishment of the operations there conducted on a basis of permanency and continuous profit. This circumstance, which naturally added much to the interest of the investigations undertaken on behalf of the State into the geology of the lead-region of the Upper Mississippi, also threw a largely increased burden of responsibility upon the person employed in the work—a responsibility which I have not sought to evade; but, on the contrary, have willingly assumed; believing, as I do, that my opinions—based, as I can affirm them to be, on careful investigations in all the more important localities, and formed without any other bias than that of a natural desire to see the resources of an interesting region fully, but at the same time economically and profitably, developed—are in the main correct, and that the future history of the workings will prove this to have been the case, even if they should not be generally accepted at the present time.

Before entering into a discussion of my own observations, it will be proper, under the circumstances, to furnish a brief review of what has been done by others in the lead-region, and some historical notices of the development of the mining interests of the Mississippi valley.

In the first place, however, it will be necessary to notice the geographical position of the lead mines of the West, and to limit the field to which the present Report is confined. There are two great divisions of the western lead-producing district, which are frequently distinguished in the Mississippi valley as the Upper and the Lower Mines. The Lower Mines, or the Missouri Mines, as they may properly be called, are situated chiefly within the limits of Washington county, Missouri, near Big River and Mineral Creek, branches of the Maramec River. There are a few others in Franklin county, on the last named river, and one or two in Jefferson county, not many miles south of St. Louis. Quite recently, discoveries of lead ore have also been made on the western borders of Missouri, in Newton and Jasper counties, and mines have been worked in this region to a considerable extent: these mines are, however, geologically as well as geographically, quite distinct from those of the well-known lead-region of Missouri, which are situated, as before indicated, in the angle formed by the Missouri and Mississippi rivers at their confluence, and on the south side of the former. As these deposits of lead ore have many features in common with those of the Upper Mines, or the Upper Mississippi lead-region, as it may more properly be designated, they will occasionally be referred to in the course of the following Report for the sake of illustration and comparison. The principal object, however, of our work is to describe that particular district which is included within the States of Wisconsin, Illinois and Iowa, forming a well characterized and distinct lead-producing region, and one which greatly exceeds in importance and extent that of the Lower or Missouri Mines.

The first mining operations in the West were commenced in 1720, under the authority of the patent granted by the French government to the famous "Company of the West," which was organized by Law. In that year Renault, the son of an iron-founder, and probably supposed to be acquainted with mining operations, came to Missouri with a large company of miners, and a mineralogist, named La Motte; these immediately commenced their explorations, in the course of which numerous discoveries of lead ore were made, but none of the precious metals, to obtain which the expedition had been organized. The Mine La Motte was one of the first and most important localities opened by the person whose name it still bears. Some lead was smelted under Renault's direction, and shipped down the river to New Orleans, and mining was commenced in a rude way at numerous localities, as is evidenced by the extent of the old workings of which traces still remain. After Renault's return to France, which took place in 1742, the object of the expedition having entirely failed of accomplishment, mining ceased in the Missouri region. Some forty years later, it was resumed again, and carried on in the rudest possible manner, while this part of the country was under Spanish government.

About 1798, the regular mining business may be said to have been established by Moses Austin, from the Wythe County Mines, in Virginia; he obtained a grant of land from the government, built reverberatory furnaces, to take the place of the rude log-heaps on which the ore had previously been smelted, and commenced mining on a somewhat more systematic plan than had before been pursued. He also erected a shot-tower and a manufactory of sheet-lead, and a considerable quantity of the produce was exported to the West India islands, and lead mining soon began to be a regular business.

According to Mr. Schoolcraft, from whose work on the Missouri mines the principal portion of the above information in regard to their discovery has been taken,* there were, in 1819, forty-five mines at work, or which had been worked, up to that time; the amount produced by them was estimated by the same authority at nearly 5,000,000 lbs., or about 2200 tons, of metal per annum. From 1834 to 1837, Mine La Motte produced on an average about a million of pounds per annum. Mine à Burton and Potosi Diggings together produced, in the eighteen years from 1798 to 1816, 9,630,000 lbs. of lead, or an average of half a million of pounds per annum. The amount of lead smelted from the produce of the Missouri mines seems to have reached its maximum between 1830 and 1840, since which it has been gradually declining. What the extent of the new discoveries in the western portion of the State is likely to be, or how great their production, we are not yet accurately informed.

* A View of the Lead Mines of Missouri, by H. R. Schoolcraft, New York, 1819.

Whether the lead deposits of the Northwest were known to the aboriginal inhabitants of the region, and ore mined and smelted by them, previous to the first visit of white men, seems to be a matter of considerable doubt. As it is well ascertained that very extensive mining operations were carried on for a long series of years, and explorations made, over the whole extent of the Lake Superior copper region, by the former inhabitants, previous to the appearance of the white race, it might be inferred that the lead ore of the not far distant territory of the Upper Mississippi would not have failed to be observed; and it would seem probable that a race possessed of sufficient perseverance and skill to sink shafts to a depth of over 50 feet in the hard trap rock of Lake Superior, and to detach and raise to the surface masses of copper weighing seven tons, would have also had the ability to mine the deposits of lead lying so near the surface, and ingenuity sufficient to smelt the metal out of the easily reducible ore.

It is almost certain, however, that no such extensive mining operations had ever been carried on in the lead region by the aborigines as we everywhere discover traces of on Lake Superior, and the fact, reported by Messrs. Squier and Davis, that fragments of galena, but no metallic lead, have been frequently found in the ancient mounds of the Northwest, while copper ornaments and utensils are known to be of somewhat common occurrence in those widely distributed earth-works, would seem to indicate that metallic lead was, to say the least, not in common use among the mound-builders. It may be said with truth that lead, from its softness, would be a metal far inferior in value to copper for the ordinary purposes to which an uncivilized people would put such substances; while the fact that the copper of Lake Superior occurs in the native state, and of course requires no smelting, or even melting down, to bring it into many kinds of useful forms, would give it a preference over any metal that required smelting, however great the facility with which the operation would seem, to us at least, to admit of being performed. I have not been able to gather from any of the accounts of the earliest travellers in the Northwest any definite information on this point; but, in the absence of evidence, should incline strongly to the belief that the use of lead was not known to the aborigines until it was taught them by the white race.

The first account of the discovery of lead ore in the Northwest seems to be due to Le Sueur, who made a voyage up the Mississippi, as early as 1700 and 1701. On this expedition, which was got up expressly for the purpose of finding ores, Le Sueur noticed numerous indications of lead ore along the banks of the river. He ascended as far as the St. Peter's River, and went up that stream to the mouth of the Blue or Mukahto River, where he supposed that he had made the most astonishing discoveries of copper ore, a cargo of which he took back with him to France, after having wintered at the locality where it was found. The whole thing seems to have been a delusion; but what the substance was which was thus mistaken for a valuable ore, I have never been able to ascertain.

The first mining in the Upper Mississippi lead-region seems to have been by Julien Dubuque, a half-breed Indian trader, who had settled on the site of the city now called after him, and who, in 1788, obtained a grant from the Sacs and Foxes, which was confirmed by Carondelet, then governor of Louisiana, of a large tract of land, including the rich deposits of lead ore on the west side of the Mississippi; he remained here, engaged in mining, until his death, which took place in 1809. The land occupied by him was relinquished to the United States by the Indians in 1832; and although Dubuque's representatives claimed it, they were forcibly ejected.

No considerable amount of mining was done in the lead-region of the Upper Mississippi by American citizens until about the year 1827: the attention of the inhabitants of the adjacent States began to be drawn in that direction about the year 1821, and settlers began to come in from Missouri, Kentucky, Pennsylvania, and other States; but it was not until 1827 that the miners began to spread themselves over the Wisconsin lead-region; from that period the quantity of ore went on rapidly increasing.

As early as 1834, the first strictly geological expedition or survey ever undertaken under authority of our General Government was instituted, by the appointment of G. W. Featherstonhaugh, Esq., by the War Department, to make a geological survey, or reconnoissance, "of the elevated country lying between the Missouri River and Red River, known under the designation of the Ozark Mountains."

In the course of this gentleman's geological tour, he visited, in the winter of 1834–5, the lead mines of Missouri. His remarks on them and the geological structure of the district in which they occur occupy seven or eight pages, and are characterized by extreme vagueness and evident want of even a rudimentary knowledge of mining matters. In regard to the theory of the formation of the lead veins, he has no doubt, apparently, that the ore was "injected from below," and the horizontal deposits of ore he conceives to be "lateral jets from the main lode, after the manner that Mr. M'Culloch has described the structure of the horizontal injections of trap rock into sandstone at Trotternish, in Scotland." He instances a locality where the ore was associated with red clay and occurred in *pockets*, "at the bottom of each of which there was a thick bright plate of sulphuret of lead, *that seemed to have sunk to the bottom by its specific gravity.*" He adds immediately after this: "All these circumstances seem to point to a projection of this metallic and mineral matter from below." He furthermore adds that "this mineral of lead, to judge from obvious appearances, exists in such inconceivable profusion in the metalliferous region of the south of Missouri and the north of Arkansas, that it may be relied on for countless ages as a source of national wealth, and an interminable supply of the most useful metals."

Mr. Featherstonhaugh was, after producing the report from which the above extracts are taken, again employed by the Government during the next year, with the title of U. S. Geologist, to make a geological reconnoissance in the Northwest, especially in the region between the St. Peter's River and the Missouri. The whole series of Lower Silurian rocks developed through the lead-region of Wisconsin, up to the Falls of St. Anthony and beyond, Mr. Featherstonhaugh refers without hesitation to the Carboniferous limestone. Although he passed down the Mississippi river, on his return, from Prairie du Chien to Galena, and visited several mining localities, his notices are confined to about a page of general and theoretical remarks, which are of the same character as those cited above in reference to the Missouri mines. One only may be quoted, without comment: "When the veins are exhausted, shafts will be sunk still deeper."

From the above, it will be seen that this so-called "geological reconnoissance" was about as worthless rubbish as could well be put together, neither correctly describing any facts which came under this author's observation, nor giving any theoretical views worthy a moment's notice except from their absurdity.

By the Act of March 3rd, 1807, all government lands containing lead ore were ordered to be reserved from sale, and a system of leasing was adopted. No leases were issued, however, until the year 1822, and but little mining was done previous to 1826, when the production of lead began to increase with great rapidity. For a few years the rents were paid to the United States officers with considerable regularity; but, after 1834, in consequence of the innumerable fraudulent entries of lands as agricultural which should in reality have been reserved as mineral, the smelters and miners refused to make any farther payments, and the

United States officers were entirely unable to enforce the claims of the Government.

In consequence of these difficulties, a resolution was adopted in the House of Representatives, on the 6th of February, 1839, "that the President of the United States be requested to cause to be prepared, and presented to the next Congress, at an early day, a plan for the sale of the public mineral lands, having reference as well to the amount of revenue to be derived from them, and their value as public property, as to the equitable claims of individuals upon them; and that he, at the same time, communicate to Congress all the information in possession of the Treasury Department relative to their location, value, productiveness, and occupancy; and that he cause such *further* information to be collected, and surveys to be made, as may be necessary for these purposes." To carry out the objects of this act, Dr. D. D. Owen was selected by the Commissioner of the General Land Office, to take charge of a geological survey of the lead-region of the Upper Mississippi, and, with the aid of 139 assistants, the field work of the survey was begun in September, 1839, and finished before the setting in of winter. A report, accompanied by maps, sections, and drawings of fossils, &c., was transmitted to the Land Office by Dr. Owen on the 2d of April, 1840, and printed in June of that year, but without the maps and other illustrations. A revised edition of the same report, with some additional statistics, and the plates before omitted, was ordered to be printed by the Senate in 1844.

In Dr. Owen's report, the geographical extent of the productive lead-region was, for the first time, delineated with any approach to accuracy, and the geological character of the district was also, with some exceptions, correctly indicated. The shortness of the time which could be given to the work, and the fact that the assistants were young men destitute of any acquaintance with geology before entering upon this work, are sufficient reasons why minute accuracy should not have been expected in the execution of this survey. The fact that Dr. Owen had had, previously to the undertaking of this work, but little experience in the investigation of the phenomena of mining districts, will account for his having been led to form exaggerated and erroneous opinions in regard to the value of some of the mineral productions of the region in question; but there were probably few, if any, persons in the country, at that early period of our geological culture, who could have executed the survey with the ability and energy which were displayed by this gentleman.

In 1847, a geological survey of the Chippewa Land District was authorized by the United States Government, and Dr. D. D. Owen was appointed to take charge of it. In his preliminary Report, entitled "Report of a Geological Reconnoissance of the Chippewa Land District of Wisconsin, &c.," furnished to the Treasury Department in April, 1848, Dr. Owen gives some additional information in regard to the lower formations occurring on the borders of the lead-region; and especially in reference to the discoveries of lead ore in the Lower Magnesian limestone. The different opinions advanced by him at various times on this subject will receive attention in a subsequent portion of this Report. No special examinations were made in the lead-region during the progress of this survey; the general geological map accompanying the final Report, published in 1851, does, indeed, include the whole of the State of Wisconsin, but necessarily on too small a scale, from the great extent of territory embraced on it, to show anything more than had already been given in the map accompanying the Report published in 1844, before noticed.

The next geological exploration undertaken in the lead-region was made under authority of the Legislature of the State of Wisconsin, in accordance with an Act approved March 25th, 1853, authorizing a geological survey of the

State, and requiring that the lead mining district should be first examined. Mr. E. Daniels was appointed by the Governor, State Geologist, and his first Report, without date, but printed in 1854, of about 50 pages, is chiefly taken up with matters connected with the lead-region, the views and opinions of Dr. Owen being, in the main, those advanced by Mr. Daniels.

After Mr. Daniels had been engaged in this survey about a year, he was removed; Dr. J. G. Percival was appointed in his place August 12th, 1854, and continued to hold the office until the time of his death, with took place at Hazle Green, May 2nd, 1856. Dr. Percival was in the field during two seasons, publishing under his own supervision one Report of 100 pages, and leaving the manuscript of another, of about the same length, in a nearly complete state; this was afterwards published (in 1856).

In his instructions with regard to the prosecution of the survey, Dr. Percival was required to give his time first to the examination of the lead-region. In accordance with this, he visited during the first season "all the considerable diggings from the south line of the State to a line drawn from east to west, north of Cassville, Beetown, Potosi, Platteville, Mineral Point, Yellow Stone, and Exeter, and from the Mississippi to the east part of Green county." The report of this season's work is chiefly devoted to the "surface arrangement" of the mineral ranges, or lead-bearing crevices, and contains a large amount of accurate and valuable information in regard to the minute details of the mode of occurrence of the mineral substances which they contain. A map or diagram, "representing the surface arrangement of the diggings" in that portion of the mineral district examined during the first season and previously, on a scale of about four miles to one inch, accompanies this report, and is valuable as being the first attempt to represent the position and direction of the lead-bearing crevices; but as these were not laid down from actual survey, while the scale of the map was too small to admit of their being represented with any detail, even if such survey had been really made, the work could only be considered as a sort of preliminary reconnoissance, and as pointing out the way to what needed to be done on a more extensive scale and with much greater precision.

A part of Dr. Percival's second season was devoted to an examination of that portion of the lead district which had been left unfinished the year before, and the remainder "to a reconnoissance of the State, for the purpose of forming a general idea of the geological arrangement."

While acknowledging the untiring energy with which Dr. Percival, even when enfeebled by disease, carried on his investigations, and gladly bearing testimony to the minute accuracy with which he observed and noted such facts connected with the mineral deposits as could be gathered without the aid of other persons (his peculiar temperament making him very unwilling to apply to strangers for information), yet I shall be obliged to differ *in toto* with him in the general conclusions which he drew from his observations, especially in regard to the feasibility of deep mining in the lead-region, the most important point, practically, to those interested in that district. The whole matter will be discussed, at length, in a subsequent portion of this Report, and the evidence on both sides will be presented in full, so that all persons may have the means of judging for themselves.

The geological survey of Wisconsin having been left, by the death of Dr. Percival, in an unfinished state, a new Act was passed by the Legislature, during the session of 1856–7, by authority of which Professors James Hall, E. S. Carr, and Edward Daniels were appointed Commissioners to execute a geological, agricultural and mineralogical survey of the State, and the sum of $6000 per annum, for six successive years, appropriated for the purpose of defraying the expenses. As there seemed to be, on the part of those interested in the lead-region, a desire to have farther explorations carried on in this part of the State, two of the Commissioners, Messrs. Hall and Carr, were led to employ the author of this Report to execute the work, and the following extract from Prof. Hall's Report to the Governor, presented during the session of 1858–9, will explain the motives and wishes of the Commissioners in taking this step. Prof. Hall remarks as follows:

"I had also proposed to secure for the State Report the completion of a carefully surveyed map of the lead-region, already begun and much advanced by Prof. J. D. Whitney. I conceive this to be a very important object, since, notwithstanding the long time that this region has been known and worked for its lead ores, there is yet no map on which the lead crevices are shown, or the extent and direction of the workings heretofore carried on. It is very evident therefore that the completion of such a map must be the first step towards a correct knowledge of the relations of the veins or crevices to the strata which they occupy, and a preliminary measure to any future plans of exploration or mining by a different mode from that heretofore proposed. The propositions that have from time to time come before the Legislature of the State, for extensive boring, or sinking of shafts to great depths, can only be prudently acceded to after an accurate map of this kind shall have been completed, and the subject well considered, with the information derived from the experience of all the previous workings. I shall urge, most emphatically, that means be taken for obtaining such a map; and, so far as in my power, will make arrangements for the prosecution of the work."

An engagement having been effected with the author of this Report, by Messrs. Hall and Carr, in the spring of 1859, the work was commenced in April; the principal object at first being the completion of a general geological map of the lead-region of the Upper Mississippi lying within the States of Wisconsin, Illinois, and Iowa, commenced several years before and already partially completed from explorations and surveys made at my own expense, at various times since 1852, when I first visited the lead-region, in company with I. A. Lapham, Esq. This general map, which is intended to embrace the whole productive lead district, was drawn on a scale of one-half an inch to the mile, which makes the map as large as could be printed from one stone; the great additional expense which would have been incurred in the engraving and printing, had it been made so large that it would require to be drawn and printed on two sheets, making it expedient to adopt this scale. After explorations had been carried on for some time, however, it became evident that the number and complication of the crevices in the extreme southeastern corner of the State were too great to admit of their being represented with any approach to accuracy and completeness on so small a scale as that of one-half an inch to the mile; and as it seemed likely that more could be learned with regard to the origin and distribution of the lead-bearing fissures, or crevices, by the more careful study of that portion of the district where they are most numerously and regularly developed, and where the amount of ore raised is greatest in proportion to the surface occupied by the diggings, a second map was commenced, on a scale of two inches to the mile, of the district between Dubuque, Galena, and Shullsburg. On this map, which is appended to the present Report, and which will be referred to in the succeeding pages as the "crevice map," no attempt is made to exhibit the geology, which is shown with sufficient accuracy on the general map; but the principal productive crevices are laid down, so far as possible from actual survey, and with the intention of representing their "surface arrangement"—to use the very suitable term adopted by Dr. Percival—as accurately as could be done with the time and means placed at my disposal by the Commissioners.

For the completion of these maps, and for the purpose of collecting additional information concerning the lead-region, to be embodied in a special report, provision was made by the Legislature, by an Act approved April 2d, 1860. By the terms of this Act, Prof. Hall was appointed Principal of the geological commission, and authorized to make a contract with the author of this Report "providing for the completion within the present year of his survey and maps of the lead mines of the southwestern portion of the State" &c. In conformity with this requisition of the Legislature, a contract was drawn, and approved by the Governor June 13th, 1860, by which an additional sum of $2500 was secured for this branch of the survey, in addition to the $1950 appropriated by the Commissioners, making the entire sum available for the resurvey of the lead-region $4450. Under the above conditions, and with the necessary hindrances and drawbacks to the rapid progress of the work caused by the entire uncertainty from the beginning of the amount of money which could be appropriated to this branch of the survey, and the consequent minuteness of observation with which it could be carried on, the work has been prosecuted during the past year and up to the present time, making in all a period of about 15 months. During the spring of 1859 and a portion of 1860, I have been assisted by Dr. J. P. Kimball of Schenectady, N. Y., in the field work. I have also had the aid of several surveyors, each in the district with which he was best acquainted; among these I may mention Mr. J. Burrill of Benton, Mr. J. Wilson, Jr., of Cassville, and Mr. John R. Gray of Fairplay.

To all these gentlemen, as well as to others who by advice or information have aided in the progress of this survey, I desire to return my most hearty thanks. I may be allowed to mention the names of I. A. Lapham, Esq., of Milwaukee, Rev. J. Murrish of Linden, Capt. E. H. Beebe and A. Estey, Esq., of Galena, as having accompanied me at various times in my excursions, and done all in their power to assist in the work.

During the progress of the State Geological Survey of Iowa, from 1855 to 1858, to which survey I was attached in the capacity of State Chemist and Mineralogist, I had an opportunity to collect considerable information in regard to the occurrence of the ores of lead in the small fraction of the mining region included within the limits of that State, and I prepared a map showing the position of the lead crevices in that district, which map, drawn on a scale of four inches to the mile, is incorporated in the Iowa Geological Report, Vol. I, published in 1858. The information contained in that map is embodied on the large crevice map herewith presented, with numerous additions and corrections, made by Messrs. C. Childs and H. De Werthern of Dubuque, at my own private expense. My thanks are due them for the zeal with which they have labored in this cause.

A still further contribution to the history of the lead-region has been made, in this connection, by the State of Illinois, under the direction of A. H. Worthen, Esq., State Geologist; by an arrangement made with the writer to furnish a crevice map of the region around Galena, with a report on the same, to be laid before the Legislature at their next session, with other materials forming the State Geological Report. The map will be constructed from surveys made under my direction by U. G. Scheller, Esq., of Galena, and will be on a scale of four inches to the mile.* The information thus obtained has been incorporated on the large crevice map accompanying this Report, so far as was possible on the reduced scale to which it is necessarily limited. Thus the map in question shows the most important portion of the lead-region, and gives the results obtained at the joint expense of the three States interested.

The question will be naturally asked, whether after all these surveys, the long list of which has been given above, the work may now be considered as complete, and whether all has been done which it is in the power of the geologist to accomplish. In answer to this, we would reply, that if

* This map has not been ordered by the State Geologist, but one on a smaller scale has been substituted.

the ideas advocated in this Report should be adopted by the mining community, we believe that much useless expenditure might be avoided; but that a great deal remains to be done before all has been ascertained which might be worked out with advantage to those interested in the lead-region, or engaged in developing its hidden treasures.

If we consider the history of geological explorations in the lead regions of the West, including both the Missouri and the Upper Mississippi, and at the same time keep in view what has been done by the miners in the way of developing the resources of these districts, it will be evident that the great question to be answered, by one taking up the investigation of a region which has been for so long a time the field of both scientific and practical operations, is this: can any change be made in the system pursued, which will place the mining interest on a more permanent basis; or, if not, can such general principles be laid down as shall limit expenditures in the region in question to the strictly necessary, remove the incentives to hazardous speculation, and prevent the wasting of money in undertakings which are sure to end in disappointment.

It is not to be denied that the element of chance or uncertainty enters in a greater or less degree into all mining enterprises; it is this which gives such a fascination to this branch of business, and causes a thousand schemes to be originated, where only a half-dozen can ever be put into successful operation. The history of mining adventures in the Atlantic States shows a melancholy catalogue of failures. Of all the mines opened in New England, with the exception of those of iron, not one has ever been worked with profit for any length of time, or repaid the money invested. We speak now of mines of the metals and their ores, but not including iron, which occurs in such abundance in nature, and so widely distributed, that the successful working of such mines does not usually depend on the abundance or quality of the ore, but rather on distance from market, abundance of fuel, cost of labor, and such other circumstances as are questions rather of political economy than of practical geology. The more thoroughly a mining district is studied, and the more facts in regard to the occurrence of its metalliferous deposits are accumulated, the less ought to be the risk of commencing new enterprises, since the experience of the past is, after all, the surest guide in all matters connected with mineral deposits. Hence the immense importance, in every mining country, of keeping as perfect a record as possible of all the discoveries which are made, and of the peculiar conditions met with. It would have been greatly for the interest of the lead-region if the miners could have preserved careful surveys of all the excavations, and kept a record of the exact position of the ore in the crevices.

As a preliminary to a thorough survey of the lead mines, an accurate map of the region would be absolutely indispensable. The whole mineral district should be carefully levelled over, and an exact representation obtained of the shape of the surface, a topographical map made on a large scale, and bench-marks established, so that every miner would know, at once, by referring to well ascertained data, precisely at what geological level he was working. This might seem a very great undertaking; but enough money has been repeatedly thrown away in ill-directed mining enterprises, at a single locality, to more than pay the expenses of the most accurate topographical survey of the whole region.

In looking over all that has been published by those who have examined the lead regions of the West, we find that one idea has been insisted on by all, without exception; namely, that the prosperity of the lead-region was to be attained by deep mining: that is to say, that all that is necessary to increase the production of this metal to an unlimited extent is to sink to greater depths. According to most of those who have written on the subject, this new source of ore and of consequent profit is to be found in the Lower Magnesian limestone, beneath the barren Upper sandstone; others would go still deeper, and find in the crystalline rocks below the much-desired continuation of the lead-bearing crevices. These points, therefore, have received careful consideration during the progress of this survey, and the results will be found embodied in the following pages, to which this chapter may be considered as forming the introduction.

In endeavoring to give as correct an idea as possible of the geological character of the lead-region, and of what has been done towards the development of its mineral wealth, we shall pursue the following order.

In the first place will be described the physical geography of the region, under which we include all that has been ascertained in regard to the configuration of its surface, the distribution of its highlands and vallies, the course of its streams, the position and elevation of its water-shed, &c.: to this will be appended a discussion of its surface geology, or of those causes which have given the region its peculiar contour, and originated the unconsolidated materials with which the solid rocks are covered. This will form the second chapter.

In the third, the rocks themselves will be described in their stratigraphical order, beginning with the lowest in the series, and going up to the highest observed in the region; under this head, the lithological and chemical characters of the different beds will be noticed, and their thickness given, with sections at different localities as illustrative of the changes which take place in them. Some allusions will be made to their fossil contents, which will be elaborated more fully by Prof. Hall, in a Report especially devoted to that subject. In short, all will be given in this chapter which is requisite to enable the reader to understand what are the different groups of strata which occur in the mining district.

In the farther development of the subject, the fourth chapter will be devoted to the mineralogy of the region. Here the simple minerals occurring accidentally in the rocks, or not forming an essential part of them, will be noticed in a systematic order, and such particulars given of their composition, mode of occurrence, and mutual association, as may be of interest either scientifically, or in connection with the economical geology, or with the application of this branch of science to mining, quarrying, &c.

The last chapter will contain as complete a statement of what has been done in the way of mining in the lead-region as can be given, and a discussion of the mode of occurrence of the useful ores found there, with special reference to the development of the mining interest in a manner suited to the nature and position of the mineral deposits with which the district is provided.

CHAPTER III.

PHYSICAL GEOGRAPHY AND SURFACE GEOLOGY.

Extent of the Productive Lead-region—Division of the State of Wisconsin into Districts on Geological and Topographical Grounds—Sketch of their Physical Geography—Topography of the Lead-region—The Water-shed—River System—Elevation of Various Points—Bottom Lands—Bluffs—Character of the River Vallies—The Mounds—Prairies—Surface Geology of the Lead-region.

The productive Lead Region of the Upper Mississippi, or that portion of the Northwest over whose surface ores of lead have been mined in noticeable quantity, is the field embraced in the present Report; and before proceeding to a consideration of its strictly geological characteristics, it will be necessary to give some idea of its physical geography. We shall therefore briefly notice some of the more important facts connected with its extent, the configuration of its surface, the size and distribution of its rivers, the form of its vallies, and, in general, such conditions of the surface as are the external manifestation of the long series of geological causes which have been in action since the beginning of time. The geographer takes note of the surface, and describes it as it at present exists, in its manifold relations to man, while the geologist looks beneath the surface, and finds in a multitude of new facts recorded within the rocky strata the explanation of much that was before incomprehensible with regard to the exterior of our earth. Thus, any investigation of the geological structure of a portion of the earth's surface must necessarily be preceded by a careful study of its external configuration; while he who would thoroughly understand its geographical conditions must acquaint himself, to a certain extent at least, with the history of the changes it has undergone, and the present relations of exterior to interior—or, in other words, with its geology.

The Upper Mississippi Lead Region is included within the boundaries of three States; namely, Wisconsin, Illinois, and Iowa. Fully five-sixths of the lead-producing district, however, belong to the State of Wisconsin, although the richest portion of the region lies near the point where the three States come together, so that Illinois and Iowa each produce more lead than Wisconsin, in proportion to the extent of surface over which more or less mining is carried on.*

An inspection of the general geological map of the lead-region of the Upper Mississippi will show the limits within which the productive mines are comprised; this map includes all the localities where lead ore is known to have been profitably mined for any considerable length of time. It extends, on the east, as far as Exeter, in the valley of Sugar

* As so much the largest extent of lead-producing territory belongs to Wisconsin, it is in every respect proper that, in describing the geology of the Wisconsin lead-region, the whole lead-region should be taken into consideration, and its character investigated as a whole, without regard to the fact that a portion of its western and southern extension runs over the borders of the State under whose authority this Report is published. It is proper, in this connection, to remark, that the facts in regard to the Iowa portion of the lead-region were chiefly collected by me while engaged in the Geological Survey of that State, from 1855 to 1858, as well as in several previous visits made at my own expense; while, on the Illinois side of the line, I have had, in addition to information obtained in previous years, the benefit of a small appropriation from the funds of the Geological Survey of that State, now carried on under the direction of A. H. Worthen, Esq., to enable me to lay down the geology with more accuracy than I could otherwise have done.

In the forthcoming Report of Mr. Worthen and his assistants on the geology of the State of Illinois, which will probably be published early in 1861, will be found a short notice, by myself, of the lead mines situated within the boundaries of that State, accompanied by a detailed map, on a scale of two inches to the mile, of the principal lead-bearing crevices of that district, from surveys made under my direction by Mr. U. G. Scheller. This crevice map, together with the one I had previously prepared, and which is published in the Iowa Geological Report, Vol. I, will, together with those herewith presented, be found to include all the more important facts in regard to the whole lead-region of the Upper Mississippi, and should all be consulted by those desirous of forming a clear idea of the whole of this important mineral district.

river, range eight east of the fourth Principal Meridian. A little ore is reported to have been found still farther east, at various points between Sugar and Rock rivers, but in no instance in sufficient amount to encourage extensive explorations, or to justify the extension of the limits of the map any farther east than Exeter. To the southeast, the farthest point where I have heard of lead having been found is at Freeport, where a few thousand pounds of ore were raised some years since; but no recent discoveries have been made in that vicinity, and we are not aware that any considerable bodies of ore have, for many years past, been found to the southeast of Warren. On the south, the mines near Elizabeth, in the valley of Apple river, are the last of any importance in that direction, although some ore is reported as having been found near the mouth of Plum creek, the farthest point south at which the lead-bearing beds show themselves. On the west, the geological formations to which the lead ore is restricted are exposed on the west side of the Mississippi river, along its banks and to a short distance inland, in the vallies of the small tributary streams, especially in that of Tête des Morts; it is but a narrow belt of productive or mineral-bearing rock, however, which is thus made available for mining purposes on this side of the Mississippi, since we soon rise to higher ground, occupied by rock of a different character, in which no lead ore has ever yet been discovered; or if in faint traces, according to vague reports, certainly not in any workable quantity. From Bellevue as far north as Dubuque, therefore, the Mississippi is very nearly the Western boundary of the lead-region; but to the northwest of the last-named city, the productive mining ground widens out, so as to embrace an area six or seven miles in width, and which extends to the northwest some fifteen miles in length, but is soon narrowed down again by the change in the direction of the Mississippi, which has an almost easterly course between Cassville and Potosi. Above Cassville, where the river assumes its north and south direction again, the width of surface covered by the lead-bearing formation is increased to about twelve miles, but the thinning out of the principal lead-bearing beds in this direction renders the chance of finding ore in them very uncertain;* and up to the present time there is no evidence of any valuable deposits beyond Gutenberg in a northwest direction, although a few discoveries have been reported on Turkey River and its northern branches. On the north, the water-shed line between the streams flowing into the Wisconsin to the north, and those directly tributary to the Mississippi to the south, forms almost exactly the limit of the mining district in that direction; but there are a few important localities of ore a little to the north of the water-shed, on the head-waters of Blue river, particularly those in the vicinity of Centreville and Franklin. As will be noticed farther on, the very rapid falling off of the surface to the north, after passing the water-shed, combined with the general southerly dip of the whole series of strata, brings us to rocks which are lower in their geological position than those in which lead ore occurs in any considerable quantity, almost immediately after passing the dividing ridge and commencing the descent towards the Wisconsin river.

The productive lead-region, as thus limited, includes an area of about 2200 square miles within the limits of Wisconsin, or just that of the State of Delaware; and its entire extent, within the three States, is not far from 3000 square miles, while the whole district represented on the general geological map, all of which has been carefully explored, so as to lay down its geological structure, is about ninety miles in length, east and west, by fifty-five broad, north and south, covering a surface almost exactly equal to that of the State of Connecticut. †

* The Blue limestone is, to be sure, well developed in this region; but it is only over a small area of the mineral district that this formation has been found productive; no trace of ore has ever been found in it in Iowa.

† The size of the map has been slightly reduced, since this was written, to allow of its being drawn on one stone.

The parallel of 42° 30′ forms the boundary between the States of Illinois and Wisconsin, and the longitude of the fourth Principal Meridian, which passes through Galena, is 90° 26′ 42″ west of Greenwich. The latitude of the Milwaukee and Mississippi Railroad station Prairie du Chien, according to Col. Graham, is 43° 2′ 1″.35, and its longitude 91° 8′ 38″.7. The geographical position of the Capitol at Madison has been also recently determined by the same high authority as follows: latitude, 43° 4′ 40″.3; longitude, 89° 22′ 56″.25.*

The State of Wisconsin may, for the purposes of geographical description, be naturally and conveniently divided into four different sections or districts; and these four divisions will be found each to be characterized by its own peculiar geological structure. They are as follows: 1st. The Northern and Northern Central; 2nd. The Western and Southern Central; 3rd. The Southwestern; and 4th. The Southeastern and Eastern.

Following this order, we pass from the lowest rocks in the geological series up to those which are the highest which occur in the State.

The Northern and Northern Central division includes all the region underlaid by the crystalline, non-fossiliferous rocks, or those to which the term Azoic may be properly applied, as indicating the probable absence of any traces of organic life on the earth at the time of their formation or deposition. This section of the State is marked by a mineral and agricultural character as distinct from that of other portions of the State as possible. Its surface is very rough and broken, intersected by numerous low ridges of granitic, hornblendic, and feldspathic rocks, which have a general easterly and westerly direction; these ridges are often covered with soil and forest trees,

* See a valuable article by Col. J. D. Graham, in the Wisconsin Historical Collections, Vol. IV, p. 393.

but not unfrequently present a precipitous rocky face on one side or the other. This region is drained by streams running in every direction, into Lake Superior, Lake Michigan, and the Mississippi. By far the larger portion of it, however, contributes its waters to feed the Wisconsin and Chippewa rivers, as the water-shed between the streams flowing north and those running towards the south is very near Lake Superior, so that the general inclination of the country is to the southward. The elevation of this water-shed above the level of Lake Superior is very imperfectly known, but appears from various barometrical measurements, made under unfavorable circumstances for accurate determination, by the U. S. Geological Surveys in that region, to be about 1000 feet on the eastern side of the State, and to diminish gradually towards the west. The fall of the Ontonagon, Montreal, Bad, and other rivers flowing into Lake Superior is much more rapid than that of the streams running in the opposite direction.

The whole of this division of the State is densely wooded, with the exception of the comparatively small surface occupied by the beds of former lakes, which, having become drained and filled with fine sediment, are incapable of supporting the growth of forest trees. Hence this is the great lumber region of the West, and a vast extent of territory is supplied with pine from the Wisconsin and its tributaries, as well as from the Chippewa, St. Croix, and other smaller streams heading in this great, and, apart from those engaged in lumbering, almost uninhabited region.

Another feature of the district in question is the vast accumulation of drift, or superficial detritus, which has been scattered over this portion of the State by currents of water, rushing across it from the north, and piling up immense accumulations of more or less water-worn materials, in alternating beds of sand, gravel, and boulders, with occasional heavy deposits of clay, indicating periods of comparative repose in the action of the currents. This region has been designated by geologists as pre-eminently the "head-quarters of the drift."

Many years must elapse before this district, situated as it is in so high a northern latitude, will become a thickly settled country, and it will be a long time before the details of its geology will be worked out. The principal mineral substance of value which it is known to contain in abundance is iron ore, which occurs in inexhaustible quantity, especially in the vicinity of Lake Superior.

The Western and Southern Central division of the State includes the region lying south of the great central nucleus of granitic and slaty rocks which forms the district just noticed, and, bending around it to the west, occupies a belt fifty to sixty miles wide along the eastern side of the Mississippi river. A line drawn from Madison to Prairie du Chien would indicate pretty nearly its southern boundary. The greater portion of this very extensive region, which covers not less than 10,000 square miles, or an area considerably larger than that of the State of Maryland, is underlaid by the Lower sandstone, the first or lowest member of the series of fossiliferous strata, succeeded, along its southern and western border, by the Lower Magnesian limestone, the next formation in order recognized in the Northwest.

The eastern side of this division of the State has been to some extent invaded by the drift, and the sandstone is there pretty well covered by the overlying detritus. A very large extent of territory, however, to the north and west of the Wisconsin river, is entirely destitute of any indications of ever having been swept over by the drift currents, and the loose materials which cover the surface seem to have been exclusively derived from the decomposition of the underlying rocks.

The surface of the "sandstone region," as it might with propriety be called, is diversified by no high mountains or regular ranges of elevations, but is in general in the form of a plain, gently declining towards the south and west. Its inequalities of surface are chiefly due to irregularity of denudation, or unequal weathering of alternate strata of different degrees of hardness. The rivers have cut for themselves channels of greater or less width and depth in proportion to their size, and are, consequently, bordered by precipitous bluffs, which increase in elevation, while the valley between them widens out, as we follow them downward.

The extremely silicious character of the underlying rocks, and the absence of the drift, impress upon this portion of the State a character of sterility, as compared with that of the adjacent country on the east and south : hence it is as yet but sparsely settled, and chiefly valuable for its timber.

The third district into which we have imagined the State to be divided lies south of the Wisconsin river and west of Rock river, and occupies its southwestern corner; it forms a division of the State which is characterized by some peculiarities, and especially by the fact of its being the district in which lead ore is extensively mined. Forming, as it does, the subject of the present Report, we shall turn to the detailed consideration of its geographical and geological structure, after briefly noticing the last remaining division, namely the fourth, or the Eastern and Southeastern.

This includes all the region which borders on Lake Michigan, and which is chiefly underlaid by rocks higher in the geological series than those found in any other portion of the State, except in a few scattered outliers through the lead-region. The larger part of the district in question is occupied by the Niagara limestone, the same member of the series which caps the mounds in the southwestern corner of the State. A very small portion of its extreme eastern edge, near Racine and Milwaukee, exhibits the only rocks found in the State which are more recent than the Niagara. These belong to the Devonian system, the next group below the coal, Wisconsin having through all its extent no rocks as high up as the coal measures.

The eastern side of the State is well covered with drift

materials, and presents quite a uniform surface, which falls off gently toward the east. The soil is generally good; and this portion of Wisconsin, together with the Lead Region, contains a much larger population to the square mile than will be found in the central, northern, and northwestern districts.

Having thus briefly noticed the characteristic features of the topography of the State as connected with its geology, we proceed to the special subject of this Report, namely, the

LEAD REGION.

The region enclosed between the Mississippi, Wisconsin, and Rock rivers, which are the approximate boundaries of the productive lead district to the west, north, and east, respectively, within the limits of the State of Wisconsin, is, on physical and geological grounds, to be considered as united with small portions of the States of Illinois and Iowa, as explained in the preceding pages; no regard will be paid, therefore, to State boundaries, in the following topographical notice of the Lead Region. The district in question is not one broken by lofty elevations, or traversed by anything which could be dignified with the title of mountain chain. The highest points scarcely rise 500 feet above the average level of the ground at their bases, although very conspicuous objects on account of the prevailing flatness of the country. The general relief of the region is indicated by the position and direction of the main water-courses, and of the water-shed between them. These may be more satisfactorily made out from a small diagram, like the one here introduced (Fig. 1), than they could be from a large map encumbered with geographical details. The dotted line indicates the water-shed between the streams flowing north into the Wisconsin and those which run to the south and empty themselves directly into the Mississippi. This last named river flows very near the western boundary of the Lead Region, but its course is not really in any way to be taken as being along the line

Fig. 1.—River-system and Water-shed of the Lead Region.

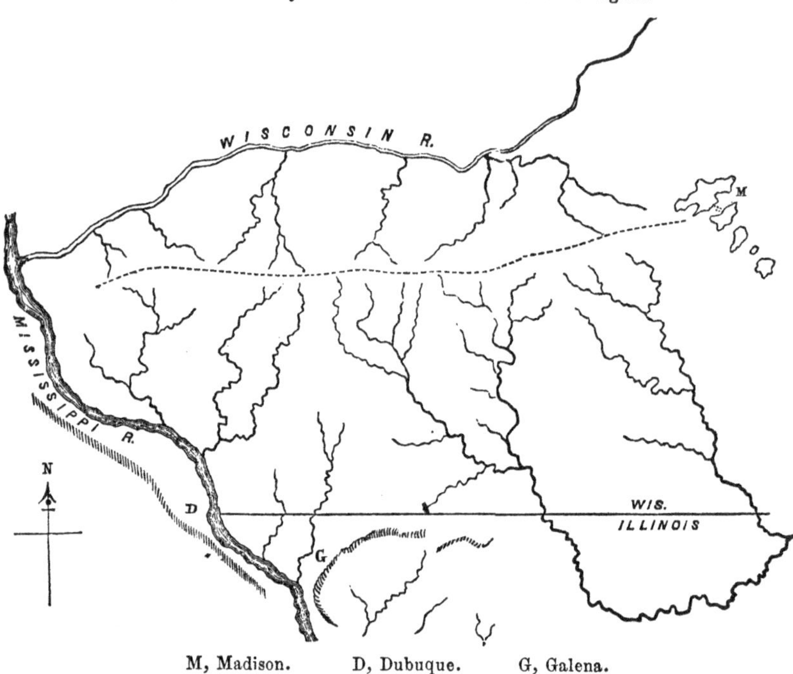

M, Madison. D, Dubuque. G, Galena.

of junction of two dissimilar formations, except between Dubuque and Bellevue, where it marks pretty nearly the outcrop of the Niagara limestone, which is itself the most marked topographical feature of the region. This outcrop is indicated by the line of heights represented on the south and west of the diagram. It forms a series of elevations, or, more properly, the edge of a plateau or table-land, which has been worn away by denuding agencies in a very irregular manner, so as to present an exceedingly complicated outline, when followed out in detail, while numerous outliers, or detached masses of the same form and elevation, but completely severed from their original connection, lie irregularly scattered in advance of the principal outline, like sentinels posted for observation. These outliers are universally known in the region under consideration as "mounds," and their geological character will be described in the chapter devoted to the general geology and description of the formations which are developed in the Lead Region. On the general geological map, the outcrop above referred to will be observed, marked by a narrow band of green, which is succeeded by one of purple, or neutral tint, on which it will be seen that no mines are indicated as occurring. The formation indicated by the green color on the map is the Hudson River group; that by the purple color is the Niagara limestone; and, at the time of their deposition, the causes which produced the accumulation of lead ore in the underlying strata had entirely ceased to act, and were never afterwards renewed; so that the outcrop of these rocks on the south and west is a topographically well marked and geologically necessary limit of the Lead Region in those directions.

The line of water-shed, as represented on the above diagram, between the streams flowing north and those running to the south, is almost exactly a straight east and west line from the Blue Mounds nearly to Prairie du Chien, and for a distance of almost sixty miles. Along this water-shed runs the military road, formerly laid out by the United States government from Fond du Lac, on Lake Winnebago, to Prairie du Chien. No one observing the position of this line could fail to recognize the fact that its origin was due to some general geological cause, as will be explained farther on.

The distance from the water-shed to the Wisconsin river on the north is from 12 to 15 miles, while the streams running in the opposite direction have a much longer course to follow before reaching the Mississippi. More than half of the Lead Region is drained by the numerous branches of the Peccatonica, which flow through it with a course a little to the east of south; but which, on entering the State of Illinois, bend to the east, and soon enter Rock river, which follows a southwest course for more than 100 miles after their junction, before finally reaching the Mississippi. Sugar river, with its numerous branches, is also a tributary of Rock river. Fever river, the Platte and Grant rivers, are the other important streams which drain the southern slope of the region, and these flow directly into the Mississippi. On the north side of the water-shed, the streams flowing into the Wisconsin are all small, and have, of course, a quite rapid descent.

The elevation of the Wisconsin river above Lake Michigan, which may conveniently be taken as the base from which to reckon the elevations in Southern Wisconsin, and which is itself 583 feet above the sea level, may be given as follows, from the surveys of the Milwaukee and Mississippi railroad:

ELEVATIONS OF THE TRACK ON THE LINE OF THE MILWAUKEE AND MISSISSIPPI RAILROAD.

Name of Station.	Elevation above Lake Michigan.	Elevation above Sea-level.	Distance from last station.
Milwaukee	5	588	
Wauwatosa	73	656	5
Elm Grove	166	749	5
Junction	245.5	828.5	4
Forest House	240	823	3
Waukesha	225	808	3
Genesee	325	908	8
North Prairie	363	946	3
Eagle	364.5	947.5	5
Palmyra	260	843	6
Whitewater	240.5	823.5	8
Milton	293	876	12
Edgerton	241.5	824.5	8
Stoughton	278.5	861.5	10
M'Farland	289	872	9
Madison	274.5	857.5	6
Middleton	347	930	7
Black Earth	232	815	13
Mazomanie	195	778	3
Arena	154.4	737.4	6
Spring Green	144	727	8
Lone Rock	126	709	6
Avoca	117	700	7
Muscoda	109	692	6
Boscobel	89	672	14
Wauzeka	60	643	10
Prairie du Chien	41	624	17

These elevations were obligingly furnished by C. H. Edgerton, Esq., Chief Engineer, through the kindness of Dr. Lapham, of Milwaukee; as also the following, on the line of the road from Janesville to Monroe:

	Elevation above		Distance from last station.
	Lake Michigan.	Sea-level.	
Janesville	240	823	
Hanover	209	792	7
Orford	312.5	895.5	5
Broadhead	221	804	6
Juda	353	936	7
Monroe	....	....	8

The elevations of various points near the south line of the State, as determined by the surveys of the Southern Wisconsin railroad, have also been furnished me by Mr. Lapham, and are as follows:

Name of place.	Elevation above	
	Lake Michigan.	Sea-level.
Mississippi river, at the mouth of the Platte river	13	596
Jamestown, high ground N. E. of, on line of road	422	1005
Benton, crossing of Fever river	156	578
Shullsburg, high ground east of	516	1099
Peccatonica river crossing, near Gratiot	206	789
Peccatonica river crossing, in Town. 1, Range 6, Section 7	196	779
Monroe, high ground S. of	500	1083

The following heights, in Illinois, near the Wisconsin line, are obtained from a section along the Illinois Central railroad, prepared in the office of the Company, and furnished by the politeness of J. W. Foster, Esq. The figures give the heights of the points specified, in feet, of the railroad track at the Stations, above the Ohio river at Cairo, and also above Lake Michigan, the difference of level between the two being, by railroad surveys, 308 feet:

Station.	Elevation above Cairo.	Elevation above Lake Michigan.	Elevation above Sea.
Freeport	480	172	755
Lena	678	370	953
Nora	715	407	990
Warren	723	415	998
Apple river	738	430	1013
Summit level, west of Apple river	805	497	1080
Scales Mound	656	348	931
Council Hill	450	142	725
Galena	307	—1	582
Menomonee	312	4	587
Dunleith	306	—2	581

The elevation of the Mississippi river at various points on the western border of the Lead Region is as follows :

ELEVATION OF MISSISSIPPI RIVER.

At	Elevation above Lake Michigan.	Elevation above Sea-level.
Prairie du Chien	24	607
Mouth of Platte river	13	596
Dunleith	—2	581

There are some discrepancies in the railroad levels, which I have not yet been able to adjust satisfactorily ; but they are probably due partly to inaccuracy in the work itself, and partly to the uncertainty in regard to the exact level of low water mark in the rivers and on Lake Michigan. The results given above, however, are sufficiently accurate for the ordinary purposes of the geologist. They show that the lake surface on the one side does not differ materially in level from the Mississippi on the other; the river at Dunleith being at low water a few feet lower, and at high water a little above, the general level of Lake Michigan. They also show that the general level of the highest prairie region along the southern tier of townships, or near the State line between Illinois and Wisconsin, is about 500 feet above the lake; also that there is a gradual rise of the surface towards the north and northeast, but that this rise is not quite 200 feet, as the average elevation of the surface at the base of the Blue Mounds is about 675 feet above Lake Michigan. Going west from the Blue Mounds, along the line of the military road, which follows the water-shed, the decline of the surface is very gradual, and indeed hardly perceptible, until we arrive within 15 or 20 miles of the Mississippi. The surface of the Lead Region would, therefore, be a gently undulating plain, elevated from 600 to 700 feet above Lake Michigan, on its northern border, and very gradually declining towards the south and southwest, where it has, on the borders of the State, an elevation of from 400 to 500 feet. But, besides the gentle undulations above referred to—which are caused by unequal denudation partly, and also in some degree by flexures of the strata themselves, which are bent up into low arches, so as to modify the relief of the ground, and to have a perceptible influence on the direction of the drainage—the character of the surface has been most essentially affected by the erosion of the river vallies, so that their peculiar form is the most marked feature in the topography of this portion of the Northwest, as it is also in much of the adjacent region of Illinois, Iowa, and Minnesota. The river "bluffs," as they are termed, give a force and character to the landscape in this part of the Mississippi valley, which would without them be entirely wanting.

The three divisions of the surface everywhere recognized in the Lead Region are the *bottom-land*, or valley, the *bluff*, and the *upland*, or prairie, where the higher ground is destitute of arborescent vegetation. The river bottom is that portion of the valley which is enclosed between the bluffs, and which is usually nearly level, or gently sloping towards the stream from either side. In most cases it is so nearly level that the river which runs through it, in its serpentine course, now touches the bluffs on one side and now on the other; for it is everywhere in this region a peculiar feature of the streams, especially of the smaller ones, that their courses are exceedingly tortuous; even if the valley through which they run be straight, they will themselves meander from side to side with a thousand convolutions in a short distance. Thus a considerable absolute fall is gained, without a very rapid current. The bottom lands are usually well covered with forest trees, especially on the Mississippi, where the elm, linden, black walnut, white and burr oak, poplar, and ash are the most abundant, and form a vigorous growth. The breadth of the river bottom is variable, but is usually proportioned to the size of the stream which flows through it: thus, on the Mississippi, the valley expands to six or eight miles in width in some places, while in others it contracts so that there is hardly more than room for the river to pass at high water. On the smaller streams the vallies are narrow at their heads, and gradually widen out as the amount of water passing through them increases with the accession of their tributaries, and at the same time the height of the bluffs on each side increases, so that a stream may have a rapid descent for a considerable distance, while the general level of the region through which it flows remains about the same. This peculiar relation of the size of the valley to that of the stream flowing through it is especially characteristic of the driftless region, in which the mineral district is comprised, as will be noticed under the head of "surface geology," farther on in this chapter: when we reach the region which has been invaded by the drift currents, we find a different state of things: thus, the valley of Sugar river is nearly as wide as that of the Mississippi itself. There are no indications of terraces in the river bottoms of the Lead Region: everything indicates a gradual and uninterrupted action of the eroding forces, and not a succession of periods of drainage alternating with epochs of repose, which would allow of the formation of terraces.

From the river bottom we come directly to the river bluff, which is the term universally applied at the West to the precipitous and sudden rise of ground which connects the bottom with the upland, and which is so marked a feature in the topography of the Northwest. Through all that portion of Wisconsin, Minnesota, Illinois, and Iowa which is not underlaid by the hard crystalline or metamorphic rock, the rivers flow in vallies, which are sometimes so narrow as to become almost ravines, imitating on a small scale the cañons of New Mexico, and which were undoubtedly, like those, eroded by the action of water, since their depth and breadth increase with the magnitude of the stream and the distance from its source. These vallies do not connect with the upland, or general level of the region, by gently sloping hill-sides, as we might expect; but by precipitous, sharply defined, and usually rocky ascents, or bluffs. These are often perpendicular, or nearly so, for a considerable portion of their height, if the rock is exposed at all, as is almost always the case if the valley has any considerable depth. More generally, however, a steep talus of rocky fragments, more or less covered with soil, is crowned by a precipitous ridge of rock, which is often worn into a variety of fantastic castellated forms, giving origin to the peculiar and picturesque scenery of the Northwest, so well known to travellers and tourists on the Upper Mississippi. It is peculiarly the great dolomitic beds of this region which assume these attractive forms under the eroding influences; the sandstones exhibit a much more uniform aspect in the bluffs, although occasionally leaving a picturesque outlier, or broken by ravines so as to imitate the character of the magnesian beds. The pure limestone strata, which, however, in the Northwest are comparatively insignificant in thickness, wear away so gradually and uniformly as to leave an undulating surface, without precipitous slopes or striking forms.

In the northwest corner of the Lead Region, in the vicinity of Prairie du Chien, the general level of the high prairie is between 400 and 450 feet above low water mark in the Mississippi, and there is an almost vertical rise in the bluffs of over 300 feet. All along the Wisconsin river, on the northern boundary of the district, the bluffs are precipitous and lofty, being from 200 to 300 feet in height, and the same is true of the streams coming down into this valley from the south. On the Mississippi, the height of the bluffs gradually declines from Prairie du Chien towards the south. At Cassville, they are about 275 feet high; at Dubuque, 200 to 210; and at Dunleith, on the opposite side, from 125 to 160 feet; this is, in each case, the elevation from the river up to the upper edge of the precipitous cliff forming the bluff: there is almost always a rapid, although gradual rise, with a grassed or timbered surface, beyond the portion where the rock is exposed. On the smaller rivers, the elevation of the bluffs is proportionally less than on the Mississippi and Wisconsin: thus on the branches of the Peccatonica, in the vicinity of Mineral Point, the ascent from the river bottom to the upland is usually from 125 to 150 feet, of which there may be from 20 to 40 feet of ledge, or nearly vertical rock. But on all the streams running to the north of the water-shed, the bluffs are higher and more precipitous than on those of the same size on the other side; owing, as it would seem, to their more rapid fall. Thus the Blue river, near Wingville, on its very head-waters has its vallies hemmed in by lofty walls of almost perpendicular rock more than 100 feet in height. The same is the case to the north of the Blue Mounds, where we have only to follow the streams a very short distance on their course northward to find ourselves already hemmed in by precipitous bluffs.

Passing from the bluffs on to the upland, we are first struck with its undulating surface: no such thing as a "dead level," as it is called, can be found. The view from any one of the mounds exhibits this most strikingly, but especially from those in the vicinity of Galena. Here we see each valley giving off its side vallies, each side valley branching again, and so on until the highest ground is reached, each ridge being furrowed by a thousand water-courses, which ramify in every direction, like the branches of a tree. The ridges which have been left by the denuding agencies are sometimes long and narrow, and are intersected by ravines, exposing the rock, even where no water now runs, except just after a violent rain storm. Many of the larger water-courses are sometimes entirely dry during a part of the summer.

There are no elevations within the boundaries of the Lead Region which can with propriety be called mountains, but several isolated, conical or flat-topped hills, which are conspicuous features in the topography of the district, and which, as before mentioned, are called "Mounds."

The most elevated of these are on the extreme north-eastern outskirts of the Lead Region, and are called the "Blue Mounds:" from their peculiar isolated position, they are visible at a considerable distance, although the highest is hardly 500 feet above its base. There are two elevations included under the term "Blue Mounds," of which one is called the East, and the other the West Blue Mound: the western one is the higher. As this is the most elevated point in Southern Wisconsin, its height was determined barometrically, with as much accuracy as was possible without a very extended series of observations. With the aid of an assistant stationed at the base of the mound, who observed with one barometer, I made a corresponding series of observations at the nearest point on the Milwaukee and Mississippi railroad, namely, Mazomanie, the height of which was accurately known by the railroad surveys (see table above). These observations were continued during a whole day of remarkably fine weather for such operations, there being a fine breeze, cloudless sky, and very slight and regular fluctuations of the barometric pressure.

These observations, on calculation, give for the elevation of the platform of Arnold's hotel at the base of the West Blue Mound, above the railroad track at Mazomanie, 469.8 feet. By a series of observations made the previous year, this station at Arnold's was known to be 486 feet below the top of the West Blue Mound; hence we have the whole elevation of the Mound as follows:

Elevation of Arnold's above railroad at Mazomanie.........	469.8
West Blue Mound above platform of Arnold's hotel.........	486.
Railroad track at Mazomanie above Lake Michigan.........	195.
Total elevation of West Blue Mound above Lake Michigan ..	1150.8

This result may be set down as, in all probability, quite near the truth, since the circumstances under which the measurements were made were as favorable as possible for this kind of work, the distance between the stations, about eleven miles, being of course to be taken into account in considering the probable accuracy of the work.

A short series of observations was taken also at Arena, and another at Madison, but as both these points are more distant from the Mound than Mazomanie, the results given above are most to be relied on, especially as the observations were kept up much longer at the last-named place. It may be mentioned, however, that the mean of all the observations taken differs less than three feet from that given above as the result of the Mazomanie observations.

The elevation of the West Blue Mound was measured in 1839, by Dr. Locke, his base being the Wisconsin river at Arena; the height of the Mound above the river is given by him at 1000 feet; if we deduct from this 31 feet, which he also gives as the elevation of the plain of Arena above the river, we have 969 feet for the difference of level of Arena and the Mound, and 1123 feet as the elevation of the Mound above Lake Michigan according to Dr. Locke's measurement. As his results were obtained with only one barometer, they could not of course lay claim to great accuracy, however skilfully the observations may have been made. The agreement is quite satisfactory, considering the limited means and time at Dr. Locke's command.

The East Blue Mound was not measured, but was estimated by the eye to be about 150 feet lower than the west mound.

The Platte Mounds are three eminences on and near the north line of Town. 3 north, Range 1 east of the meridian, near Belmont, and from 6 to 9 miles northeast of Platteville. The East and West Mounds are nearly of the same height: the Central, or Little Platte Mound, is a low and very diminutive conical hill, on which no rock is exposed, excepting several large loose blocks lying upon its sides. Observations were made at the base of the Platte Mounds, with corresponding ones at Mineral Point; but as the weather was very unfavorable, and as they could not be repeated, the results can only be taken as approximations. They gave the height of the general level of the surface at the base of the mounds as 553 feet, and that of the west mound at 703 feet, the mound being about 150 feet above its base.

The elevation of Sinsinnewa Mound was also measured, and found to be 591 feet above the Mississippi river at Dunleith, and about 225 feet above the general level of the country at its base; it is 129 feet above the college.

The following table gives the height of all the principal mounds in the Lead Region, above Lake Michigan:

	Feet.
West Blue Mound	1151
Platte Mounds	703
Sinsinnewa Mound	591
Sherald's Mound, Iowa	600
Table Mound, Iowa	472
Waddell's Mound, Illinois	484
Pilot Knob, Illinois	429
Scales Mound "	582
Charles Mound "	657

Under the head of Stratigraphical Geology, further remarks will be made in reference to the form of the mounds and their distribution.

A portion of the Lead Region is occupied by those tracts destitute of arborescent vegetation which are known at the west as *prairies:* perhaps one-seventh of the area south of the Wisconsin and west of the Sugar river is prairie, while a large portion of the remaining six-sevenths is only thinly grown over with trees, which are chiefly different species of oaks. The peculiar distribution of the prairie lands in the State of Wisconsin, considered with reference to the meteorological conditions there prevailing, show clearly that the absence of moisture is not the principal reason why so considerable a portion of the surface is so scantily provided with arborescent vegetation. I have discussed this subject in the first chapter of the Iowa Geological Report, to which I need here only refer the reader, with the remark that during the progress of the Wisconsin survey many additional facts have been observed bearing on this subject, and that I am strengthened in my conviction, that the physical condition of the soil is the predominating cause of the existence of the prairies in this region, and that climatic conditions have little to do with it. It is proposed to take up this subject at another time, and to discuss it more fully than the limits of this Report would allow. We pass next to a division of the subject closely allied with its topography, namely its Surface Geology.

SURFACE GEOLOGY OF THE LEAD REGION.

By the term "surface geology" is here understood, the character, position, and origin of the loose or unconsolidated materials, the superficial detritus, as it may be called, which lies upon the surface of the solid rock, and which is the result of those agencies which have last been in operation, connecting themselves most closely with the present epoch; so closely, indeed, that in many cases it is quite impossible to draw any line of separation between what is now taking place and what has been going on through an immense lapse of time. Within the limits of the Lead Region, this identity of the causes which have given the present relief to the surface and covered it with detrital materials, and the unbroken progression of the series of events which characterize the most recent geological epoch, is something of very great interest, since it differs in this respect completely from what is known to have taken place in all the rest of the northern and northwestern United States, and most especially in the region of the Great Lakes and the valley of the St. Lawrence. In the most hasty examination of the surface, through all the vast region of Canada, New England, the western States north of the Ohio, and far to the west and northwest of the Mississippi, we cannot fail to notice that the rocks in place are covered by accumulations of detrital materials, often of great thickness, which we perceive at once not to have originated from the decomposition of the underlying strata, but, on the contrary, to have been brought from a distance, and sometimes a very great distance, by a cause or series of causes quite different from any now in action. Thus we find, in New England, the summits of the highest mountains scored, grooved, and polished by the friction of heavy bodies of material passing over them, and loose blocks or boulders carried to a long distance from their native bed, and often deposited at an elevation far above their starting-point.

A little more attentive study of this class of facts soon shows us clearly that the great bulk of the loose materials which cover the northern United States has been carried from the north toward the south, or approximately so, and that this is true across the whole breadth of North America, and that the same general facts hold good with reference to the northern part of the European Continent. These transported materials are called "drift," and the period during which those causes were in operation by which the transport was effected is called the epoch of the drift, or the diluvial period.

From the time of the cessation of the great movement of abraded materials to the southward, another series of changes has been going on, binding the drift epoch with the actual condition of things, as now existing on the surface, by a closely interwoven chain of events; the continents have been depressed beneath the ocean level and again raised above it; while the drainage of the elevated land, either effected gradually or at intervals, with more or less rapidity, has scooped out the vallies, worn their sides into terraces, and re-arranged the previously existing detrital materials into their present condition and position. Thus we pass from the drift epoch to the alluvial; the whole series of events included since the tertiary up to the present time being frequently designated as the "quaternary period."

In no part of the United States are the phenomena of the drift displayed on a grander scale than in the Lake Superior region, and on the northern borders of Wisconsin. Here we have a great thickness of detrital deposits, covering the whole region, so as almost entirely to conceal the underlying rocks, and extending across the Mississippi as far to the west as has been explored. The lower portion of this drift material consists usually of red or bluish clay, succeeded by sand and gravel with some large boulders imbedded, very irregularly heaped together, but still bearing, on the whole, distinct marks of stratification. Scattered over the whole surface, even on the tops of the highest ridges, the boulders are found, in greater or less number, and of all sizes, up to that of a small house.

If we consider the magnitude and universality of the drift deposits in the northern United States, and especially in northern Wisconsin, we shall be the more astonished to learn that throughout nearly the whole Lead Region, and over a considerable extent of territory to the north of it, no trace of transported materials, boulders, or drift can be found; and, what is more curious, to the east, south, and west, the limit of the productive Lead Region is almost exactly the limit of the area thus marked by the absence of the drift.

The conclusions to which we have been led by the study of this driftless region are as follows:

1st. That there has existed, ever since the period of the deposition of the Upper Silurian, a considerable area, chiefly in Wisconsin and near the Mississippi river, which has never been sunk below the level of the ocean, or covered by any extensive and permanent body of water, and which, consequently, has not only not received any newer deposit than the Upper Silurian, but has also entirely escaped the invasion of the drift, which took place over so vast an extent of the northern hemisphere.

2d. That the extensive denudation which can be shown to have taken place in this region, as witnessed by the outliers of rock still remaining, and the general outline of the surface, has not been occasioned by any currents of water sweeping over the surface, under some great general cause, but that it has all been quietly and silently effected by the simple agency of rain and frost, acting uninterruptedly through a vast period of time.

3d. That during a long period this island, as it may be called, remained uninhabited by animals, but that at the close of the drift epoch, when the surrounding region itself became peopled with numerous animals and plants, it was the residence of a variety of species, some of which are now extinct, while others still exist.

4th. That a large portion of the superficial detritus of the West, even in those regions where drift boulders are met with, must have had its origin in the subaërial destruction of the rocks, the soluble portion of them having been gradually removed by the percolating water, while that which remains represents the insoluble residuum, the sand and clay, which was originally present in smaller quantity in the strata thus acted on.

The facts which have led to these conclusions will next

be set forth, so that the reader can form for himself an opinion of their probability.

In proceeding south and southwest from the Wisconsin river into Illinois and Iowa, we find the southerly dip of the strata gradually bringing to the surface newer formations, until we soon come upon the coal-measures, which constitute the highest member of the series, until we approach the Ohio to the south, and the Missouri to the west. The observations of the geological corps of Iowa and Illinois show that, during the deposition of the carboniferous limestones, the whole of the area south of the Lead Region was gradually rising from the water, so that each group occupies a less width in that direction than the one deposited previously. As the tops of the highest points in and about the Lead Region, the "mounds" as they are called, are made up of the Niagara limestone, and as no higher rock is found anywhere in that district, or to the north for a great distance, it may be assumed that this region rose from the water, and was thus rendered inaccessible to any further deposits, soon after the deposition of the Niagara limestone.

That it was not again submerged during the drift epoch is rendered certain by the following facts:

1st. The entire absence of boulders or pebbles, or any rolled and water-worn materials, which by their nature would indicate that the region in question had been exposed to the action of those causes by which the drift phenomena were produced.

The boulderless district on the south of the Wisconsin is, as has been already remarked, almost exactly coincident in extent with the productive Lead Region. The annexed map, necessarily on a small scale, will show approximately the outlines of the area which is absolutely devoid of boulders and gravel.

Within the limits of the region south of the Wisconsin river, the outline of the boulderless district, as shown by the dotted line on the map, is laid down with a pretty near

Fig. 2.

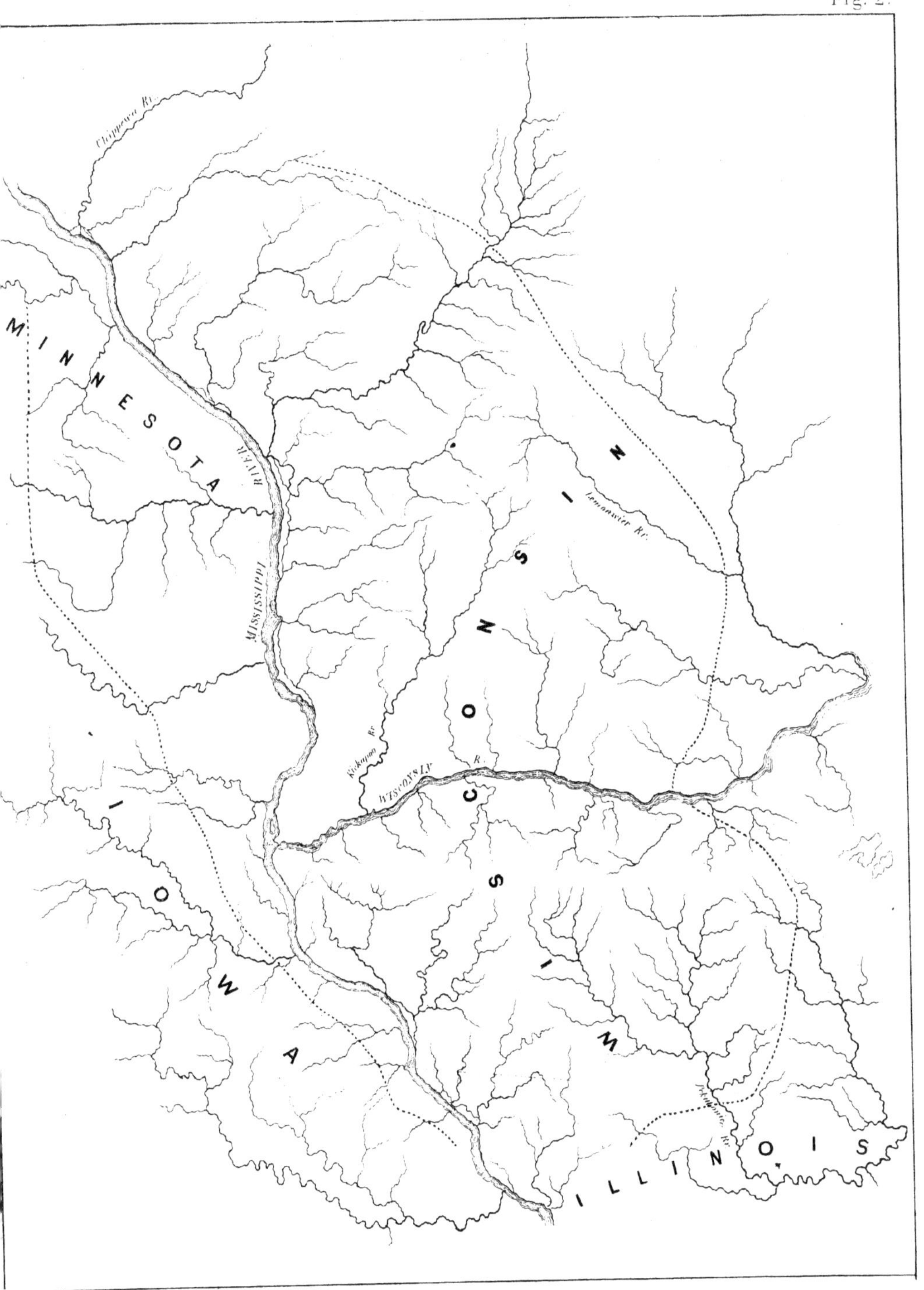

DIAGRAM OF THE REGION DESTITUTE OF DRIFT AND BOULDERS IN WISCONSIN, IOWA AND MINNESOTA.

approach to accuracy, as that part of the country has been carefully explored. The line has been continued to the north, in a fainter dotting, chiefly on the authority of Mr. Lapham, who has not, however, made any minute exploration for the purpose of defining the boundary of the drift, so that it must be accepted as only approximately correct.

Within the area thus inclosed by dotted lines, the only approach to water-worn materials to be observed is in the beds of some of the streams, where there are, occasionally, fragments, more or less rounded, of the adjacent rocks, forming imperfect gravel beds; but nothing which would indicate any different action from that which is now taking place in the beds of the rivers. The appearance of the deposits thus formed is very different from that which is presented by the accumulations of modified drift which fill the river vallies, as soon as we cross the line into the drift-covered region. Most of the smaller streams of the driftless district have no pebbles in their beds, but flow between low banks of sand, loam, or clay. The large rivers, as the Wisconsin, have their bottoms made up chiefly of sandy materials.*

2d. The absence of any signs of stratification in the superficial detritus covering the district indicated on the map, and designated as the driftless region.

We can conceive that, over a district of limited area, at least, depositions from water might have taken place without the introduction of any boulders, or the formation of gravel, or even the presence of detrital matter in any form. Thus the Upper Sandstone of the Lead Region offers an instance of a thick and wide-spread sheet of silicious mate-

* It appears from Mr. Kimball's observations that there is coarse drift in the valley of the Wisconsin, at some points, so that it is possible that north of that river it is only the higher ground which is destitute of boulders. Mr. Kimball describes a bed of water-worn materials on the Wisconsin, 15 or 20 feet above the river, and 20 feet thick, in which boulders, some as large as 2 or 3 feet in diameter, were observed. These observations would appear to limit the driftless region almost exactly to the area of the Lead Region. This subject should receive farther attention in the progress of the survey.

rials without a single pebble ever having been found in it, or any foreign detrital matter. When deposition has taken place by chemical precipitation, there may be no detrital matter present; but in all cases where masses of sedimentary or chemically precipitated matter have been thrown down from water, we may expect to find the characteristic bedded structure, or stratified arrangement, which is common to all sedimentary deposits. For instance, a lake may become filled up so quietly that not a pebble will find its way into the accumulating materials; yet the evidence of previous suspension in an aqueous medium will be found in the differences of color, texture, or composition of the different layers, which may be minute, yet will always be capable of being made out.

All the evidences of a stratified arrangement being wanting in the superficial detritus of the boulderless region, we are justified in asserting that the material of which it is composed can never have been in aqueous suspension, and although it may have been produced by the action of water, it could not have been either by mechanical or chemical precipitation.

Wherever we examine the materials which overlie the rocks in place in the Lead Region, we find the following condition of things. In the first place, the surface of the rock is uneven and irregular, bearing the marks of chemical rather than of mechanical erosion. This is especially the case where limestone or dolomite forms the rock in place. There are of course no glacial furrows or striæ, no drift-scratches, and no evidence of the rock having been planed down to a level, as is so beautifully seen in many localities where the drift has been moved over the surface; as at the mouth of the Menomonee river, or in western New York, where the dolomitic rocks have preserved most perfectly the evidence of this kind of operations. The annexed wood-cut (Fig. 3), showing the character of the surface of the rock, and a section of the overlying loose materials, as seen in the vicinity of Warren, and as might be observed in a thousand other localities, will serve to illustrate the above remark.

Fig. 3.—Section of Galena Limestone and Superficial Detritus, near Monroe.

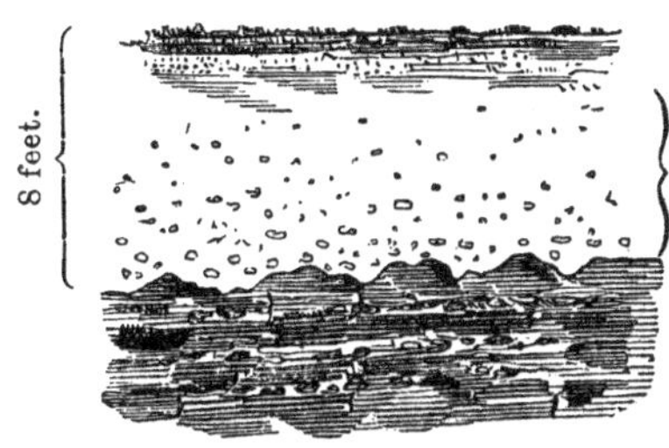

Above the surface of the rock thus irregularly eroded, we find almost always in the Lead Region a varying thickness of a dark reddish-brown clay, not very pure, however, but containing more or less sand; this clay is usually intermixed with flints, which are more abundant towards the bottom of the bed, and frequently make up a large portion of the mass for several feet in thickness. The clay is not always dark colored: it may be of a light yellowish color; but the brown ferruginous varieties are more frequent in the mineral region. The thickness of the stratum of clay and flints is very variable, as is that of the whole mass of the surface materials. I have found it very difficult to fix on the average amount of detritus accumulated on the solid rock in the Lead Region. It is sometimes quite thin, and at others equals at least 30 feet; probably there is not less than 10 feet, on the average, of detrital material spread over the surface of this district. Of this the larger portion would come under the denomination of red clay; although the amount of sand intermixed is quite variable, and the exact term by which it would be most proper to designate the mixture might not always be certain.

The disposition of the flints in the clay is quite irregular, but they are generally accumulated in greater abundance towards the bottom of the deposit.

The occurrence of the flint nodules in the clay is most noticed in those districts which are covered by the lower beds of the Galena limestone, as it is in the middle and lower portions of this rock that they are most abundant. Where the Blue limestone occupies the surface, this rock is frequently observed to be covered by fragments of the same material mixed with clay or loam, and gradually decreasing in abundance upwards. This may be illustrated by the annexed wood-cut (Fig. 4), which represents the character of the superficial detritus in many places near Mineral Point.

FIG. 4.—Section of the Blue Limestone and Overlying Detritus, near Mineral Point.

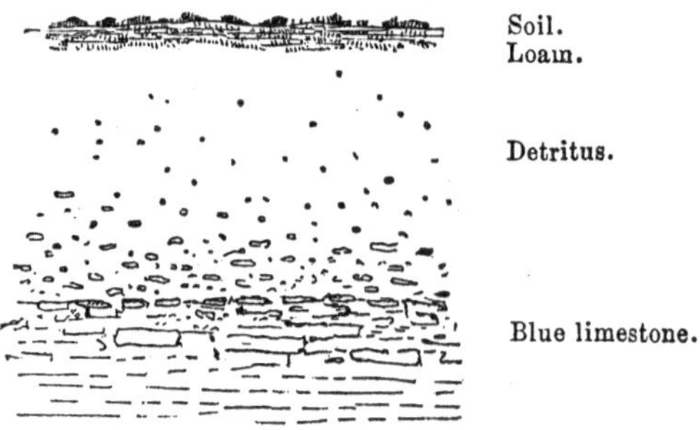

These fragments, in all cases, are seen to be very little removed from the original position which they occupied before the rock became broken up. The character of the loose pieces of rock in the clay or loam, their shape and position, everything connected with them, in short, indicates most conclusively that there has been no motion or transportation of the detrital matter: it must lie on the very spot where the quiet disintegration of the stratum to which it belonged has left it. Of course, on a steep side-hill, or the edge of a bluff, there may have been considerable sliding down of loose materials after the wearing out of the valley: but such partial and very limited transferences of material are not at all to be confounded with those caused by any general agencies like the drift currents.

But whatever the nature of the materials resting on the solid strata beneath, we never find them assorted in layers, or divided by well-marked lines of stratification, or showing any indication of the action of currents of water, or any other phenomena which are everywhere the result of deposition from an aqueous medium. In view of these facts, therefore, we are justified in asserting that the region in question can never have been under water since the epoch of the Upper Silurian, and that it must have formed an island at the time when the great currents from the north were bringing down the detrital materials which are spread over so vast an area in the northern hemisphere.

3d. The entire absence of all traces of marine or fresh-water animals in the superficial detritus of the region in question. The occurrence of fossil remains in the drift is something which is very rarely observed, the causes in action during the diluvial period having been highly unfavorable to the development of animal or vegetable life; the absence of any traces of marine or fresh-water life in the most recent formations is certainly no proof that they may not have been deposited from water; on the contrary, we know that in all the great thickness of stratified drift clays in the Northwest, on Lake Superior, not a vestige of an organic form has ever been found. In numerous instances, however, marine or fresh-water shells have been found in the deposits formed during the later periods of the quaternary, which have been called by various names, such as Laurentian, which includes deposits more recent than the drift and older than the alluvial, and characterized by marine shells of existing species; or in the "loess," or Algonquin formation, which is of fresh-water origin. If the superficial detritus of the Lead Region were a sedimentary deposit, as it would have been, if the equivalent of the "loess," it would, in all probability, have been found to contain fresh-water shells; this we infer, because the superficial deposits of the adjacent region have been proved, by the discovery of animal remains of this character, to have been formed at the bottom of a lake or inland sea of fresh water.

The only remains of animals or plants found up to this time, however, in the surface deposits of the Lead Region, all belong to species living on the land, and not a vestige of a shell has ever been discovered except in the very limited and peculiar beds in the neighborhood of the Mississippi, which will be noticed more particularly farther on. Bones and teeth of land animals of various kinds, among which the mastodon was the most conspicuous, are so abundantly found buried at different depths in the clay and other loose materials of the Lead Region and in the lead-bearing crevices, that it would be difficult to come to any other conclusion than that the region must have been dry land during at least a very considerable portion of the time when these detrital deposits were accumulating. The nature of these animals, and the circumstances under which their bones were accumulated and preserved, will be the subject of discussion in another part of this Report. It is sufficient here to have noticed the fact of the terrestrial character of all these remains, as bearing on the question whether the beds in which they are found could have been deposited from water.

2d. If, as we think has been demonstrated above, the region in question has never been covered with water, or subjected to the action of the drift currents, the question arises, how could the denudation of the rocky strata which were once continuous over the whole region, and have since been removed, have been effected?

Not only have the river vallies been excavated to a very considerable width and depth over the whole region, as has been explained in the section on physical geography, but there is every reason to believe that a comparatively great thickness of rock has been removed over the whole extent of the Lead Region. By referring to what has been said of the position and elevation of the mounds in a preceding chapter, and to the next succeeding one, on stratigraphical geology, it will be seen that there is the strongest reason to assume that the Niagara limestone once extended in a nearly continuous mass over the larger portion of the districts south of the Wisconsin river, and east to some distance beyond the Blue Mounds. The same is the case with the Hudson-River group, of which so few traces remain except under the harder limestone, which caps the mounds, and has protected the softer underlying materials. Of these two groups, at the very least, an average thickness of from 200 to 250 feet must have disappeared, over a surface of several thousand square miles; besides, as it is only over a small portion of the district that the whole thickness of the Galena limestone has been preserved, and as the denudation has often gone so far as to remove the whole of this rock, and a portion of the underlying Blue limestone, even on the more elevated portions of the region, it is thought that the total average diminution of the thickness of the strata caused by some denuding or eroding agency can hardly be less, over the whole area south of the Wisconsin river, than from 350 to 400 feet of vertical thickness. If, as we have already seen, the region in question has never been submerged, then this vast mass of matter can only have been removed by the natural drainage: that is to say, it must have been carried off in solution, by the rain falling on the surface and flowing off charged with the soluble substances contained in the rocks, while the insoluble must have remained behind, and gradually accumulated, so far as force was wanting in the river currents to carry them away mechanically.

Almost the whole mass of strata thus removed by percolation, as it would perhaps be most proper to call it, consists of calcareous and calcareo-magnesian rocks; in the whole thickness of 350 feet estimated above to have been denuded, at least 300 must have consisted of dolomite or limestone, and not over 50 feet of silicious rock—chiefly shales, somewhat calcareous, and extremely liable to decomposition or disintegration. As all the rivers of the Northwest are known to hold a large quantity of lime and magnesia in solution, it will not be difficult to comprehend that, although the process may be slow, yet, if time be allowed, any amount of material may thus be carried off, chiefly in the form of the bicarbonate of lime and of magnesia. The quantity of material mechanically displaced by the river currents must be quite small, since the surface of the country is of such a form that it is only in the immediate vicinity of the river vallies that there can be any considerable mechanical action. The larger portion of rain falling percolates through the solid rock, and finds its way out at a lower level, clear: that is, free from mechanically suspended sediment; but hard, or, in other words, charged with lime and magnesia.

The great mass of superficial clay, loam, and other loose materials lying on the solid rock in this region is therefore simply the residuum left after the more or less complete solution and removal of the soluble portion of the rock. We have learned from numerous analyses of the various rocks which occur in the Lead Region, that the Galena and the Niagara limestones contain, in addition to the carbonates of lime and magnesia, from two to ten per cent of insoluble matter, and one or two per cent of carbonate of the protoxide of iron. The insoluble matter is chiefly clay and sand, the former predominating. As the rocks of these groups are acted on by the percolating water, the protoxide of iron is converted into peroxide and remains behind, intermixed with the clay, and is gradually carried downwards, so that the more ferruginous portion accumulates at the bottom. The nodules of flint, also, which are contained in such abundance in some portions of the Galena and Niagara limestones, being exceedingly indestructible, remain behind in the clay, sometimes forming a considerable portion of the mass.

The character of the river vallies, and the geological causes which have influenced their formation, are subjects well worthy of examination in this connection. Referring back to what has been said, in the chapter on topography and physical geography, about the distribution of the vallies, some additional considerations in regard to their origin will be most appropriately introduced at this point, in connection with the phenomena of erosion and denudation.. That there have been no great currents of water sweeping over the Lead Region in one direction, and scooping out the vallies anew, or modifying the form of pre-existing ones, is not only evident from what has been advanced in the preceding pages, but is equally clearly shown by the form and distribution of the vallies themselves.

We have shown, in the Iowa Geological Report, that the drainage of the interior of that State is dependent on or has been determined by two sets of flexures or narrow ridgings of the strata, which are nearly at right angles with each other: one set running northwest and southeast, and the other southwest and northeast. Thus long, and proportionally very narrow, vallies have originated. Thus the Wapsepinicon river has a length of some 250 miles, following its meanderings, while the width of the area drained by it and its tributaries is, for a considerable part of its course, not more than from eight to twelve miles. These systems of foldings of the strata, which may be traced over a great extent of surface on the west of the Mississippi, do not appear to have extended to the eastern side; at least, not to the north of the Illinois line. Within that State, the courses of the Illinois and Rock rivers seem to belong to the northeast and southwest system above referred to. In the Lead Region, as already remarked, the line of water-shed is an exact east and west one, and the drainage, although very irregular, is, in the main, at right angles to this direction. It seems pretty evident that this portion of the surface of the State has been elevated parallel to the great north and south axis which has determined the geological features of the eastern half of the State, while a secondary, or subordinate series of ridges, at right angles to this, has had an important influence in giving its present contour to the Lead Region, as well as in originating the best developed and richest mineral-bearing crevices.

The entire absence of terraces in the river vallies of the district in question is one of its striking features, indicating very clearly that it has not been submerged in recent times. Throughout the northern United States, after the general depression of the country, during which the vast deposits of clays and sands extending over so large a region were formed, when a rise of the land took place again, it was not in one uninterrupted and gradual succession, but by a paroxysmal or oscillatory action, which gave rise to the terraces bordering all the vallies where this depression and elevation occurred. If anything of the kind had ever affected the Lead Region, we should not fail to observe somewhere in the river vallies some evidences of terraces at a level above that reached by the streams flowing through them.

As mentioned above, there is an exceptional occurrence of stratified materials near Galena and Dubuque, which must here be noticed, although so limited is the area covered by these deposits as not to affect the general statements made above. In the valley of Fever river, up to a point about two miles above Galena, we find a deposit of red and yellow clay in very thin layers, with fine gravelly materials intermixed, extending for a very short distance on each side of the river, and rising to a height of 40 to 50 feet above the highest level at present reached by the river at its highest stages. The same kind of beds may be observed up the Catfish valley, near Dubuque, but not by any means so extensive as those near Galena. These clay beds have not been noticed at any other points near the Lead Region. They contain numerous fresh-water shells, of forms now living in the river, such as *Planorbis*, *Lymnea*, *Paludina*, &c., and identical species. It appears that these stratified clays were deposited in a sort of lake formed by the temporary damming up of the rivers near their mouths, by some local cause. The same formation could not have been deposited generally in the Mississippi valley, or it would have been noticed at other points, since it is hardly possible to imagine it entirely swept away if it ever had existed there.

The character and mode of occurrence of the remains of animals and vegetables found in the superficial detritus of the Lead Region may next receive attention, as illustrating the third proposition enunciated above, namely that in reference to the existence of life after the close of the drift epoch.

If, as we have endeavored to prove, the region in question was never under water after the close of the palæozoic period, then of course no organic remains, except those of land animals or plants, could be expected to be found in the superficial detritus. Such is really the case; for, as will be shown, one of the most interesting features of the Lead Region is the great abundance of the bones of land animals of various species, found imbedded in the loose materials which cover the surface.

The occurrence of bones in the crevices with the lead ore, as well as in the clay and sand on and near the surface, has been repeatedly noticed by those who have been engaged in investigating the geology of the Lead Region. The remains of the mastodon, that giant among animals, have been found in very numerous localities, and, from their great size and abundance, have attracted more attention than any others. The elephant, formerly as widely, although perhaps not as abundantly, distributed over the territory of the United States, was also once a resident of the Lead Region; but the bones of this animal are found much less frequently than those of the mastodon, and never in the crevices, so far as I have been able to ascertain.

Ever since the first settlement of the western country, the finding of new localities of bones of the mastodon and elephant has been a matter of common occurrence. The famous Big Bone Lick in Kentucky, according to J. W. Foster,* was noticed as early as 1744, and at this place portions of the skeletons of at least a hundred mastodons have been found, besides very many remains of the elephant, buffalo (or bison), and other large animals. In Ohio, Illinois, Iowa, and Missouri, as well as in the eastern States, portions of skeletons of the same animals have been dug up from time to time, in such numbers as to indicate conclusively that they were once as abundant over the whole of the northern United States as the buffaloes now are on the great plains at the base of the Rocky Mountains.

The exact geological period during which these animals flourished on our continent has been a matter of considerable discussion. That they belong to the post-tertiary epoch is of course admitted by all, but whether they began to exist before the close of the drift period—that is to say, whether of alluvial or diluvial age; or, in other words, whether belonging to the past or the present epoch in geological history—has remained a matter of some doubt. It seems, however, at present, that the weight of evidence is strongly in favor of the mastodon not having appeared until after the close of the northern drift period. No instance has ever been observed in this country where the remains of this animal were found in the drift proper: they have always been obtained from the peat bogs, swamps, and morasses on the surface of the drift, or in the modified or valley drift, or in some analogous position. Indeed, it would seem *a priori* that no portion of the northern hemisphere could have been inhabited by living beings during the drift period, except under exceptional circumstances, and in limited areas.

In general, the elephant and the mastodon have been found throughout the northern States under the same circumstances, indicating that they made their appearance contemporaneously, and lived through the same period of time. In Ohio, however, according to Mr. Foster, the

* Proceedings of the American Association, Albany meeting (1856), p. 161.

remains of the elephant have been found in the vicinity of Zanesville, in the coarse "valley drift," under such circumstances as to indicate that this animal must have been living while a portion at least of the detrital covering of the northern hemisphere was being transported towards the south. Mr. Foster concludes from his examination that the mastodon did not appear until after the elephant, as there is no instance on record of his bones having been observed in a position implying such antiquity as that mentioned as belonging to the environs of Zanesville. The exact age of the "valley drift," or rather its relations to the great drift period, however, are among the mooted points of geology; but it seems as if the discovery of elephant bones in it, taken in connection with all the other facts observed in reference to their position, was sufficient proof that these accumulations of detritus were intermediate between the drift period and the alluvial. The facts reported by Mr. Foster are sufficient to show, at all events, that the elephant lived through a period of great length, and one in which considerable changes were made in the form of the surface and the arrangement of the superficial detritus upon it. It is clear, also, that the transportation of boulders continued to be effected after the appearance of the elephant and the mastodon, although there could not have been an entire submergence of any very extensive area at any one time.

As the elephant and mastodon, with the other large animals accompanying them, belong to the post-tertiary epoch, and as the Fauna of the driftless region of the Northwest is of this character, it is evident that, although this portion of the United States remained dry land during an immense period of time, yet it was not peopled by living land animals or plants until after the whole of the adjacent territory, which had been submerged during the drift epoch, was again elevated from the water, and had itself become the abode of the gigantic proboscidians. At least, we have no evidence from organic remains of any other Fauna than that of the post-tertiary period ever having existed in that region: nor is it probable, although possible, that if anything living had existed there in previous geological epochs, some evidence of this fact would not have been detected before this time. It will be a legitimate conclusion, therefore, that the conditions prevailing during the long period of time between the Palæozoic and the Post-tertiary were unfavorable to the development of organic life.

Let us now examine more minutely what were the different animals living during the mastodon period, and what the exact conditions under which their remains have been found in the Lead Region.

The most abundant relics of the ancient Fauna of this district are those of the mastodon, the *Mastodon giganteum* of Cuvier. Of this animal, fragments of bones and more or less perfect teeth have, as appears from my notes, been found in more than twenty different localities within or near the limits of the Lead Region. Of course, but a portion of those which have been discovered have ever come to my knowledge, and when one considers how small a proportion of the surface of the district has been dug over, and in how many instances fragments of bones are thrown out by the miners and left to decay without having been noticed — or, if noticed, not recorded—we are safe in placing the actual number of individuals which were embedded beneath the surface under circumstances favorable to preservation as very great, even within the limited area of the lead district. But, of the animals which inhabited the country, and died there, how few, comparatively, could have been so protected by a covering of suitable material, before decay or destruction, as that they should be preserved down to our time! The inference is unavoidable that the region in question must have been most thickly inhabited by these animals, and that they must have roamed over it during a period of immense length.

Owing to their greater durability under exposure, the teeth are the portions of the animal which have been most perfectly preserved: they are found in all stages of decay, from those which are hardly to be distinguished from the tooth of the still living animal, down to a crumbly, incoherent mass, which falls to pieces and is destroyed soon after being exposed to the air.

Among the most interesting remains of the mastodon observed was a set of the three first deciduous molars, or milk-teeth, of the same individual, found at the Blue Mounds: these were in an exquisitely perfect state of preservation, and not at all discolored. The largest quantity of bones of the mastodon found in one locality seems to have occurred near Sinsinnewa Mound, but I have no exact particulars of the depth or position. Some of them were preserved at the locality for several years; others, to the amount of several bushels, were carried off and lost or destroyed. The localities where such bones and teeth have been found are scattered all over the Lead Region, and not confined to any particular part of it.

The elephant would appear to have been by no means so abundant in the Lead Region and its neighborhood as the mastodon. It has never happened, within my knowledge, that its bones have been found in the crevices, as so many of those of the mastodon have been. The only elephant remains which I have seen myself from the district in question are some teeth and bones in the collection of I. G. Potts, Esq., of Galena. One of the teeth was found near the surface, and not far above the river, within the limits of the city of Galena. This fact, as far as it goes, would indicate that the elephant was more recent than the mastodon in this region.

Perhaps the peccary, or Mexican hog, was more abundant during the epoch of the mastodon than any other animal: certainly, its remains have been found in a larger number of localities than those of any other animal, unless the mastodon itself be excepted. The individuals found in this region, which were formerly referred to several different genera by the naturalists who had examined them, are now all considered as belonging to one genus, *Dicotyles*, and to a single species, to which the name of *compressus* has been given. This is an extinct species. The common peccary, or Mexican hog, is now found, according to Baird, in Mexico and Texas, and as far north as the Red river of Arkansas, in latitude 34°. Its western limit, according to the same authority,* is not well ascertained, although it is said by some to occur in California. The species still living in the United States is called *Dicotyles torquatus*, the chief difference between this and the extinct species once so abundant in the Lead Region being, according to Leidy, in the form of the skull.†

The extinct peccary of the Northwest was first described by Dr. J. L. Le Conte, in 1847, from specimens obtained near Galena: these were bones and teeth found in the lead crevices worked in that vicinity, but of the exact circumstances of their occurrence I am not informed. It is stated, however, that the bones in question were found at a depth of 50 feet below the surface, in a mixture of clay and sand cemented by oxide of iron.‡ These were referred by Dr. Le Conte to several distinct genera, but they have since all been recognized as being one and the same species.

Dr. Leidy, some years later, also obtained a large number

* Report of the Pacific Railroad Surveys, vol. viii, p. 627.

† Dr. Leidy remarks as follows, in his description of the extinct Peccary of North America (Transactions Am. Philos. Soc., xi. 19): "The extinct *Dicotyles compressus* was a little larger than the existing *D. labiatus*, and its other more important differences from this and the more common species, *D. torquatus*, chiefly observable in the skull, are as follows. The face is more prolonged and narrower, the upper outline of the head is less inclined from the horizon, the forehead is much broader, the cheeks deeper, the orbits have a more supero-posterior position, the sides of the ixion are less oblique, the technical angle of the lower jaw is strongly everted, and the symphysis is narrow and keeled; the incisor teeth are smaller, and the principal lobes of the molar teeth possess a greater proportionate degree of development."

‡ See Abstract of Proceedings of American Association of Geologists and Naturalists, in Silliman's Journal, (2) v. 102.

of specimens of the peccary, through his own investigations and those of Dr. Kittoe of Galena, from the crevices of that vicinity. These are described by him in vol. xi of the Transactions of the American Philosophical Society.*

In the same crevice in which the bones and teeth of the mastodon were found at the Blue Mounds, as noticed above, several fragments of jaws and some teeth, with a variety of other bones of the peccary, were obtained by me in 1856. These remains were in an excellent state of preservation. A number of teeth and bones of the same animal were excavated by Mr. C. Childs and myself from a crevice near Dubuque, on the Mississippi, a few rods below Lorimiai furnace.

As the bones of this animal are small, compared with those of the mastodon, they do not excite so much attention among the miners, and, naturally enough, it may be inferred that they are generally overlooked: yet the great number of individuals which have been already met with in the Lead Region would indicate that the animal must have been very abundantly diffused over its surface.

The remains of the extinct peccary have also been found near Burlington in Iowa, in Benton county, Missouri, and also in Virginia.

The remains of the mastodon and peccary seem to have been more abundantly preserved in the lead crevices than those of any other animals, and these are the only extinct species which are proved to have been very common in that region during what may perhaps be called the *mastodon period.* A considerable number of other animals have been found at different times in connection with the mastodon, &c.; and although some of these may belong to extinct species, there is reason to believe that most of them are identical with such as are now living in the Northwest, so that it may

* Since the above was written, specimens of teeth obtained by me from a crevice near Dubuque have been examined by Wyman, and referred to the living species of peccary: these teeth were associated with those of the megalonyx, and found at a depth of about 10 feet below the surface, in a flat crevice in the Galena limestone, embedded in clay.

be safely inferred that the mastodon and elephant formed part of the actual epoch, and that their disappearance did not take place until after the Fauna of the region was mainly that which it now is. Thus, although there is as yet no evidence of the coexistence of the mastodon and man, yet it is not impossible that such may be found, or that human remains may be found in the lead crevices, exactly as those of the large proboscidians have been.

Among the animals found associated with the mastodon and the peccary, the following have been mentioned at different times:

Dr. Le Conte speaks of an extinct species of raccoon (*Procyon*), which he calls by the specific name of *priscus*, of which several teeth and phalanges were found near Galena. The same author has described* a single tooth from the same district, which he considered to have belonged to a large insectivorous animal allied to *Scalops* (the mole family), and to which he has given the generic name of *Anamodon*.

Dr. Leidy found among the specimens brought him by some miners from a deserted lead crevice, in connection with the peccary, a few fragments of bones and numerous incisor and molar teeth of four species of rodents, of which he remarks as follows: "these latter may, on subsequent investigation, prove to be extinct species, but the remains are not distinguishable in anatomical character from the corresponding parts of the recent *Arctomys monax* (woodchuck), *Pseudostoma bursarius* (gopher), *Lepus sylvaticus* (hare), and *Arvicola* (field mouse)."

In the very interesting crevice explored by me at the Blue Mounds, already referred to as containing the mastodon and peccary, bones and teeth of the buffalo (*Bos Americanus*) and the wolf (? *Canis latrans*) were also found, in such connection as to show almost beyond the possibility of doubt that these various species must have lived at the same time.

* Silliman's American Journal, (2) v. 106.

The exact depth at which the bones were obtained could not be ascertained, but it may have been about 40 feet; they were embedded in reddish clayey loam, the usual crevice dirt, and some galena was found in the same association.

All the bones and teeth which have been obtained by me since my first explorations in the Lead Region have been placed in Dr. Jeffries Wyman's hands for description: his remarks on them are intended as a supplement to this Report.

We have already, in the preceding pages, fully set forth the fact of the absence of boulders or transported materials over almost the entire area of the Lead Region. A single exceptional case has, however, been noticed, which is of great interest, and in regard to which it is difficult to offer a satisfactory explanation. The locality to which we here refer is one near Mineral Point, a little to the southwest of the Dreadnaught diggings. Here, between two small affluents of the Legate branch, on a ridge of the Galena limestone, and at an elevation of about 125 feet above the sandstone, which is exposed at the base of the bluff or ridge something over a quarter of a mile distant to the west, is a group of loose blocks of sandstone, a phenomenon entirely without a parallel in the Lead Region This group is represented in the annexed wood-cut (fig. 5): the principal central mass of sandstone (*a* on the figure) is five feet long and two and one-half broad, and is buried in the ground even with its upper surface; an excavation for ore at one end enables us to see that it is at least four feet deep in the ground: *b* is also sunk deep in the ground, and is four feet in length; *a* and *b* lie nearly in an east and west line with each other. The remaining fragments are scattered on the

Fig. 5.—Group of Sandstone Blocks near Mineral Point.

surface, or partly buried in the soil: they are all angular, or not at all rounded on the edges, and are exactly similar in character to the sandstone lying below the Blue limestone, which is the uppermost layer of silicious material in the Mississippi valley until we reach the coal-measures, which do not occur within a hundred miles of this place.

There can be no doubt that these masses of sandstone have been raised, either artificially or by natural means, 125 feet above their original place of deposit: a circumstance which would be of easy explanation, if the drift had ever swept over this region; but as this is not the case, as has been already shown, the solution of the problem of their transportation is much less simple. The most natural supposition would be that there was a silicious layer in the Galena limestone, from the breaking up of which these fragments were derived. This, however, seems improbable, as I have never observed anywhere an instance of a sandstone bed intercalated in the Blue limestone, or in any of the groups above.

The only natural agents capable of effecting these changes of position of large fragments of rock are either currents of water, or floating ice masses. But to apply either of these causes in this case, it would be necessary to make the phenomenon a strictly local one, since there is nowhere else in the region any evidence of either currents or transportation by ice. It is not impossible that, ice having been formed in the bottom of the valley, a damming up of the outlet may have taken place, so as to raise the stream, form a temporary lake, and thus float sheets of ice, having masses of sandstone attached to them, up to the present level at which they are deposited, where they would be left when the barrier gave way, and the water was drained off. Since there is but little in the shape of the ground, as at present situated, to favor this idea, inasmuch as the neighboring valley is in no respect differently formed from any other one in the neighborhood, this is only suggested as a possible explanation.

One might be tempted, perhaps, to refer the presence of these masses of sandstone to human agencies; and that they were placed there by the hand of man is, of course, not impossible, since the weight of the largest is by no means so great as to forbid such a supposition. But although we might see a reason for a preference given to sandstone over limestone for building purposes—inasmuch as it would be so much more easily quarried by a race destitute of steel or iron tools, and as loose blocks of it might easily be got from the base of the cliffs with a little aid from wedges and levers—yet the whole history of discovery respecting the former inhabitants of this region affords little to warrant one in believing that they ever built anything of stone.

CHAPTER IV.

STRATIGRAPHICAL GEOLOGY.

Potsdam Sandstone—Lower Magnesian Limestone—Upper or St. Peters Sandstone—Buff Limestone—Blue Limestone—Galena Limestone—Hudson River Group—Niagara Limestone.

In this chapter it is proposed to discuss briefly the character of the different rock formations which come to the surface in and near the Lead Region, and to give such facts in regard to their lithological character, chemical composition, thickness, and geographical distribution as may be necessary for understanding the relations of the rocky masses to each other, and more especially to the useful minerals and ores of which they are the repositories. For this purpose, the rocks of the region in question will be taken up consecutively, in chronological order, beginning with the lowest, or first deposited group of strata, and ascending to the highest. The reader is farther referred to the section of the rocks exposed in and near the Lead Region for a concise view of some of the principal facts in relation to the groups of strata developed in this portion of the State.

POTSDAM, OR LOWER SANDSTONE.

Throughout the whole Northwest, the lowest sedimentary fossiliferous rock which is recognized by geologists is a sandstone, which is usually, and conveniently, called the Lower sandstone, to distinguish it from another, but thinner mass of sandstone, which lies above it, and which is separated from it by the Lower Magnesian limestone. The Lower sandstone occupies the same position as the Potsdam sandstone of the New York Geological Survey, and is the exact equivalent of it. As developed in the Northwest, and especially in the State of Wisconsin, where it occupies a large extent of surface, it is made up of an almost chemically pure silicious sand, in minute grains, hardly larger than a pin's head, which are held together by the minutest possible quantity of a calcareous or ferruginous cement. Frequently even this small quantity of cementing material is wanting, so that the rock can be readily crumbled between the fingers, like a crystalline, granular sugar. Where the ferruginous material, which is the peroxide of iron, becomes more abundant, so as to form two or three percent of the mass, the sandstone acquires a dark brown color, and frequently affords a solid and durable building stone.

The Lower sandstone forms a continuous series, extending from the State of New York through Canada, and along the south shore of Lake Superior, as far as Chocolate river, where it divides into two branches, enclosing between them the great central mass of azoic, or non-fossiliferous rocks, which forms the northern half of Wisconsin. The northern division of the sandstone extends along the south shore of the lake, and, becoming associated with rocks of igneous origin, has its thickness greatly increased, and its lithological character materially changed. In the vicinity of the trappean rocks, the whole series of sandstones and associated beds of conglomerate acquires a development of several thousand feet, some single masses of the latter rock being not less than 2000 feet thick. On receding, however, from the trap, in either direction, we soon find the beds of conglomerate thinning out and disappearing, and the sandstone loses its firm texture and dark ferruginous color, its dip gradually becoming less in amount, showing that these abnormal conditions were due to the peculiar circumstances under which the deposition of the sedimentary rock took place, owing to the vicinity of a line of intense volcanic or igneous action.

In the undisturbed districts of central Wisconsin, the Lower sandstone has a thickness probably not much exceeding three or four hundred feet; but we have no data for an exact determination of this element. The material of which it is composed was undoubtedly accumulated on an irregular floor of azoic rocks, filling pre-existing depressions; hence its thickness would be likely to vary considerably at different points not very distant from each other. Besides, the passage of the sandstone into the overlying dolomite, or magnesian limestone, takes place through a series of alternating beds of dolomitic and silicious material, or of the two mixed together in varying proportions, so that it is not easy to say where one group begins and the other ends.

The Lower sandstone occupies a vast extent of surface in central and northwestern Wisconsin, forming a wide belt, which completely encircles the great central nucleus of azoic rocks. It is finely exhibited along a large portion of the course of the Wisconsin river, which, for sixty or seventy miles before uniting with the Mississippi, flows through a wide valley, enclosed between bluffs of this rock, which are from two to three hundred feet in height.

The annexed sketch (fig. 6) will serve to show the irregular mode in which this sandstone weathers, and the curious conical and mound-like forms which it occasionally assumes. It represents a view looking up the valley of the Wisconsin river, from a point above, and not far distant from, Helena.

FIG. 6.—Outcrop of Lower Sandstone near Helena.

Within the limits of the Lead Region proper, the Lower sandstone nowhere comes to the surface; but on the north side of the water-shed, in the vallies of the streams running down into the Wisconsin, it soon makes its appearance after we begin to descend them. At Prairie du Chien the top of this sandstone lies pretty nearly on a level with the Mississippi river. On the opposite side of the river, at M'Gregor, it shows itself in a ledge some 30 feet thick; and a short distance farther down the river, nearly opposite the mouth of the Wisconsin, it sinks below the level of the water, and is seen no more. Ascending the Wisconsin river from Prairie du Chien, we soon find this sandstone emerging from beneath the level of the water, and rapidly rising as the river changes its course, from a west-southwest to a directly westerly course.

There is no doubt that the Lower sandstone underlies the whole Lead Region, and that, if borings were executed, this rock would everywhere be reached after passing through from 200 to 250 feet of the Lower Magnesian limestone which lies above it. Probably, if the borings were continued 400 or 500 feet below the top of the sandstone, the older crystalline rocks would be reached.

This sandstone shows itself everywhere exceedingly deficient in minerals and metalliferous ores, except in the Lake Superior region, where, as has been already noticed, its whole character has been changed by the presence of rocks of igneous origin. There it is traversed by well-developed veins of calc. spar, which bear ores of copper as well as the native metal; but they are not productive except in the trappean rocks, no working ever having been profitably carried on for any length of time in the sandstone or conglomerate. The occurrence of stains of carbonate of copper in this sandstone is not uncommon, even at a great distance from the trap; but I have never observed in it anything like a regular vein of any kind of ore. Masses of peroxide of iron of considerable size are occasionally seen in the formation, but never in sufficient quantity to be of economical value.

Farther remarks on the mineral contents of this sandstone will be found in another portion of the Report, where the subject of deep mining is discussed. The details of its fossiliferous contents and local peculiarities will be furnished in the Report upon these branches of the survey.

LOWER MAGNESIAN LIMESTONE.

This is the next great natural division or group of strata to the Lower sandstone throughout the Northwest, and it is extensively developed, and covers a large area, in Wisconsin. It is the geological equivalent of the Calciferous sandstone of the New York Geological Reports, although this name cannot with propriety be applied to it in the West, since it is almost entirely made up, everywhere in the valley of the Mississippi, of an almost chemically pure dolomite, or a mixture of carbonate of lime and carbonate of magnesia, in the proportion of one atom or equivalent of each. Some beds, however, near the bottom of the mass, are made up of a mixture of sand and dolomitic material, and to these the name of calciferous, or rather dolomitic, sandstone might properly be given. Thus, a specimen with an oolitic structure from near Prairie du Chien, and at the base of the formation, was found on examination to contain nearly equal quantities of silicious sand and dolomite. Another specimen of the rock from the quarries at the same place, and a fair sample of the valuable building-stone obtained there, was found to have the following composition:*

Silicious sand	14.26
Carbonate of iron and a trace of peroxide of iron	.67
Carbonate of lime	46.98
Carbonate of magnesia	37.55
Traces of chlorine, sulphuric acid, soda, &c., and loss	.54
	100.00

*Quoted from Iowa Report, vol. I, p. 334.

Other specimens from the same region proved, on examination, to contain less than one percent of silica or sand: one from M'Gregor gave only one and one-half percent of substances other than the double carbonate of lime and magnesia.

The lithological character of the Lower Magnesian limestone is somewhat variable in different portions of the mass. In its normal development, however, it is made up of rather heavy-bedded and irregular layers of a light greyish-yellow or greyish-white rock, finely crystalline or compact in its texture, brittle, breaking with an irregular and rather shelly fracture, and usually resisting well the action of the weather. The different layers of rock do not, however, maintain exactly the same structure and appearance over any very considerable extent of surface.

Near the junction of this formation with the underlying sandstone, the beds of rock present an admixture and alternation of dolomitic and silicious materials, showing a gradual passage of one group into the other. The annexed section, taken at the first railroad bridge across the Wisconsin above Prairie du Chien, where the lower beds of the Lower Magnesian are well exposed, will illustrate this remark:

	Feet.
Light-yellow porous dolomite, with obscure traces of fossils	3½
Dolomite, growing more compact and quite arenaceous,	4
Dolomite, thin-bedded and arenaceous	5
Dolomitic sandstone, a nearly equal mixture of dolomite and silicious sand	5
Dolomite, regularly stratified, &c.; good building stone, and quarried extensively	7
Dolomite, irregularly bedded, in layers from seven to eight inches in thickness	4–5
Slope to the Wisconsin river, made up of sandy dolomitic beds, not regularly bedded, partly covered by detritus, about	60

On the Iowa side of the Mississippi, the Lower Magnesian is well exposed, in the vicinity of Prairie du Chien, and especially up the valley of the Upper Iowa river. On Bear creek, a branch of this stream, there is a thickness of 198 feet of dolomitic beds to be observed, in an almost perpendicular cliff, and 30 feet of beds of passage into the sandstone below, which may with as much propriety be referred to one formation as the other. It is often quite difficult to distinguish by the eye, unaided by chemical examination, the purely dolomitic beds from those which are quite arenaceous. Some of the layers which have a sharp gritty feel, and all the external appearance of a very sandy limestone, consist in reality of almost pure dolomite, being made up of an aggregation of minute rounded crystals, or crystalline grains, of that material, with no more than two or three percent of sand intermixed.

The almost entire absence of argillaceous matter in the Lower sandstone and Lower Magnesian limestone is a very striking fact connected with the origin of those rocks. Hardly a trace of clayey material found its way into the ocean from which they were being deposited. It is not until we rise considerably higher in the geological series that, in this region at least, we find argillaceous deposits intermixed with the silicious or calcareo-magnesian.

At Prairie du Chien, in the bluffs which are so finely exposed and form such a picturesque back-ground to the city, we have a very complete section of the whole or nearly the whole thickness of the Lower Magnesian, together with the Upper sandstone, which itself is capped by the Blue limestone; the whole thickness exposed in a nearly perpendicular bluff is 321 feet, of which the lower 221 belong to the Lower Magnesian, the 82 next above to the Upper sandstone, and 18 at the top of the bluff to the Buff limestone, or base of the Blue or Trenton limestone. Above this, the ground slopes gradually upwards for the height of 50 feet or more, and is occupied by the thin-bedded fossiliferous beds of the Blue limestone. The details of the section are as follows:

	Feet
Grassed surface, covering blue, thin-bedded, highly fossiliferous layers of limestone, gradually sloping upwards: nearly the whole thickness of the Blue limestone is still remaining: thickness about	50
Buff limestone; a heavy-bedded, somewhat impure, and slightly argillaceous dolomite	18
Upper sandstone	82
Hard, crystalline, white dolomite, the upper portion graduating into sandstone, and containing layers of pure silicious materials	51
Greyish dolomite, growing less arenaceous	24
Very cherty and irregular layers of dolomite	15
Irregularly bedded, white dolomite, with cherty layers and occasional concretionary structure; a few faint traces of *Orthocerata*	26
Dolomite, hard and crystalline, stratification very irregular and indistinct, occasional layers of flints	65
Not exposed	5
Dolomite, color light greyish-yellow, in heavy but tolerably regular layers, quarried as a building stone	21
Arenaceous dolomite, in regular and handsome layers, color light straw-yellow, extensively quarried for building, a handsome and durable material, (see above, for an analysis)	14½
Entire thickness exposed, to the bottom of the bluff, which is about 60 feet above the Mississippi river	371

The base of the bluff is probably near the bottom of the Lower Magnesian limestone, as the change of the character of the rock from a pure dolomite into a more silicious one indicates. The different members of the series, as developed at this point, have, therefore, the following thicknesses:

	Feet.
Blue limestone	50
Buff limestone	18
Upper sandstone	82
Lower Magnesian	221—250

The lower portion of the Lower Magnesian is frequently rather thinly bedded; but the strata in this position are usually the only ones which can conveniently be used for building purposes, as the central and upper beds are too irregularly stratified, and too much mingled with nodules of chert, to be easily split and dressed into a handsome form. The central portion of the formation is characterized by an abundance of these flinty masses, which are disposed in irregular layers a few inches in thickness. Where the flint is abundant, the rock is usually hard, white, brittle, and very irregularly bedded, the original lines of deposition being almost entirely obliterated. The layers of silicious material vary considerably in texture and appearance. They sometimes take the form of cellular quartz, the cavities being small and irregular, and often lined with minute crystals of the same material, a fact which I have never observed in the lead-bearing dolomite, or Galena limestone, as it is now called.

While the lines of stratification are often nearly obliterated, as noticed above, there is another peculiarity which distinguishes the Lower Magnesian from the Galena limestone, which is, the concretionary and brecciated structure which it often displays, especially in the upper portion of the group. Where this condition of things is manifest, the layers appear as if they had been subjected both to chemical and mechanical disturbances while being deposited, or shortly after their formation. At several localities where lead ore has been obtained in some quantity from the rock, this peculiar disturbed condition of the strata has been noticed as existing in a very marked degree.

The evidences of the existence of organic life during the deposition of the Lower Magnesian are but faint: still, fossils do exist in this rock, although in a very imperfect condition; their structure having been almost obliterated by the rearrangement of the particles of the rock in which they were embedded, subsequent to its deposition. At several localities, however, distinct traces of *Orthocerata* have been noticed, projecting from the weathered surface of the rock; these are quite frequent in the vicinity of Cross Plains and Mazomanie, and in that region, south towards the Blue Mounds. A few specimens of what appeared to be *Euomphalus* were also observed in the same vicinity. A single very fine and large specimen of the *Dikelocephalus*, a trilobite described by Dr. D. D. Owen from the Lower sandstone, was dug up in Madison, near the capitol, and about three feet below the surface, in a loose angular fragment of rock, which closely resembles in lithological character that of some of the beds near the junction of the Lower sandstone and the Lower Magnesian.

Within the limits of the Lead Region, the Lower Magnesian limestone is frequently exposed in the vallies of the streams; but nowhere south and east of Prairie du Chien does it rise high enough to permit its whole thickness to be observed. As we ascend the Wisconsin river from its mouth, we find the Lower sandstone soon emerging from beneath the water, and gradually rising higher in the bluffs which border the valley, until their whole height is occupied by this rock, which continues to be the case for a long distance up the river. Following the Milwaukee and Mississippi railroad, however, as it leaves the Wisconsin and ascends Blackearth creek, the sandstone begins to fall again, and at Mazomanie we have a thickness of 50 to 75 feet of the Lower Magnesian on the bluffs in the vicinity. Ascending any of the streams which flow into the Wisconsin from the south, we soon come upon the Lower Magnesian, and rise above it to the succeeding higher formations, with the gradual but rapid rise of the country to the south. Following the same course, and descending the rivers on the south side of the water-shed, we find this rock exposed at different points in the vallies of almost all the principal streams flowing south, brought to the surface by the undulations of the strata, combined with the deep cutting down of the river vallies beneath the general level of the country. The head-waters of Grant river show the Lower Magnesian, from the centre of Beetown township nearly up to their sources. On the Platte river it is exposed from about the centre of Liberty and Clifton townships down as far south as opposite Potosi. At Ellenboro it forms a cliff 50 feet high, and there is a thickness of at least 100 feet above the level of the river at that point. It is not brought up on either the Little Platte or Fever rivers. On the Legate branch of the Peccatonica, near Mineral Point, it forms a low cliff, rising to the height of about 30 feet above the river, and extending for from one-third to one-half a mile, while around it the sandstone forms a low arch, as represented in the annexed figure (fig. 7):

FIG. 7.—Outcrop of Lower Magnesian on Legate Branch.

(a) Sandstone.
(b) Level of the Legate Branch.

The Lower Magnesian is nowhere else exposed on the main branch of the Peccatonica; but it comes to the surface in several places on the East fork of that river. At Moscow, sixteen miles east of Mineral Point, and for some distance up and down the branch on which that town is situated, this rock is elevated from 35 to 40 feet above the level of the river. It sinks beneath the river again a few miles below Moscow, but re-appears in a low swell at Argyle, on Dougherty branch, about one-half mile southeast of the town, where it forms an elevation of about 20 feet above the stream, but cannot be traced to any considerable distance in either direction. It also emerges again, and for the last time in this region, on the Peccatonica, south of Wyota, on the road from Wyota to Winslow, rising only a few feet above the river.

On Sugar river it is exposed at a few points near its headwaters in Primrose township; but I have nowhere observed it in the main valley of the river to the southeast of this. Beyond the line of the branch of Sugar river which heads in Springdale and Cross Plains townships, and flows through

Verona and Montrose, the Lower Magnesian occupies the surface of the country for a great distance to the northeast.

The mineral contents of the Lower Magnesian limestone, and the possibility of the lead mines being extended down into this rock, will be made the subject of careful investigation in another portion of this Report. No other ores than those of lead have been observed in it, and these only in small quantity.

UPPER SANDSTONE.

This formation is one which is very distinctly marked throughout the valley of the Upper Mississippi, wherever this portion of the geological series is exposed; it is the lowest member of the series which occupies any considerable extent of surface in the Lead Region proper, and is everywhere a sort of horizon, from which calculations as to geological position may be conveniently made.

In the Eastern States, and even as far west as Lake Superior, there is no mass of silicious rock in exactly the position of the sandstone in question, which begins to be first recognized as a distinct formation, in coming from the east, to the south of Winnebago Lake, so far as is yet known. It may be observed, however, far up the Mississippi, to the vicinity of St. Paul and St. Anthony: it is also well exposed on the streams of northeastern Iowa, especially the Upper Iowa.

In lithological character the Upper sandstone closely resembles the Lower, or Potsdam; like that rock, it is made up of an almost chemically pure silicious material, in the form of minute rounded grains, held together by the merest trace of a ferruginous or calcareous cement, or indeed by mutual cohesion under pressure, so that the mass may usually be easily moved with shovel and pick, as is everywhere done for the purpose of obtaining sand for mortar. This rock is generally so friable that it is difficult to preserve specimens of it, as the smaller fragments crumble rapidly when handled.

Still, there are portions of the sandstone which, owing to the presence of a little more ferruginous matter than usual, are sufficiently firm to be valuable as a building material. The size of the grains of silica, of which the rock is made up, is wonderfully uniform, and exceedingly minute, varying from the two-hundredth to the four-hundredth of an inch. Although this sandstone is abundantly exposed throughout the Lead Region, I have never yet observed in it a single pebble or grain of any other substance than quartz, the only variation in its character being the more or less considerable coating of ferruginous matter with which the grains of sand are surrounded. When entirely pure, the sandstone is of course white, the single grains being quite transparent and colorless: when contaminated by the presence of iron, the rock assumes a great variety of shades of brownish-yellow and red, according to the quantity and degree of oxidation of the iron. The dark and bright red varieties are made up of grains of quartz in which the oxide of iron exists in chemical combination, diffused equally through the interior of each grain; the dark-brown specimens are shown by examination with the microscope to owe their color to a thin coating of the hydrous peroxide on the exterior of each minute particle of which the mass is made up, and which is the result of infiltration, subsequently to the deposition of the rock.

A remarkable fact in connection with the Upper sandstone is its uniformity of thickness throughout the whole extent of the northwest. Near Fort Snelling, at the mouth of the St. Peters river—which is the farthest point to the north, apparently, where its whole thickness has been observed—it amounts to 92 feet, according to Dr. Shumard: at Prairie du Chien, as already noticed in the section at that place, given under the Lower Magnesian limestone, its thickness is 82 feet: on Grant river, at the crossing of the road from Lancaster to Prairie du Chien, it is 72 feet: in the vicinity of Mineral Point it is about 100 feet, there being no exposure there where its exact thickness can be measured.

The farthest point to the south where the Upper Sandstone has been recognized is at La Salle, Illinois, where it is brought to the surface by a low axis of elevation, and where its development appears to be somewhat greater than it is in Wisconsin; but it does not much exceed one hundred feet. Thus we see that this layer of silicious material was spread over a space at least 400 miles in length, and 100 miles in width, with the most extraordinary equality of thickness, when we consider how thin it is in comparison with the other members of the series of which it forms a part. Its persistence in development is equally remarkable with its wonderful uniformity of lithological character, especially when taken in connection with the everywhere noticeable fact of the abrupt transition from sandstone to dolomite, both above and below, there being no beds of passage either into the Lower Magnesian below, or the Buff rock, also a dolomite, above. Neither have I ever observed a trace of any dolomitic or calcareous bed included within the mass of the Upper sandstone, such as have been noticed in connection with the Lower sandstone. The whole series is of uniform texture and composition throughout. These facts prove conclusively that a universal and abrupt change in the character of the material deposited took place over a great extent of country: that it continued without break or interruption for a certain period, and was then succeeded by another change, equally sudden and general, back into a condition of things closely resembling that which had before prevailed, except in the character of the organic life developed before and after the period of silicious deposition, which we have reason to suppose was very different.

In looking for facts connected with this sandstone, as bearing upon its probable origin, I have sought especially for indications of ripple marks and cross-stratification, as well as for beds of pebbles, or single instances of pebbles, or masses of material other than quartzose. Marks of wave-action, or ripple-marks, as they are commonly called, I have never observed: and those appearances which are usually regarded as evidences of deposition in shallow and shifting currents of water are almost equally wanting. On the Legate branch of the Peccatonica, however, along which this sandstone forms nearly perpendicular bluffs from 50 to 100 feet in elevation, at numerous points, indications of something which appears to be identical with cross-stratification, or discordant stratification, may be observed on a large scale. The annexed wood cut (fig. 8) will show a marked instance:

Fig. 8.—Section on Legate Branch, exhibiting Cross-stratification of the Upper Sandstone.

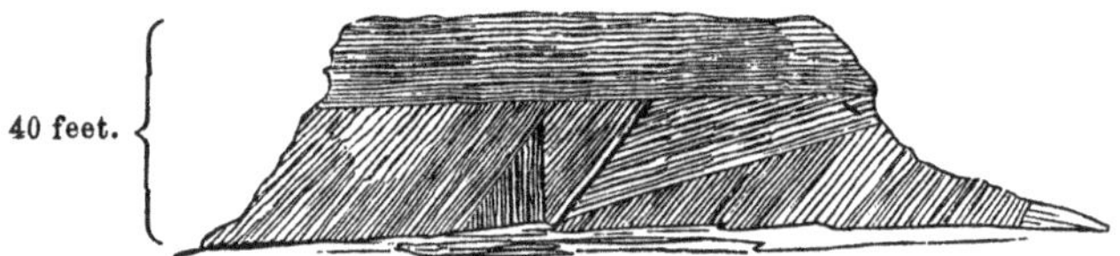

Another point, a mile lower down the river, shows a bluff of sandstone, 70 feet high, of which the whole mass appears to have a dip of about 45°, from the bottom to the top: the lines of stratification, however, are but faintly indicated, although plainly to be seen at those times when the light falls at a favorable angle on the face of the rock (fig. 9).

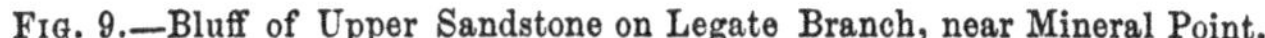

Fig. 9.—Bluff of Upper Sandstone on Legate Branch, near Mineral Point.

It is difficult to find a plausible solution of the question how this fragment of the sandstone, connected as it is on both sides with masses of the same rock horizontally stratified, could have acquired its present position. Some farther remarks on this point, as well as on the source of the materials of which this sandstone is composed, and the mode of its distribution, will be found in the latter portion of this chapter, in which the variation in the physical conditions prevailing during the deposition of the successive members of the geological series in the Lead Region will be discussed.

No trace of anything like an organic form, either vegetable or animal, has, so far as I know, ever been discovered in the Upper sandstone: and this is the only division of the series of which this can be said, since neither the Lower sandstone, nor the Lower Magnesian, are entirely destitute of fossils, although traces of life in these groups are, except in a few circumscribed localities, very rarely to be met with.

The distribution of the Upper sandstone in the Lead Region will be best made out from the general geological map, where this formation is represented by a bright yellow color. It will be seen that there is hardly a stream of any magnitude north of the Wisconsin line which does not, in some portion of its course, cut down to this rock. It usually forms quite precipitous bluffs along the streams, and is rarely found to extend back from them to any considerable distance, with gradually sloping surface, like the Blue limestone which lies above it. This is due to the fact that the sandstone, although yielding so readily to mechanical causes of disintegration, is almost entirely proof against chemical ones, being absolutely insoluble in water. Large blocks may be split off from the parent mass by the action of frost, but this tends to leave a highly inclined face to the outcrop, while the quantity of material thus removed is but a trifle as compared with that which is carried away in solution from the calcareous and dolomitic masses, by the quiet but ceaseless action of water. We have repeatedly noticed instances where water running over beds of sandstone had lent additional hardness to it, by causing this rock to become permeated with calcareous matter, so as to form a smooth, hard, and very enduring calcareo-silicious crust upon its surface, over which currents might glide for ages without removing any sensible amount of material.

In some of the vallies leading down from the water-shed towards the north, the sandstone exhibits itself in picturesque outliers, and curiously worn forms, which present many attractive scenes for the artist's pencil. One of these curious isolated eminences, which seems to have escaped the denuding forces which have worn out the valley, owing to its position in a kind of eddy formed by the meeting of the currents, is represented in the annexed wood cut (fig. 10). It is situated in Dark Hollow, north of Wingville, on the head waters of the Blue river, near the junction of Badger Hollow.

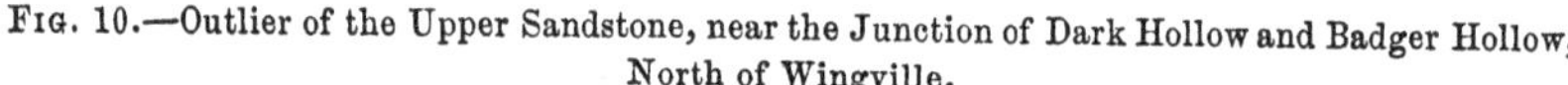

Fig. 10.—Outlier of the Upper Sandstone, near the Junction of Dark Hollow and Badger Hollow, North of Wingville.

Another sketch (fig. 11) will show the irregular manner in which this sandstone weathers in some localities, owing to the different degrees of hardness of the different layers. It is from the immediate vicinity of the outlier represented in the preceding figure.

Fig. 11. Mass of Sandstone in Dark Hollow near Wingville.

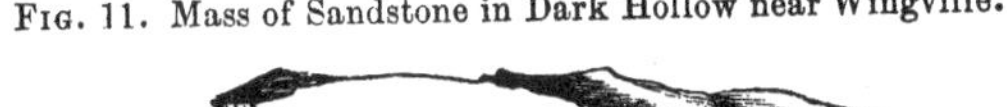

BLUE LIMESTONE.—Buff Limestone.

The beds which lie between two well-marked horizons throughout the Lead Region—namely the top of the Upper sandstone and the bottom of the Upper Magnesian, or the Galena limestone—comprising a vertical series of from 50 to 100 feet, have been heretofore designated, throughout the Northwest, as the "Blue limestone." This term refers, however, especially to the upper two-thirds or three-fourths of the series, in which the difference of color and lithological character, as contrasted with the over and underlying groups, is very marked: while the lower beds, from their thinness, were usually considered as quite subordinate, and thus escaped general notice. In Dr. Owen's Report of 1840, the lower beds here referred to are thus noticed, in describing the geological map which accompanies the work; "the buff stripe, north of the last described rock, represents a narrow belt of buff-colored limestone, of little importance: it was not detected west of the Mississippi." No other reference is made to this member of the series in the Report; but it is designated on the map as the "buff-colored stratum." As this "buff-colored stratum," or "Buff limestone," as it is generally called, constitutes a well-marked member of the series, and is everywhere in the Lead Region easily recognized, as differing both lithologically and palæontologically from the beds above and below, and as it is also of importance in its relations to the mineral interests of the district, it deserves a special and careful notice. It will be convenient to retain, for the present, at least, the term by which it has been hitherto known in the Lead Region, although it cannot be considered as very well chosen; since it is not a limestone, but a dolomite, and its color is not especially different from that of the other dolomites of the district; although, on the whole, it exhibits a greater tendency to a bluish tint than the other magnesian groups.*

Everywhere throughout the Lead Region, when the top of the Upper sandstone is exposed, a series of dolomitic beds will be found overlying it, of which the whole thickness is quite uniform. The same may be observed on the Iowa side of the Mississippi. Near the river, but towards the northwest, the distinction does not seem to be well maintained; although, perhaps, the want of good exposures, and of sufficiently minute observations, may be the reason why this subdivision of the series has not been traced out in that direction.

Beginning, therefore, at the northwest corner of the Lead Region, and referring to the section at Prairie du Chien, it will be seen that the Buff limestone is there well exhibited, having the character of a heavy-bedded, somewhat argillaceous dolomite, with a thickness of eighteen feet. At the crossing of Grant river, on the Lancaster and Prairie du Chien road, there is also a good exposure of this rock: it is of a light yellowish-brown color, mottled with shades of blue; its texture is irregular, as well as its composition, varying from earthy to crystalline in proportion to the amount of

* The same objection may be made to the names "Galena limestone" and "Niagara limestone:" they should properly be "Galena dolomite" and "Niagara dolomite."

argillaceous matter it contains, the different layers being not very homogeneous in composition.

The annexed analysis of the rock at this locality is quoted from the Iowa Geological Report:

Insoluble in acids	22.86
Carbonate of iron	4.56
Carbonate of lime	42.97
Carbonate of magnesia	29.49 (by loss)
Alumina, in soluble portion, with a trace of peroxide of iron	.12
	100.00

The insoluble portion was analyzed by itself, and found to have the following composition:

Silica	63.7
Alumina	14.7
Peroxide of iron	3.5
Potash and soda, with a trace of magnesia	18.1 (by loss)
	100.00

The composition of this residuum is therefore nearly that of orthoclase (common feldspar), a small portion of the alumina being replaced by peroxide of iron.*

Another specimen from Clayton, Iowa, from the same geological position, gave 7.07 per cent of insoluble substances. Both this and the Grant river specimens were found to contain a little excess of carbonate of lime over that required to form dolomite with the carbonate of magnesia present.

A specimen of this rock from Mineral Point had the following composition:

Insoluble in acids, (clay and sand)	15.54
Carbonate of iron	1.01
Peroxide of iron	trace.
Carbonate of lime	45.77
Carbonate of magnesia	37.42
	99.74

* Orthoclase contains: silica 64.8, alumina 18.4, potash 16.8.

In the vicinity of Mineral Point the Buff limestone is well exposed in its whole thickness, and is quarried very extensively, both for building materials and for lime. At a quarry behind the mill near the railroad station the following section of this rock was measured:

	Stratum	Thickness
	Greyish, brittle, highly fossiliferous limestone, in layers from one to three inches thick, with shaly partings......exposed	10 to 12 feet.
	Yellowish-brown dolomite, decomposing irregularly, with blotches of calcareous spar; lines of stratification obscure....	3 feet 2 inches.
Buff limestone—thickness 14 feet 2 in.	Yellowish-brown, argillaceous dolomite...	1 foot 1 inch.
	Mottled brown and buff argillaceous dolomite, somewhat porous, the lower portion rather shaly	2 feet 1 inch.
	Thin band of yellowish shales...........	2 inches.
	Blue dolomite, with buff bands of color along the lines of parting between the beds, splitting into layers 8 or 9 inches thick, the principal quarry stone.......	4 feet.
	Buff and blue layers, but not regularly stratified, and therefore not so valuable as those above, the upper portion more so than the lower	2 feet 3 inches.
	Buff and blue dolomite, in thin rather shaly layers, floor of the quarry, and probably within a few inches of the top of the sandstone..........................	1 foot 5 inches.

Another section, half a mile farther up the Mineral Point branch, at the lime-kiln, shows 21 feet of a heavy-bedded yellowish-brown rock, which when cut into displays a tendency to a thin-bedded structure, and a bluish tinge in the interior layers. The lower three feet, however, are very thinly and irregularly bedded, and contain considerable argillaceous matter, as is usually the case in close proximity to the sandstone. Above the twenty-one feet of Buff rock, there are five feet of very much the same kind of material as that below, but more calcareous: these are the beds which are burned for lime: they seem to be beds of passage into the purely calcareous layers above (see analysis of the rock from this quarry, above).

The larger portion of the rock quarried about Mineral Point, where the Buff limestone is almost exclusively used when stone is required for building material, is of a light greyish-blue color. This is always the color of the interior of the layers, when they are quite thick; but for some distance into the stratum from the thin shale or line of parting which separates two adjacent beds, the blue color is almost always converted into a yellowish brown, or buff, owing to the oxidation of the iron contained in the rock, which takes place wherever air and water can find access—and that is, of course, between the strata. Hence it is evident that the buff color of the rock is only an accidental alteration of its natural bluish tinge.

Some portions of this rock contain a sufficient amount of silicious and argillaceous substances to form good hydraulic lime, if properly burned. No use is yet made of it for this purpose, so far as could be learned; but its use may be recommended. It is also a good building stone, and much used around Mineral Point.

That portion of the Buff limestone which lies near the Mississippi river is not rich in fossils; but, as we go east, we find this member of the series more and more charged with organic remains, and in the vicinity of Mineral Point, and on some of the other branches of the Peccatonica, there are points where some of the layers are replete with a great variety of forms of marine shells, corals, and plants. The shells are chiefly preserved in the form of casts, as seems to be more frequently the case in the dolomitic beds.

The character of these fossils seems to show conclusively that the Buff limestone is the representative of the Chazy, Birdseye, and Black-river limestones of the New York system. The most conspicuous among these are the large *Orthocerata*, which are very abundant in the eastern part of the district, although not occurring as large as in the layers of the Blue limestone proper. *Lituites undatus*, or a species closely resem bling it, seems to be a characteristic fossil of the Buff, as I have not noticed it in any other beds. The specimens observed were about nine inches in diameter. *Maclurea magna* is also a fossil peculiar to this division, so far as observed: also *Columnaria alveolata*, a Black-river fossil, and the only coral observed in the Buff, except of the family of the Cyathophyllideæ, appears to be limited in its range to this member of the series. Casts of several different species of *Murchisonia* and *Pleurotomaria* are frequent in the eastern district: some appear identical with species observed in the Galena limestone, others are different, as will doubtless be fully set forth by Prof. Hall in his part of the Report. The brachiopods, so abundant in the Blue limestone proper, are not frequently met with in the Buff.

BLUE LIMESTONE PROPER.—TRENTON LIMESTONE.

Rising in the series above the Buff limestone, we find, everywhere throughout the Lead Region, a considerable thickness of strata, which are particularly well marked by the predominance of purely calcareous matter, and by the very great abundance and perfect preservation of the organic forms which they contain. The absence of magnesia is the more noticeable, from the fact that the beds in question are the first in the series in which this element is not present in large quantity, with the exception, of course, of those made up entirely of silicious materials; they are also the first during whose deposition animal life was everywhere abundantly developed.

The beds in question are those to which the name of "Blue limestone" has generally been given, as they are everywhere distinguished by their bluish-grey color, which contrasts strongly with the light yellowish-grey of the dolomitic masses above and below.

For the purpose of showing clearly the character of this portion of the series, a section will be given, in which its fullest and most characteristic development is exhibited, and which may serve as a sort of standard of comparison for the Blue limestone, as less perfectly developed or exposed at other localities in this region.

The section referred to, and of which a description follows, is that exhibited in the quarry at Quimby's mill, on the Shullsburg branch of Fever river, near Benton. Although the whole thickness of the Blue limestone is not so great in this part of the Lead Region as farther to the northwest, yet its different sub-divisions are more distinctly marked than at any other point, its distinctive features gradually disappearing in that direction, while the whole series becomes more homogeneous in lithological character.

The section at Quimby's mill is as follows:

	Feet.
A. Very fossiliferous, thin-bedded, and sometimes rather shaly and argillaceous layers of limestone; color bluish grey, but bleaching to a dirty white on exposure. Thickness not entirely exposed, but about...........	12
B. Grey, and light yellowish-grey, somewhat magnesian layers (see analysis below of a specimen from this position), with a finely crystalline texture; in rather irregular layers, about two inches thick; not valuable as a building stone, but preferred for burning to lime..	5
C. *a.* Pure limestone (see analysis below), very compact, brittle, breaking with a conchoidal fracture; color dark-grey; very uniform both in texture and color; rather heavy-bedded, but not so much so as the division next below (C. *b.*); layers from six to eight inches thick, but not very regular; fossils few in number, comparatively, and confined to the partings between the beds.......	5
Between C. *a.* and C. *b.* is a thin layer of shale crowded with fragments of fossils, trilobites, brachiopods, bryozoa, &c.	
C. *b.* Very heavy-bedded and regularly stratified layers of rock, of the same color and texture as the division next above (C. *a.*); layers eighteen to twenty-four inches thick; numerous specimens of *Strophomena alternata* between the layers; the lower portion graduates by a succession of shaly beds, six or eight inches in thickness, into the Buff limestone below......	5

	Feet.
D. "Buff limestone," a blue and buff dolomite, somewhat argillaceous, in layers twelve to thirteen inches in thickness, with numerous fucoidal markings, otherwise unfossiliferous; extensively quarried as a building stone	8
Buff and blue dolomite, more shaly and less thickly bedded than the division above, hence of much less value as a quarry stone, gradually sloping down to the branch, and not well exposed	9
Total thickness exposed of the Blue limestone	27
do do do Buff limestone	17

The chemical composition of a specimen from division B. was as follows:

Insoluble in acid	.98
Alumina, Peroxide of iron,	.80
Lime	35.03
Magnesia	17.81
Carbonic acid	45.04
Potash, soda, chlorine, and loss	.34
	100.00

A specimen from C. yielded on analysis:

Carbonate of lime	97.92
Carbonate of magnesia	1.60
Peroxide of iron and alumina	.28
Insoluble, clay	.82
	100.62

The divisions C. *a.* and C. *b.* are everywhere known in the Lead Region as the "glass-rock," a term given with reference to the very compact texture of these layers, and their peculiar conchoidal fracture, somewhat resembling that of a piece of glass. But, in the more eastern portion of the district, the term glass-rock is pretty generally applied to any portion of the Blue limestone, the lithological distinctions so well exhibited in the section on Fever river and its branches not being as well marked in the Mineral Point district.

The section given above is defective in one respect, which is, that it does not expose the whole thickness of the upper or shaly fossiliferous layers (division A.), nor show the passage of the Blue limestone into the Galena limestone above. This portion of the series, however, is well displayed at O'Brannan's diggings, on Fever river, in the immediate vicinity, as follows:

		Feet.
Galena limestone.	Grey, crystalline dolomite, layers uneven, three to four inches thick, thickness exposed........	5
	Grey and yellowish-grey dolomite, somewhat argillaceous, texture irregular, with blotches of calc. spar, quite heavy layers, no fossils...........	6
Beds of passage.	Greenish shales, with abundant fucoidal markings, and thin-bedded calcareo-magnesian layers with Trenton limestone fossils	4-5
Blue limestone.	Thin-bedded, somewhat shaly, and highly fossiliferous layers of limestone, separated by argillaceous partings crowded with fossils.........	15-20
	Slope of the hill, concealing the glass-rock, or division C. of the Blue limestone.............	15

Only one more section showing the lithological peculiarities of this member of the series need be introduced here as the subject will come up again for more detailed consideration, in connection with the mode of occurrence of the lead ore in the so-called "openings" of the Blue limestone. The annexed section will show the details of the strata between the Buff and Galena limestones as exhibited on the Mississippi river, and may be compared with those given above on Fever river. It is that exhibited at Cassville, at the base of the bluff directly in the rear of the town, where the rocks are freshly exposed in the quarries.

Galena limestone, in an almost vertical cliff, exposing of that rock a thickness of about	200 feet.
Blue and green, somewhat argillaceous, calcareo-magnesian layers, stratification broken and irregular..............................	2 feet

Greenish-blue, heavier-bedded layers, with some Trenton fossils, showing on the weathered edge a tendency to a division into thin and irregular layers (this is the upper portion of the Blue limestone)	4 feet 6 inches.
More argillaceous stratum	1 foot 6 inches.
Bluish-grey limestone, rather thick-bedded, but irregularly stratified, fossiliferous, separating into thinner layers on weathering	7 feet 9 inches.
Thin beds of crystalline limestone, including some very fossiliferous layers, stratification somewhat irregular, with shaly partings	4 feet.
"Pipe-clay opening," marked here by a seam about ten inches thick, filled with clay and irregular fragments of limestone, in elongated nodules	10 inches.
Glass-rock, in rather heavy but very irregular beds, a pretty regular layer at the bottom one foot in thickness	6 feet 1 inch.
Shale, decomposed argillaceous stratum	2 inches.
Blue limestone	13 inches.
Blue shaly matter at the base of the cliff, not well exposed, but evidently marking the place of the "glass-rock opening"	2–3 feet.
The whole thickness here exposed, which may properly be reckoned as belonging to the Blue limestone is	27 feet.

The terms "pipe-clay opening" and "glass-rock opening" will be explained in the chapter on the mode of occurrence of the ores of lead.

The whole thickness of the Blue limestone in the Lead Region is somewhat variable. At Gutenberg, on the west side of the Mississippi, a few miles above Cassville, there is a series of calcareous beds exposed in the bluffs behind the town, nearly 100 feet thick, which must be considered as belonging to the Buff and the Blue together. In the vicinity of Mineral Point there is not much more than 35 feet, of which the Buff occupies the lower 20 feet, and the glass-rock the remaining 15. Perhaps the average thickness throughout the Lead Region may be put at 70 feet for both members of the series.

The Buff limestone occupies so little space on the surface that it was not possible to represent it separately on the geological map: it must be assumed as everywhere overlying the Upper sandstone, and is indicated by the blue color, which includes both the Buff and the Blue divisions of that portion of the series between the Upper sandstone and the Galena limestone. As will be seen by referring to the map, these groups are exposed in the bluffs which border almost all the streams running through the Lead Region. To the north and northwest of Lancaster, the Blue limestone occupies a large extent of surface, being the uppermost rock all around the head-waters of the Grant and Platte rivers. It extends across the Wisconsin, and forms the highest portion of the bluffs in the vicinity of Prairie du Chien. On the Little Platte, on Fever river, and on the main Peccatonica, from Calamine to Riverside, the Blue limestone is on the level of the bottom of the valley, that being the lowest rock exposed along these streams. There is also an extensive district around the head-waters of the east Peccatonica and some of those of Sugar river, on the northwest side, where the Blue limestone occupies the larger portion of the surface.

The Blue limestone undergoes decomposition rather rapidly under exposure to the air and the weather. The blue, thin-bedded, rather shaly and argillaceous layers, which form the main body of the group in the Lead Region, have their calcareous matter dissolved out by contact with water, and the protoxide of iron contained in the form of carbonate becomes oxidized to peroxide, while the argillaceous matter remains behind, so that the blue rock weathers yellowish-brown, and finally becomes converted into a yellow clay. The greater the quantity of argillaceous substance in the rock, the more rapid is its decomposition: hence the fossils which it contains, being almost pure carbonate of lime, are left standing out in relief as the surrounding rock disappears.

Although the quantity of clay which the Blue limestone contains is not very large, yet it is, in comparison with that present in the dolomitic rocks above and below, sufficiently great to impress a decided character on the soil which results from its decomposition, as will be noticed more particularly in speaking of the superficial deposits covering the Lead Region.

The Blue limestone, in some of the northern districts of the Lead Region, is a metalliferous rock, a large portion of the ore raised near Mineral Point, Linden, Centreville, Franklin, Crow Branch, and other diggings, coming from openings in this geological position, as will be more fully set forth in the succeeding chapter. In two or three instances, lead has been mined in considerable quantity in the Buff subdivision: but, on the whole, this part of the series cannot be considered as a productive rock, and we have no record of any ore raising from it at present, unless it be at Crow Branch. The openings above and below the glass-rock, however, and especially the "pipe-clay opening" above, are extensively worked. It is especially in this rock that the dry-bone, or carbonate of zinc, is found in great abundance, in the openings, and in connection with the sulphurets of lead, zinc, and iron.

The abundance, variety, and fine state of preservation of the fossils of the Blue limestone make this group of strata one of great interest to the palæontologist, and it will undoubtedly receive full attention from Prof. Hall in his Report. There is no doubt that the series represents pretty nearly the Trenton limestone of the New York survey, containing, as it does, many fossils identical with those of that rock.

GALENA LIMESTONE.

We come now to speak of that member of the series which is, of all, by far the most important in the Lead Region, since it not only covers much the larger portion of its surface, but is the chief repository of the valuable ores which are here so extensively mined. At present, however, we have to do with it only in its stratigraphical and lithological relations: the nature and peculiarities of the mineral deposits it contains will be fully investigated in a succeeding chapter.

The term "Upper Magnesian limestone" is that by which, throughout the Lead Region, the rock which we are about to describe is generally known. In Dr. Owen's Report of 1840 (it is absolutely necessary, for a correct understanding of the nomenclature of the different groups in this district to go back a few years, and trace out the origin of the names applied to them at various times), the whole series of rocks above the Blue limestone, occurring in the Northwest, as far down the river as Davenport, was described as one natural group, under the name of the "Cliff limestone"—a term adopted "because it aptly expresses its most striking external characteristic, which imparts to the scenery of any country in which the rock abounds a bold and romantic character." This Cliff limestone was subdivided as follows:

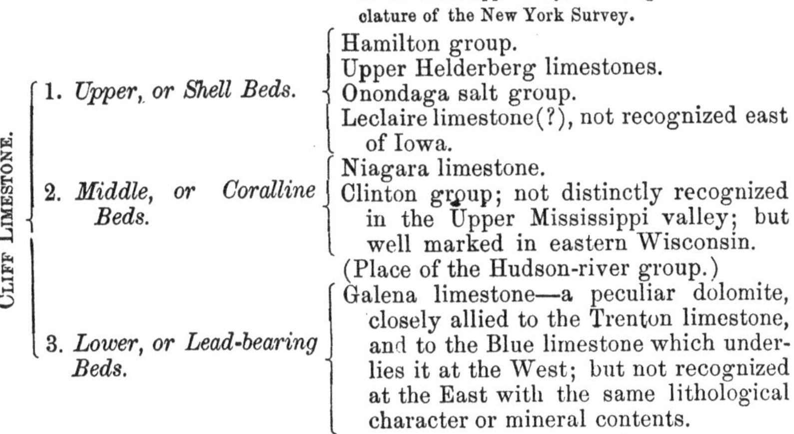

		Includes the following subdivisions, as now recognized in the Mississippi valley, according to the nomenclature of the New York Survey.
CLIFF LIMESTONE.	1. *Upper, or Shell Beds.*	Hamilton group. Upper Helderberg limestones. Onondaga salt group. Leclaire limestone(?), not recognized east of Iowa.
	2. *Middle, or Coralline Beds.*	Niagara limestone. Clinton group; not distinctly recognized in the Upper Mississippi valley; but well marked in eastern Wisconsin.
		(Place of the Hudson-river group.)
	3. *Lower, or Lead-bearing Beds.*	Galena limestone—a peculiar dolomite, closely allied to the Trenton limestone, and to the Blue limestone which underlies it at the West; but not recognized at the East with the same lithological character or mineral contents.

The Leclaire limestone has not been thoroughly studied, and its extension and palæontological relations do not seem to be well made out. It has been placed, with doubt, as parallel with the Galt limestone of Upper Canada, and the lower part of the Onondaga salt group.

Here we have Lower and Upper Silurian and Devonian rocks grouped together under one name, so that the term "Cliff limestone" really included six or seven different groups, each entirely distinct from the other in its organic remains; in lithological character, however, the principal groups of which the "Cliff" was composed do resemble each other, the predominant material being dolomite; but the two great dolomitic masses of the "coralline beds" and the "lead-bearing beds" are in reality separated by from 70 to 100 feet of silicious and bituminous blue shales, and the fact that the existence of these shales had been entirely overlooked, in the first surveys of the Lead Region, was one chief cause of the wholesale grouping of the rocks under the name of "Cliff limestone." Furthermore, the larger portion of the rocks included in the "Shell beds" of this series are made up of purely calcareous materials; and, as they do not even form cliffs, they are in no respect proper to be classed with any of the lower strata.

The term "Cliff limestone" is now generally dropped, and that of "Upper Magnesian" has taken its place; this was introduced by Dr. Owen in his Report of 1840, as synonymous with the "lead-bearing beds" and the "coralline beds" of the Cliff, in contra-distinction to the Lower Magnesian, or that portion of the series which lies between the Upper and Lower sandstones.

As the lead-bearing beds and the coralline beds were known to be palæontologically entirely distinct formations or groups of strata, so that the two must of necessity be absolutely distinguished from each other; as the former were not the only lead-bearing, nor the latter the only coralline beds of the region, and as neither of them was the uppermost magnesian bed, it was suggested by Mr. Hall, in the Report on the Geology of Lake Superior, that the name of

GALENA LIMESTONE should be given to the lead-bearing beds above the Blue limestone; while that of Niagara limestone would naturally be applied to the coralline beds, as these are the direct continuation of the group known under this name in New York, in Canada, and on Lake Michigan; and identical with this, or nearly so, in the fossils they contain. The discovery of the Hudson-river shales, between the lead-bearing beds and the coralline beds, completely separating the two members from each other, made the necessity and propriety of this new nomenclature apparent. The name "Galena limestone" is doubly appropriate, as designating at once a locality where this rock is displayed to great advantage, and the ore which occurs in it, and gives it so much economical importance.

The Galena limestone, as usually developed, is a rather thick-bedded, light grey, or light yellowish-grey dolomite, quite crystalline in its texture, although the crystalline particles are frequently so minute as to make the rock appear quite compact. The coarsely granular portions not unfrequently contain small cavities, lined with minute crystals of brown spar or dolomite.

There is a very great uniformity in the character of the Galena limestone, throughout the entire series of beds of which it is made up, and over the whole district in which it occurs. It contains the two carbonates of lime and magnesia in almost exactly the required proportion to form dolomite (carbonate of lime 54.35, and carbonate of magnesia 45.65), with a varying proportion of substances insoluble in acid, chiefly clay, but which does not generally amount to more than two or three per cent.: there is also a small quantity of iron, partly as the peroxide, but chiefly as the protoxide, and in combination with carbonic acid.

The annexed analyses, made at various times, will show the composition of the Galena limestone :

	i	ii
Insoluble in acid	2.46	4.43
Carbonate of iron	1.35	.93
Soluble alumina and peroxide of iron	trace.	trace.
Carbonate of lime	52.00	52.01
Carbonate of magnesia	43.93	42.25
Carbonates of soda and potash	.26	.38
	100.00	100.00

No. i. is from Dubuque, collected at an elevation of 150 feet above the river.

No. ii. is a specimen from Clayton county, Iowa.

The above analyses were made for the Iowa Survey, but they indicate accurately the composition of this rock over the whole Lead Region, taking it as in its normal development, in the crystalline, heavy-bedded portions of which it is in so large a part made up. Other analyses, by different chemists—Dr. Owen in particular—give the same results in regard to the composition of this member of the series.

The whole thickness of the Galena limestone, where it can be measured, from the top of the Blue up to the overlying Hudson-river shales, may be set down at about 250 feet; this is in the vicinity of the mounds, and along the Mississippi river at Dubuque, at Fairplay and Hazle Green, and from Galena east to Warren, and Waddam's Grove; towards the north, this formation gradually thins out, and soon disappears after crossing the water-shed. In noticing the different mining districts, the details of the thickness of the Galena limestone will be given.

The differences in the character of the different portions of the series are chiefly such as are connected with the bedding of the rock, and the greater or less abundance of silicious nodules, or flints, disseminated through the layers. The upper fifty feet of the Galena limestone are usually more regularly bedded, and in thinner layers, than the middle and lower portions; hence the best quarries are in this position, and the rock is not much used as a building stone, except where it can be quarried from the upper beds. At Dubuque, in the principal quarries, the layers are seven or eight inches in thickness, and quite regular; they are extensively used for common building purposes. The middle portion of the series is quite heavy-bedded, crystalline, and somewhat less argillaceous than the beds above. The lower division is more irregular in its lithological character than either the upper or middle; some portions are somewhat argillaceous, and not unfrequently there is a gradual passage, by a series of calcareo-magnesian and argillaceous beds, into the Blue limestone beneath. This is especially the case in the region west of the Mississippi river, where there is much more difficulty in drawing the line between the Galena and the Blue limestone than there is in the Lead Region proper. The same thing is true of the upper portion of the upper division of the Galena limestone, which passes into the Hudson-river shales by a series of thin shaly beds of a yellowish color, containing a somewhat larger proportion of clay than the main body of the rock below. The shaly partings of the beds throughout the series are usually quite thin, sometimes a mere varnish on the surface of the layer, at other times, although quite rarely, as much as a few inches in thickness, and forming by their decomposition green and blue clays, which have various designations among the miners, by whom their position is carefully noted, with reference to the position of the ore above or below.

It will not be necessary to dwell on the minute differences of lithological character which are exhibited in different portions of the Galena limestone, as they will all be carefully noted and described in discussing their relation to the mineral deposits which are connected with this division of the series.

One feature of the Galena limestone, by which this rock is most distinctly characterized, and especially in the vicinity of the Mississippi river, is its peculiar mode of weathering.

There are very great differences in the rapidity with which different beds and different portions of the same bed disintegrate and decompose, when exposed to the weather; so that the bluffs, where the vallies have been deeply cut down into this rock, and the points of the ravines, where two unite with each other, are frequently worn into the most picturesque and curiously formed masses. The line of bluffs, with its salient and reëntering angles, will frequently resemble the half-mined walls of some old fortified city, while the outlying masses which have escaped denudation, and remain scattered up and down in the vallies, may well be compared to ancient watch-towers. There is no portion of the Lead Region where more curious instances of this kind of weathering may be observed than on the branches of the Little Makoqueta, near Dubuque: the farther we go east from the Mississippi, the less the thickness of the Galena limestone exposed in the vallies, and, consequently, the less marked the condition of things here alluded to. Not only do we meet the most fantastically-shaped outliers of the Galena on the Little Makoqueta, but even the crests of the ridges are frequently crowned with a narrow wall of rocks, whose resemblance to an old half-ruined wall may be well illustrated by the accompanying plate (Plate II.), which represents the outcrop of this rock on one of the side vallies leading down to the river, in the vicinity of Burton's furnace. On the left hand of the scene, a series of workings rising up the side of the hill may be observed, which will illustrate the way in which these ridges are sometimes crossed by the mineral ranges.

This irregularity of weathering shows itself wherever the surface of the rock has been long exposed to the elements; it then has a curious, irregular appearance, which can only be unsatisfactorily designated as "honey-combed;" "worm-eaten" would perhaps be more expressive. This peculiarity of the Galena limestone, which is in a less marked degree shared by the Niagara limestone also, is due, as nearly as can be ascertained, to its irregular crystalline texture. Those portions of the rock which have the greatest tendency to disaggregation are found to be made up of a mass of minute dolomite crystals, held together by a small amount of argillaceous matter, which is soon washed out on exposure, and then allows the crystals to fall apart; in which condition they are rapidly dissolved by the rain water, and the calcareous and magnesian portions are carried off in solution, while the clay and sand which the rock contained remain behind. Those parts of the rock which are less crystalline in their structure resist decomposition better, from the closeness of their texture, which does not permit the ready penetration of the dissolving agent into the interior of the mass.

The Galena limestone is strongly contrasted with the underlying Blue limestone in respect to the variety of its fossils, and the degree of perfection with which they have been preserved. In the first-named of these groups, the highly crystalline character of the material is, of course, very unfavorable to perfection in the organic remains it encloses. It is difficult to say how much may have been obliterated as the crystallizing process went on; many layers show on their weathered surfaces abundant, although obscure, indications of organic life, when the interior of the same specimens appears to be homogeneous and destitute of fossils. There is reason to believe that marine vegetation may have flourished extensively during the deposition of a considerable portion of the Galena limestone, although the forms are now with difficulty to be made out, the interior structure being apparently entirely gone. The surfaces of the strata, especially in the upper and lower portions of the series, are completely covered, in many localities, with branching forms, closely resembling those described by Prof. Hall as occurring in the Lower Silurian rocks of New York. Although these have been considered by some as merely of concretionary, or inorganic origin, I think that every palæontologist will agree with me, after inspecting a few specimens, in pronouncing them the remains of marine plants. It is, indeed, probable that the materials of which the rock itself is composed may have been largely indebted for their origin to the agencies of plant life, flourishing with luxuriance, during the early period of geological history. As a good locality for observing these remains of sea-weeds in the rock, Dubuque may be mentioned: in examining the quarries near the town, one can hardly fail to be struck with the immense number of branching forms which cover the surface of almost all the layers, especially in the upper portion of the series of rocks exposed. In this connection, it may be noticed that there are carbonaceous layers occasionally met with in the body of the Galena limestone, which are not only so impregnated with organic matter as to take fire and burn with flame when heated, but which show distinct impressions of a vegetable character, although perhaps those thus far collected are too imperfect to allow anything more to be made out than that they are undoubtedly plants.

These vegetable remains are not the only forms found in the Galena limestone: there are, in certain strata, quite abundant traces of animal life, which, however, it is not within the province of this Report to describe. The most characteristic fossil of the Galena limestone in the Lead Region is the *Receptaculites*, the "lead-fossil," as it is sometimes called, or the "sun-flower coral," from its resemblance to the disk of that flower. This very interesting form occurs all over the Lead Region in the Galena limestone; and within the productive mining district it appears, so far as has been observed, to be limited to that rock: no specimens have been collected in the Blue limestone. The *Receptaculites*, which was formerly considered as a coral, is now pronounced by palæontologists to belong to the foraminifera, but not without some doubt: perhaps the specimens which have been collected during the progress of this Survey may throw some additional light on the matter, in the hands of Prof.

Hall. Almost equally characteristic of the Galena limestone with the *Receptaculites* is the *Lingula quadrata*, which is quite frequently noticed in the upper beds of this rock, but never in the Blue or Buff. There are also occasional beds with numerous casts of gasteropods, of the same genera which occur so abundantly in the Buff limestone, namely *Murchisonia*, and *Pleurotomaria*. Among the brachiopods, which are mostly found in the upper layers of the series, are *Orthis*, *Spirifer*, and *Strophomena*. A species which seems identical with *O. testudinaria* is very abundant in the shaly partings between the strata in the railroad cut near Warren, Ill.

That the same fossils which are characteristic of the Galena limestone in the Lead Region are found in the Blue, beyond the limits of our district, to the northwest, is a fact observed during the progress of the Iowa Survey; it is evident that after crossing the Mississippi, and proceeding beyond Gutenberg in that direction, the Galena and the Blue limestone become more and more merged in each other, and less distinguishable either by lithological or palæontological characters.

HUDSON-RIVER GROUP.

As developed in the vicinity of the Hudson river, where this group of strata was first recognized and described by the geologists of the New York survey, the rocks referred to this geological position are made up of detrital material, the larger portion of which is in a finely-comminuted state, while in some districts sandstones and grits predominate. They have usually a dark color, owing to the presence of bituminous matter; but, the coarser the material of the rock, the lighter the shade of color. Following this series of strata towards the west, we find it rapidly thinning out, from over a thousand feet in thickness in the immediate vicinity of the Hudson, to some four hundred in the upper part of the Mohawk valley. As we go west into Canada, the rocks in this position become more and more calcareous, without any very considerable change in thickness: thus, at Cabot's Head on Lake Huron, there are nearly five hundred feet of somewhat argillaceous limestone, referred to the Hudson-river group by Mr. Logan. Along the north side of the Grand Manitoulin and Drummond's islands—where, however, the whole of the series is not exposed—there is still a predominance of calcareous matter: but argillaceous and silicious materials in the form of shales and impure limestones begin to be more common as we go from this point westward; and, in the vicinity of the Mississippi river, a large part of the series has become again almost purely detrital, calcareous matter being present usually only in thin bands, while its thickness seems to have undergone a gradual diminution from Lake Huron westward.

Although the Hudson-river group is so well exposed on the north side of Lake Huron and on the islands which front the shore, yet, owing to its peculiar lithological character, and the topography of the country as we go west, the exposures become less and less satisfactory, as has been fully explained in the Iowa Geological Report. Indeed, its existence in the Lead Region was not suspected by the first observers in that section, and this was one of the principal difficulties in the way of recognizing in the Mississippi valley the eastern equivalents of the Lower Silurian groups. The best natural sections of the portion of the series of rocks between the Galena limestone and the Niagara group in the Upper Mississippi valley, are those observed on the Little Makoqueta and its branches, northwest of Dubuque. The greatest thickness exposed here is about 25 feet; the details of this are given in the Iowa Report.* There are several artificial sections, one of which exhibits a thickness of 42 feet, on the line of the Illinois Central railroad, near Scales Mound, and between that and Apple River station. At the first-named place, the junction of the Galena limestone and the

* See Vol. I, page 66, of that work.

Hudson-river group is admirably exhibited; but no locality has been found, thus far, which exhibits the whole of the group, or even the junction between the shales and the Niagara limestone above.

In the higher portions of the district, near Dubuque, a considerable thickness of the Hudson-river shales has to be penetrated in the shafts sunk on the ridges, before the lead-bearing rock below is reached; but the rock thus removed in sinking the shafts is always immediately covered by the materials taken out from the Galena limestone: which accounts for the fact that one may examine the workings frequently, even where there has been a considerable thickness of the shales penetrated, without discovering any traces of them in the rubbish thrown out.

The shafts sunk in the vicinity of Fairplay have many of them passed through a few feet of the Hudson-river shales before reaching the lead-bearing rock, and traces of this group are seen about Hazle Green, but there has never been a good section measured within the limits of Wisconsin, either naturally or artificially exposed. It is always present, of course, in its whole thickness, under the Mounds, which are capped with 100 to 150 feet of the overlying Niagara; but there is not a single natural section at the base of either of them which exhibits anything satisfactory, and the thickness of the series can only be made out approximately.

As a key to the lithological character of this member of the series, the section measured in the railroad cut, a little west of Scales Mound station, may be given here, since there is none within the limits of Wisconsin which can be referred to:

Alternating bands of impure argillaceous and silicious shales, with more calcareous layers, of a few inches in thickness	8 feet.
Silicio-calcareous shales....................	11 feet 6 inches.
Limestone, magnesian, rather argillaceous, and containing a little carbonaceous matter....	3 inches.
Shales, as above.........................	12 feet.

Calcareous band............................	2 inches.
Shales....................................	6 feet.
Layer filled with minute fossils, of which *Tellinomya* (*Nucula*) is the most abundant; hence the stratum is usually called the "Nucula bed." At the bottom is a thin layer containing a great abundance of *Lingula*......	6–12 inches.
Dark olive shales, finely laminated, and destitute of fossils..........................	3 feet.
Nucula bed, similar to the one above........	4–6 inches.
Whole thickness exposed belonging to the Hudson-river group, about...................	42 feet.

In the western end of the cut, the upper beds of the Galena limestone are well exposed; the strata of dolomite alternate with yellow shaly beds, which, however, are chiefly made up of calcareo-magnesian materials; these shaly partings are a few inches in thickness, and contain a considerable number of fossils, among which *Murchisonia bellicincta*, *Pleurotomaria lenticularis*, &c., were recognized. Above this alternation of limestone and shales come ten feet of a rather compact bluish dolomite, and above that four feet of a greyish-blue dolomite with numerous geodes, usually of from two to three inches in diameter, the sides of which are lined with very pretty crystallizations of pyrites, bitter spar, and heavy spar, of which the latter mineral occurs in sufficiently well-formed crystals to make quite handsome cabinet specimens. This geode bed has an irregular surface, on which is deposited the lower nucula bed. This fossiliferous layer, which is at the bottom of the Hudson-river shales, is from four to six inches in thickness, as here developed: it is strongly impregnated with iron pyrites, which soon decomposes after exposure to the air, so that the blocks which were quarried at the time the railroad was constructed, about ten years since, are now entirely disintegrated. This layer contains a great number of finely-comminuted fragments of fossils, with many individuals of *Nucula*, small orthoceratites, *Pleurotomaria*, *Murchi-*

sonia gracilis, &c., together with a great number of small pebble-like concretions of a dark slaty material, and nodules of pyrites; the larger portion of the mass is made up of the debris of organic forms. The upper nucula bed is similar in character to the lower one, being equally crowded with fossils, although not quite so pyritiferous.

At the locality where the section was obtained—near Chan ningsville, Iowa, on the Makoqueta river, about thirty miles west of Scales Mound—there are six or seven of these fossiliferous bands alternating with the shales, and all through this region the presence of small orthoceratites, in prodigious numbers, is characteristic of these layers. The sections taken at different points near each other show considerable discrepancies in the number and arrangement of the fossiliferous layers; but there seems always to be a zone crowded with fossils at or near the base of the series.

The whole thickness of the Hudson-river group in the Lead Region and its vicinity may be set down as from 70 to 100 feet: at least, this is the nearest estimate which can be given from a careful consideration of the topography of the region adjacent to the mounds.

In the elevated district between Gratiot's Grove and Scales Mound, there is a considerable area over which nearly the whole of the Hudson-river group remains undenuded. There is a considerable thickness of a light-yellowish magnesian limestone to be seen here, which differs materially from the lower portions of the Hudson-river group as exposed on the Illinois Central railroad and near Dubuque. These beds I suppose from their position and fossil contents to be the upper portion of the Hudson-river group, although I have not been able to find a good section showing their relations to the strata above and below. This rock is in some places, particularly at Gratiot's Grove, made up of a mass of coralline fragments scattered through a soft dolomitic mass. These corals appear to be *Chætetes lycoperdon*, in a variety of forms, hemispherical, branching, &c. With the corals are considerable numbers of *Orthis occidentalis*. These strata are well exposed on the road from Shullsburg to White Oak Springs, and there would appear to be something like fifty feet of the beds in that vicinity. At the summit of Paige's Mound, in Jo Daviess county, Ill. (Sec. 36, T. 29, R. 3), at a quarry used for procuring material for lime, a rock closely resembling the strata above noticed was met with. It is a soft, yellowish, magnesian limestone, with graptolitic markings, and a considerable number of fragments of *Asaphus* (*Isotelus*) *gigas*. These strata on the summit of Paige's Mound are identical with a portion of the series observed farther south, at Savannah.

An analysis of a specimen of the rock from this geological position, taken from near the summit of the ridge at Gratiot's Grove, gave the following results:

Carbonate of lime	49.75	(by loss.)
Carbonate of magnesia	27.49	
Peroxide of iron and alumina	6.54	
Insoluble, clay and sand	16.22	
	100.00	

It is, therefore, an impure dolomite, containing a considerably larger amount of clay and oxide of iron than the Niagara or Galena dolomites usually do. It is not unlikely that portions of the strata in this geological position might be valuable for hydraulic lime.

One of the most interesting facts connected with the rocks of the Hudson-river group, is the large amount of organic matter which they frequently contain: a circumstance which, in the valley of the Mississippi especially, contrasts them strongly with the other members of the Silurian system. From the State of New York westward, as far as Iowa, this same fact has been noticed at different times, and in some localities the quantity of carbonaceous matter present in these shales seems to be sufficient to make them at some future time, if not at present, of economical value.

Some investigations have been made by Messrs. Chandler and Kimball, into the quantity of organic matter present in some samples of rocks of the Hudson-river group obtained at different localities between Canada and the Mississippi river. The following is the composition of four specimens from the vicinity of the Lead Region:

		i.	ii.	iii.	iv.
Insoluble in Chlorohydric acid.	Clay and sand	80.65	73.57	48.27	76.16
	Carbon	3.97	15.03	6.99	3.97
	Hydrogen	.63	1.65	1.13	.77
	Oxygen	4.87	5.39	3.39	3.56
Soluble in Chlorohydric acid.	Carb. lime	4.77	1.29	20.30	7.19
	Carb. magnesia	3.40	.76	11.48	5.34
	Alumina and oxide of iron,	1.99	2.79	7.99	2.81
		100.28	100.48	99.55	99.80

No. i. is a dark-grey shale, with a few faint graptolitic markings, from the Catteesh diggings, a few miles south of Dubuque. It had been taken from the shaft only a short time before it was collected for examination.

No. ii. is a dark chocolate-colored shale, weathering whitish-grey on exposure, containing no traces of organic remains. It is a silicious shale, containing only one or two percent of the carbonates of lime and magnesia, but rich in carbonaceous matters. When heated in the closed crucible, it lost 14.12 percent of volatile combustible matter, and 6.84 was driven off, in addition, on ignition with exposure to the air.

No. iii. is a dark-brown shale, without fossils, from the Pitts farm, on the Little Makoqueta, twelve miles west of Dubuque. This sample contained 31.78 percent of the carbonates of lime and magnesia.

No iv. is from Hawley's mill, near the last mentioned locality. It is a dark chocolate-colored shale, with fragments of *Lingula*, &c.

For comparison, some further examinations were made of

specimens from the same geological position in Canada,* which all contain more or less organic matter, although not in so large a quantity as do some of the western shales. These analyses were also made by Messrs. Chandler and Kimball. The results were as follows:

	i.	ii.	iii.	iv.
Clay and sand	38.45	37.26	34.60	48.27
Carbon	6.83	.61	6.63	6.99
Hydrogen	.74	.83	.77	1.13
Oxygen	3.20	1.71	2.96	3.39
Carbonate of lime	45.02	52.60	49.31	20.30
Carbonate of magnesia	2.09	3.42	2.53	11.48
Alumina and peroxide of iron	2.16	3.29	2.09	7.99
	98.49	99.72	98.89	99.55

No. i. is a very dark-brown, almost black, very fine-grained rock, breaking with a somewhat conchoidal fracture, and not perceptibly laminated in its structure. It was from Cape Smith, Lake Huron; no traces of fossils observed in it.

No. ii: a dark-brown rock, with an earthy texture; indistinct traces of lamination; contains a few graptolitic impressions. From the river Ste. Anne, Lower Canada.

No. iii: dark-brown, almost black; very fine-grained earthy texture; laminated; no fossils. From the islands north of Maple Cape.

No. iv: a black bituminous shale, filled with fossils: from Gloucester, on the Rideau river; it is filled with fragments of crinoids and trilobites.

These shales are much more calcareous than those of the Mississippi valley, and might properly be called marls; they are not so magnesian as are the same rocks further west, and the quantity of organic matter they contain is more uniform.

The presence of carbon in the shales of the Hudson-river group over so extensive an area, and in such large quantity, is a matter of considerable interest, both practically and

* These were obtained from Sir W. E. Logan, Provincial Geologist, through the kindness of T. Sterry Hunt, Esq., Chemist to the Canada Survey.

scientifically; it seems hardly possible that a material existing in such abundance, and containing from one-tenth to one-fifth its weight of bituminous and carbonaceous substances, should not at some future time be utilized for lighting or heating purposes, in a region where coal does not occur. The subject is one which needs investigation. In the Upper Mississippi valley, these shales are the only rocks containing any perceptible quantity of organic matter. The great masses of dolomite and sandstone which make up the bulk of the sedimentary strata are absolutely destitute of carbon. The only portion of the series in which it is present, even in traces, with the exception of the Hudson-river group, is the calcareous beds of the Blue limestone, which are faintly tinged with bituminous matter: but this is hardly present in weighable quantity. There are, however, a few thin layers of rock intercalated in the Galena limestone which are also highly bituminous, and which will be mentioned, in their relations to the lead deposits, in the chapter devoted to the subject of the mode of occurrence of that metal.

Taking into consideration the entire absence of vegetable remains in the rocks of the Hudson-river group, there can be hardly any doubt that this carbonaceous matter must have been derived from the decomposition of animal matter enclosed in the strata as they were deposited. The exceedingly fine argillaceous sediment of which these shales are composed seems to have been suited, by its physical properties, to the retention of the gases which were generated in the underlying strata. The astonishing abundance of animal remains in this part of the series has already been spoken of. Some of the layers of Orthocerata are so crowded with these animals that hardly any detrital or sedimentary matter can be perceived among them: the whole rock is a mass of fossils. It would seem as if a large portion of the bituminous matter which occurs in strata of different geological ages at the west must have originated from the decomposition of animal rather than vegetable substances, as the bituminous strata are usually quite destitute of any traces of the latter.

M. Rivière has shown that, in the earth surrounding the gas-pipes of a city, a very large amount of carbonaceous and bituminous matters is absorbed where leakage has taken place for some time. According to his statements, argillaceous moist soils sometimes collect enough of these substances in the vicinity of the pipes to become black as coal and very combustible. Animal and vegetable substances under these circumstances become converted into a more or less bituminous coal.* It would seem as if the finely divided sediment of the Hudson-river group had a peculiar tendency to collect the gases originating in decomposition of the organic matters contained in that and the underlying groups, and it is to this physical property that we must attribute the concentration of so much bituminous matter in this geological position.

NIAGARA LIMESTONE.

The next member of the geological series above the Hudson-river group, throughout the valley of the Upper Mississippi, is one which, although it covers but a small extent of surface within the limits of the Lead Region, is found to extend east, south, and west of it, occupying a large area, and of great importance from its thickness, and the persistency of its lithological and palæontological characters. In the lead district itself it forms the upper portion of the detached eminences, or "mounds," as they are called, which are such conspicuous features in the topography of the region, and which have already been noticed in the chapter devoted to physical geography. For this reason, the rock in question was called by Dr. Percival the "Mound limestone," a name appropriate only within the limits of the Lead Region, and not at all applicable to the condition of things over the much

* See Comptes Rendus, xlvii. 646.

greater extent of surface occupied by this member of the series in other portions of the Northwest. The origin of the term "Coralline and Pentamerus beds of the Upper Magnesian limestone," as applied to what is here called the Niagara limestone, has been adverted to in the preceding pages, under the head of the Galena limestone.

The Niagara limestone has been traced from the centre of New York, where it is first recognized as a distinct formation in coming west from the Hudson river, across the river at Niagara Falls, from which locality it receives its name, through Canada, along the north shore of lakes Huron and Michigan, down the peninsula of Green Bay; thence along the east side of Wisconsin, and through Illinois and Iowa, into Minnesota. As developed at Niagara Falls, it consists of two distinct members, a shale and a limestone; the shale is of a dark-bluish color, weathering of an ash-gray, and readily decomposing into a sort of marly clay: its thickness is about 80 feet. The limestone, 164 feet thick at the Falls, is of somewhat variable character, but generally rather dark-colored, from the presence of bituminous matter; it appears to contain some magnesia, although not a pure dolomite. As we trace the group farther west, we find it considerably increased in thickness, and forming bold precipitous escarpments along the north side of Lake Huron, at the same time gradually becoming more magnesian. On the north side of Lake Michigan, the rocks of this group are almost exclusively dolomite, remarkably free from any intermixture with silicious or argillaceous matter. The same is the case in Wisconsin, Illinois, and Iowa, this rock everywhere in the Northwest maintaining a remarkably homogeneous character, although spread over an immense extent of surface. In its lithological character, as exhibited in the Northwest, it closely resembles the Galena limestone; so that, in hand specimens, it is not always easy to distinguish the two from each other Its structure, however, is rather less crystalline and more homogeneous than that of either of the two magnesian limestones below it, and its stratification is more distinctly preserved. It is also much less marked by a tendency to weather irregularly than the Galena limestone, so that it rarely presents any such ragged forms and picturesque outliers as are so often met with when the latter rock forms the bluffs. It is a characteristic feature of the outcrop of the Niagara, in the neighborhood of the mounds, that owing to the more rapid decomposition of the underlying shales, the Niagara limestone has been left in tabular overhanging masses, which have at last cracked off from their own weight, and have frequently slidden down the slope beneath, to some distance from their original position, as may be illustrated by the accompanying figure (fig. 12) sketched near Tête des Morts. In some instances, the summit of the ridge

FIG. 12. –Outcrop of Niagara Limestone near Tête des Morts.

or mound of this rock left by denudation will have become entirely grassed over, so that nothing but a smooth and regularly conical eminence is seen, while the evidence of the character of the material of which it is made up is furnished by a few huge square blocks of dolomite, scattered irregularly around its base. An outline sketch of the smallest Platte Mound may serve to illustrate this. In this case, the Niagara limestone probably occupies only a few feet of the

FIG. 13.—Little Platte Mound.

summit of the cone, the larger portion of it being made up of the Hudson-river shales.

The color of the Niagara limestone throughout the valley of the Mississippi is a light yellowish-grey, which sometimes passes into a light ash-grey or drab, and occasionally becomes almost white. It is very little changed by the action of the weather, although occasionally assuming a deeper yellowish, or even a brownish tinge.

The presence of silicious matter, in the form of nodules and layers of flint, is another peculiarity in which this rock resembles the Galena limestone. It is especially in the middle and lower portions of the Niagara that the flinty masses are found, although the tendency to silicification exhibits itself throughout the formation, in the fact that the remains of corals, with which this rock is so abundantly charged, are found invariably converted into flint or silica.

The chemical composition of the Niagara limestone, as developed in the Northwest, may be seen from the following analyses of characteristic specimens from various localities:

	i.	ii.
Insoluble in acid	.90	3.93
Protoxide of iron, Alumina,	.35	.24
Lime	30.98	29.16
Magnesia	21.05	20.66
Soda	.18	.23
Chlorine	trace.	
Sulphuric acid	trace.	trace.
Carbonic acid	46.54	44.11
	100.00	98.33

No. i. is a specimen from the upper beds of this rock, in Jackson county, Iowa.

No. ii. is from the bluffs on the east side of Big Bay des Noquets.

A specimen representing the Pentamerus beds of the Niagara limestone, obtained on the south side of Sturgeon Bay, contained only 0.57 percent of silicious residuum, insoluble in acid; the remainder was pure dolomite.

A specimen from the lime-kiln quarry, on the summit of the west Platte Mound, gave as follows:

Insoluble in acid	8.47
Carbonate of lime	49.40
Carbonate of magnesia	41.33
Carbonate of iron	.60
Loss, soda, chlorine, &c.	.20
	100.00

This is a fair sample of the quality of the limestone occurring on the mounds in the Lead Region: it contains a little more silicious matter than some varieties: but, with this exception, it is almost a pure dolomite.

The tendency to silicification, referred to above, exhibits itself in a striking manner on the summit of the west Blue Mound, where the upper portion of the mass, for a thickness of at least 200 feet, is almost entirely converted into flint or hornstone; which is probably the principal reason why this outlier has been so well preserved amid the general denudation of the region. A few of the cavities in this rock are lined with indistinct quartz crystals: a form of occurrence exceedingly uncommon in the Niagara limestone, although so much silicious matter is present in it.

The rock which caps the mound is much quarried for building purposes, as portions of it are regularly bedded, so as to split into layers of a serviceable size; it is also of an agreeable color, a very light straw or greyish tinge being predominant. It is a very durable material, and has no essential defect except the nodules of flint which occur in it, and are very troublesome where abundant. The Niagara limestone is also quarried for lime in many places, apparently partly from a preference for that variety of stone, and partly because wood is usually more abundant in the vicinity of the mounds.

The Niagara limestone everywhere in the West is emphatically a coralline limestone, and from Lake Huron to Iowa and Minnesota is characterized by an abundance of the same fossils. Among these the chain-coral (*Halysites catenulatus*) is the most conspicuous; *Favosites*, *Heliolites*, *Syringopora*, and *Lyellia* are others of frequent occurrence. These are usually preserved in the silicified condition, while the brachiopods are chiefly in the form of casts. The *Pentamerus oblongus*, which is so characteristic of this formation at the West, is limited in the vicinity of the Lead Region to the upper portion of the Niagara; hence it is not observed in that region, except on the west Blue Mound, where a much greater thickness of this rock remains than on any other of the mounds. The lower 100 feet of the Niagara seem very sparsely supplied with fossils, and the corals are hardly found at all, except in the upper layers exposed on the mounds. The most abundant and perfect specimens are obtained to the southwest of Dubuque, on the ridges where the highest portion of the formation is exposed. Here the silicified fossils, corals chiefly, collect in great numbers, remaining behind as the more easily decomposable dolomite in which they are imbedded gradually disappears.

The outcrop of the Niagara limestone to the south and west of the Lead Region is the most marked feature in the topography of that part of the country, as has already been remarked. The only vestiges of this rock left within the Lead Region of Wisconsin are those on the summits of the Blue, Platte, and Sinsinnewa Mounds. Nowhere to the north of the Wisconsin river are any outliers left remaining, although the rock covers an extensive area along Lake Michigan, on the eastern side of the State.

Economically, this rock is of little importance in the Lead Region, as it covers so small an area, and lies entirely above the lead. Excavations have been made in it on the tops of several of the mounds; but we have never been able to ascertain with certainty that even so much as a trace of metal has ever been found in this geological position. Nowhere in the Northwest has this member of the series proved itself to contain any minerals of economical value; and although it has been supposed that beds of iron ore occurred in it, which might be profitably worked, this has been proved not to be the case.

In the geological series, the Niagara limestone is the highest rock which exists in the Lead Region, and only a very limited area within the State, on Lake Michigan, appears to contain anything above it.

CHAPTER V.

MINERALOGY.

In reporting upon the geology of the Lead Region, it will be found convenient to put together under one head the principal facts which have been collected during the progress of the Survey in regard to the nature and mode of occurrence of the different simple minerals which are found in the unaltered palæozoic rocks of the Northwest, and especially in the district which forms the subject of this Report. And in this chapter, which will be devoted to the mineralogy of the Lead Region, the minerals which have been observed will be enumerated, and any peculiarities in regard to their structure, crystalline form, and composition which may have been noticed will be described—the order followed being that of the last edition of Dana's Mineralogy;—at the same time, the more important facts touching their geological and geographical distribution will be added; and, in order to present as complete an account as possible of the mineralogy of the unaltered sedimentary rocks of the Northwest, we shall not feel ourselves called on never to overstep the limits of the Lead Region; but shall add such other facts, connected with the general subject of the occurrence of the simple minerals anywhere in the Northwest, as may have come under our notice during several years of explorations carried on in the Mississippi valley.

After going over the list of minerals, some considerations

will naturally suggest themselves as to the cause of the absence of certain elements and classes of compounds which are of common occurrence in other metalliferous regions, and the general character of the accidental minerals associated with the unaltered rocks, or those which, according to geological phraseology, have not undergone *metamorphism*.

The following is the order in which the mineral species are described in the work above referred to:

I. NATIVE ELEMENTS, or elementary substances occurring in their simple, uncombined condition.
II. SULPHURETS, ARSENIURETS, &c.
III. FLUORIDES, CHLORIDES, BROMIDES and IODIDES.
IV. OXYGEN COMPOUNDS, subdivided as follows:
A. BINARY COMPOUNDS, OR SIMPLE OXIDES.
B. DOUBLE BINARY COMPOUNDS, OR SALTS.

Subdivisions under A.

A. 1. OXIDES OF ELEMENTS OF THE HYDROGEN GROUP.
A. 1. *a*. ANHYDROUS OXIDES.
A. 1. *b*. HYDROUS OXIDES.
A. 2. OXIDES OF ELEMENTS OF THE ARSENIC GROUP.
A. 3. OXIDES OF CARBON, BORON, AND SILICON.

Subdivisions under B.

B. 1. SILICATES.
B. 1. *a*. ANHYDROUS SILICATES.
B. 1. *b*. HYDROUS SILICATES.
B. 2. TANTALATES, COLUMBATES, TUNGSTATES, MOLYBDATES, VANADATES, CHROMATES.
B. 3. SULPHATES, SELENATES.
B. 3. *a*. ANHYDROUS SULPHATES.
B. 3. *b*. HYDROUS SULPHATES.
B. 4. BORATES.
B. 5. PHOSPHATES, ARSENATES, ANTIMONATES, NITRATES.
B. 6. CARBONATES.
B. 6. *a*. ANHYDROUS CARBONATES.
B. 6. *b*. HYDROUS CARBONATES.
B. 7. OXALATES.
V. RESINS, ORGANIC COMPOUNDS.

Following this order, we have, first, the

NATIVE ELEMENTS.

Native Sulphur. This substance has been occasionally noticed, in small quantity, in rocks of different geological ages, and at various points, from New York to the Mississippi. It does not occur, however, in quantity sufficient to make it of any economical importance anywhere in the Northwest. Within the limits of the Lead Region it has been found in a pulverulent form, in small fissures in the limestone. As thus occurring, it was probably the result of the decomposition of iron pyrites. The only locality where it has been noticed in anything more than mere traces was at Mineral Point.

If we except the carbonaceous matters found in almost all the rocks of the Northwest, in greater or less quantity, and especially in those of the Hudson-river group—but which are rarely pure carbon—sulphur is the only element which has been observed in that region in its native or uncombined condition.

SULPHURETS, ARSENIURETS, &c.

Following the order of Prof. Dana's Mineralogy (4th edition), we have next the combinations of elements of the arsenic group (of which sulphur, arsenic, antimony, and bismuth are the most important), with each other, and with the elements of the hydrogen group. Of the elements of the arsenic group, one, sulphur, is universally diffused, and frequently occurs in large quantity in various forms of combination: the others appear to be entirely wanting in the palæozoic series of the Northwest. So far as yet known, no trace of arsenic, antimony, bismuth, selenium, tungsten, molybdenum, or vanadium has been discovered in the *unaltered rocks*, anywhere from New York to the Mississippi. Binary compounds of these elements, therefore, are entirely wanting.

Of the compounds of the elements of the arsenic group with the other elements, of course none except the suphurets could occur: these, however, make up by their abundance for the deficiencies of the others, since sulphur seems to have been the original mineralizing agent for all the metals found in the unaltered palæozoic rocks; that is to say, those metals which are found in this geological position were originally deposited in combination with sulphur, and all the oxidized metalliferous ores associated with them are the products of the subsequent decomposition of the sulphuretted. Farther remarks on this condition of things will be made in a subsequent portion of the Report.

The following are the sulphurets found in the unaltered rocks of the northwest:

Erubescite (Variegated copper-ore; Purple copper). This is the ore to which the term "horse-flesh ore" is frequently applied by the miners. This species may be found in small quantity in some localities, in connection with the common yellow ore, which contains the same substances, but in different proportions (erubescite contains sulphur 28.1, copper 55.5, iron 16.4; chalcopyrite, or copper pyrites, sulphur 34.9, copper 34.6, iron 30.5 percent). I have never seen a well characterized specimen of it, however, in the Northwest, except in the metamorphic rocks of Lake Superior.

Galena. This being the metalliferous substance which, next to the sulphuret of iron, is most abundant in the rocks of the northwest, and also the only one which has, thus far, been extensively and profitably mined, its mode of occurrence will be, of course, carefully and minutely considered in the chapter devoted to economical geology; what will here be said in reference to it, will include only its mineralogical occurrence, or those facts which come expressly under the head of mineralogy.

Galena—universally called by the miners of the Northwest "mineral"—is a compound of sulphur and lead, in the proportion of 13.4 percent of the former to 86.6 of the metal.

This is always the exact composition of the ore, when free from any admixture of foreign, earthy and metalliferous substances. Pure metallic lead, it may here be remarked, does not occur in nature, unless it be in a few rare instances, and then only in very minute quantity. When pure, galena has a specific gravity of about 7.5: it has a very perfect cubic cleavage, a brilliant metallic lustre, and a steel-grey color, by which it may easily be distinguished from all other minerals. Occasionally it has a fine granular structure; but this is very rarely the case in the unaltered rocks; in the Lead Region it is always largely crystalline. In Illinois, however, at a locality in the Carboniferous limestone, in Hardin county, the granular, or steel-grained, variety does occur; the specimens closely resembling the argentiferous ores from the metamorphic rocks, and containing considerable silver. In its crystalline form and general habit, the galena of the Upper Mississippi mines presents a remarkable uniformity; it almost invariably occurs crystallized, wherever the crystalline faces have an opportunity to develop themselves, and in cubes, which very rarely exhibit any modifications. Occasionally, the corners of the cube are replaced by the planes of the octahedron; and, in a very few instances, the octahedron itself has been observed, but not in the Galena limestone. It is very characteristic of the galena of the Upper Mississippi region, that the surfaces of the crystals are never brilliant; on the contrary, they are almost always quite rough and corroded, so that they have little beauty as cabinet specimens. The size of the single crystals of a group is quite variable, and the miners are accustomed to give different names to the different sizes and forms of grouping: such as "dice-mineral" and "cog-mineral;" the term "sheet-mineral" is applied to masses of ore which, being enclosed between walls of hard rock, have not developed any crystalline faces; that of "chunk-mineral," to large, indistinctly crystallized specimens, or such as have very imperfectly formed faces. The largest single crystal which I have observed in the Lead Region measured about seven inches along one of the edges of the cube: it was obtained at Shullsburg. The most interesting cabinet specimens are the single crystals sometimes found in the "pipe-clay opening," at the Crow Branch diggings; which, though small, not exceeding half or three-quarters of an inch in diameter, are comparatively smooth and perfect: finely crystallized specimens, with tolerably smooth faces, are also found implanted on pyrites at Earnest's diggings, near Shullsburg.

The only perfect octahedrons ever observed by me in the Lead Region were obtained at New Galena, Iowa, in the Lower Magnesian limestone. Some curious facts were noticed at this locality in regard to the interior of the crystals. On breaking open an octahedron, about three-fourths of an inch in diameter, it was found to be a hollow shell, with the axis only remaining, as represented in the annexed cut (fig. 14), the walls of the cavities thus formed being lined with minute crystals of sulphate of lead. This would indicate, in connection with other facts observed at the same locality, that the crystal was first formed as a solid octahedron, then partially redissolved, and converted into carbonate of lead; the mineral along the line of the axes having the power to resist the decomposing agent for a longer period than the rest of the crystal. Other specimens showed, when broken, a system of concentric shells, or thin plates of galena, forming the sides of the octahedron, and held together by continuous, although thin, portions of the same material along the line of the axes, as in the instance previously mentioned. The appearance of the crystal, when broken in the plane of the base of the octahedron, is represented in the annexed figure (fig. 15).

Fig. 14.

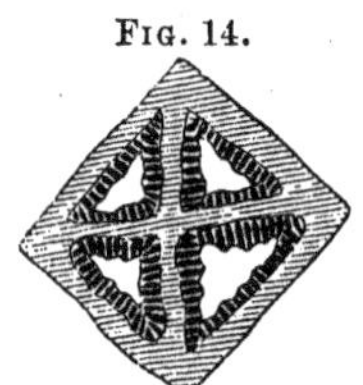

Fig. 15.

The association of silver with sulphuret of lead is a matter of very common occurrence; indeed, hardly a specimen of galena has ever been carefully analyzed without the discovery of at least a trace of silver in it. In many cases, the nobler metal is present in sufficient quantity to be worth separating, and a considerable portion of the silver of commerce is obtained from this source. In general, the older and more crystalline the rocks in which the galena occurs, the larger the amount of silver it is likely to contain. Thus, the lead ores of Cornwall average about twenty-three ounces of silver to the ton; those of the north of England, Alston Moor, Weardale, &c., yield from six to twelve ounces per ton of lead; those of Derbyshire, only one or two ounces to the ton. In the United States the same facts have been observed. The ores of lead contained in the highly metamorphic rocks of New England are usually quite rich in silver: they not unfrequently contain from thirty to seventy ounces to the ton, and in a few instances even a much larger quantity. In the western lead regions, however, both the Missouri and the Upper Mississippi, where the rocks are unaltered, the amount of silver in the galena is exceedingly small, hardly more than a mere trace. The ores of Missouri, from a number of different localities, assayed by Dr. Litton of the State Geological Survey, usually gave from .001 to .002 percent of silver, or less than one ounce per ton, even in the most argentiferous specimens. The galena of the upper Mississippi mines has been frequently assayed for silver, and, like the Missouri ore, found to contain hardly more than the faintest trace.

The analyses of a few Wisconsin and Illinois ores, by Messrs. Chandler and Kimball, gave the following results:

Locality.	Percentage of Silver in		Ounces Troy in 2000 lbs. lead.
	Galena.	Lead.	
Rockville, Wis.	0.00038	0.00043	$\frac{1}{8}$
Mineral Point, Wis.	0.0088	0.0101	3
Massac county, Ill.	0.0043	0.00496	$1\frac{2}{5}$
Rosiclare, Ill.	0.0283	0.0326	$9\frac{1}{2}$
Marsden Lode, near Galena, Ill.	0.00022	0.00025	$\frac{1}{14}$

Blende. This is the "black-jack" of the Cornish miners, a term universally current in America. It is a compound of sulphur and metallic zinc, in the proportion of 33 of sulphur to 67 of zinc. It has a highly perfect dodecahedral cleavage, and frequently occurs in very beautiful crystals. When pure, it has a white or yellowish color, and is transparent, with a fine resinous lustre: usually, it contains more or less iron, and is dark-brown, or almost black, and quite opaque. It has a specific gravity of about 4 to 4.2.

The sulphuret of zinc is, probably, next to the sulphurets of lead and iron, the most abundant simple mineral found in the palæozoic rocks of the Northwest, although in the Lead Region it is almost always associated with the carbonate of zinc, so that it would perhaps be difficult to say, taking the whole region through, which exists in the larger quantity.

In the rocks of western New York, we find blende occurring in small quantity in the Niagara limestone and the Onondaga salt-group. In the Magnesian limestone, at Lockport, it occupies small geodes, in honey-yellow crystals; but nowhere in this region does it form anything like regular veins, or possess economical importance, although quite abundant farther east, on the borders of the metamorphic region of New England. No traces of this mineral were observed in rocks of the same age on the north shore of Lake Michigan; nor does any lead ore occur in that region. It is only within the limits of the Lead Region that the ores of zinc are found in any considerable quantity anywhere in the Northwest, to the south of Lake Superior.

The black-jack of the Lead Region is rarely found distinctly crystallized: a few specimens from Bracken & Allen's mine, near Mineral Point, exhibit imperfectly formed dodecahedral and tetrahedral planes. As usually occurring, it forms imperfectly lamellar-radiated masses, with a concentric or rudely stalactitic structure; it is frequently uniformly distributed in foliated grains through a stratum of limestone, and rarely without being mixed more or less with galena and pyrites. Some interesting facts in reference to the mutual association of these minerals will be noted in the description of the mines, in a subsequent chapter.

Black-jack, from Mineral Point, was carefully tested for cadmium and antimony, but neither of these substances were found to be present in it. The specimen was analysed by Prof. Chandler, and the following results were obtained:

Zinc	66.37
Iron	.79
Sulphur	33.41
Insoluble	trace.
	100.57

It is, therefore, a very pure blende, although quite dark in color.

The localities where black-jack is most abundant in the Lead Region of the Northwest are: the vicinity of Mineral Point, especially at the Irish diggings; Mifflin or "Black-jack"—the abundance of the ore having given a name to the place; Centreville; Franklin; Norway diggings; and many other localities. It is far more common in the lower openings, or those in the Blue limestone, and in the lower beds of the Galena, than in a higher position. There is hardly any locality in the Blue limestone, producing lead, which does not at the same time yield more or less zinc, in the form of sulphuret and carbonate. These are also ores of very common occurrence in the West and Southwest.

Pyrites and *Marcasite* (*mundic*). The bisulphuret of iron occurs in nature in two distinct forms, which, although possessing the same chemical composition, differ in their physical properties. They are both called "mundic" by the miners; or, frequently, "sulphur," from the predominating ingredient. Common pyrites crystallizes in the cubic form, or some modification of it: marcasite belongs to the trimetric system, and frequently presents itself in flat crystals somewhat resembling a spear-head; hence one of its names, "spear-pyrites:" it also occurs in crested aggregations, and is then called "cockscomb-pyrites." The color of this variety is usually much lighter than that of the common pyrites: it is also very much more liable to decompose on exposure to the elements. The percentage composition of both forms of iron pyrites is: iron 46.7, sulphur 53.3.

Iron pyrites occurs in the greatest abundance in rocks of every geological period, from the oldest to the most recent. It is emphatically the predominating mineral of the unaltered sedimentary strata, and is almost invariably present in the metalliferous veins of the older crystalline rocks; being, undoubtedly, the most universally distributed of all the metalliferous minerals. Unfortunately, it is of little value, and not used at all in this country. Were sulphur not so abundant in volcanic regions, where it occurs in the pure state, iron pyrites would be of importance as a source of this very necessary substance: it is, indeed, used to some extent in Germany, for the manufacture of sulphuric acid.

In the rocks of the Northwest, pyrites occurs in large quantity; in some of the groups, however, the products of its decomposition, or the proofs of its previous existence, are more frequently met with than the undecomposed substance itself. Thus, in the Lower and Upper sandstones and the Lower Magnesian limestone, as well as in the Niagara limestone, large quantities of nodular and stalactitic masses of brown iron ore are found, sometimes thoroughly peroxidized; at other times retaining in their interior a portion of the sulphuret of iron of which they originally consisted, and which has not yet been entirely decomposed. These masses are frequently crystallized in the form of pyrites; a fact which shows conclusively the nature of the original material from which they were formed. Probably all the iron ore of the stratified rocks underlying the Lead Region was originally deposited in combination with sulphur; the specular and magnetic oxides are not found in these unmetamorphosed strata.

In connection with the lead deposits of the Northwest, there is not only found a vast quantity of ochre, as it is commonly called—namely, the impure, earthy, hydrous oxide of iron—but there is also a great amount of the undecomposed sulphuret of iron; which, however, rapidly undergoes decomposition on exposure to the air, when brought to the surface. By far the larger portion of this pyrites seems to be the white, or spear-pyrites variety, which occurs in a great variety of forms, occasionally furnishing handsome cabinet specimens, if collected before having been exposed to the air for any considerable time. It is chiefly in the lower part of the Galena, and in the Blue limestone that the heavy deposits of pyrites are to be found; in the upper portion of the Galena limestone, the ore of lead is much less frequently contaminated with this substance, and, where it has previously occurred, it is now almost always found quite converted into ochre. The Crow Branch diggings may be instanced as a locality where pyrites occurs in large quantity, and where its decomposition goes on with the most astonishing rapidity. The mineral at this place very frequently forms casts of shells and other fossils, so common in connection with the rocks of this age. At the Marsden lode, near Galena, a concentrically-aggregated variety of marcasite occurs, made up of radiated layers, with a texture as delicately fibrous as the finest silk. This variety will not endure the slightest amount of exposure to air and moisture: it cannot be preserved except in a very dry room.

Chalcopyrite (Copper pyrites, yellow copper ore). This is the predominant ore of copper in almost every part of the world where that metal is mined, and it is the only one which occurs in any considerable quantity in the Northwest. It is a combination of the sulphurets of iron and copper, in the following proportions: sulphur 34.9, copper 34.6, iron 30.5;

it has very nearly the color of iron pyrites, but may easily be distinguished from it by its greater softness.

In New York, at a distance from the metamorphic rocks, this species occurs only in very minute quantity; it does not appear ever to have been found in sufficient abundance anywhere east of the Lead Region, as far as western New York, to have been the object of mining enterprise. A few stains of green carbonate, arising from the decomposition of copper-pyrites, may be occasionally observed on the sandstone bluffs of the south shore of Lake Superior, and in the region of central Wisconsin underlaid by the same rock: but in general, it is only where the rocks are thoroughly metamorphosed, or in the vicinity of igneous rocks, that any large deposits of copper ore are to be looked for. Considerable bodies of yellow copper ore have been found at different points in the Lead Region, and mining operations have been undertaken, but not, as yet, with success, as will be fully set forth under the head of economical geology. As no crystallized specimens have been obtained, nothing farther need be added here.

No other of the compound sulphurets is known to have been discovered in the unaltered rocks of the Northwest.

CHLORIDES, FLUORIDES, BROMIDES, &c.

Next in order are the combinations of chlorine, fluorine, bromine, and iodine, which are very thinly represented in this region.

Common Salt. Chloride of sodium, that indispensable material, is abundantly but very irregularly diffused through the unaltered sedimentary strata of palæozoic age, from New York west to Michigan. The great salt springs of the first-named State issue from rocks of the Onondaga salt group, which is the body of strata next above the Niagara limestone, the highest member of the series existing in Wisconsin, except over a very small area near Racine and Milwaukee. No salt springs are known to exist in Wisconsin, or in eastern Iowa, where the saliferous groups of New York are but very thinly represented. A trace of chlorine, however, has been detected in almost or quite every specimen of limestone examined from the Mississippi valley, and this is probably in combination with sodium, which is also found to be present in minute quantity in all these rocks. A few hundredths of one percent is the amount of chlorine usually present in the limestones of the Lead Region; between one and two-tenths of one percent is the largest quantity found in any specimen examined: this was from the Niagara limestone, near Green Bay.

Fluor. The element fluorine seems to be very scantily and irregularly distributed through the palæozoic rocks of the Northwest. Even where these have been partially metamorphosed by igneous agencies, as on Lake Superior, fluor-spar is of very infrequent occurrence: indeed, we are not aware of its having been discovered in more than two or three localities.

In New York, fluor-spar has occasionally been found in small crystals in the Niagara limestone, associated with calcite and celestine; also in the Lower Helderberg group: the mode of occurrence is that of small crystals in geodes, and also in seams of calcareous spar traversing the limestone.

No traces of this mineral have been observed in any of the unaltered rocks of Silurian age farther west than New York, so far as can be ascertained. The Lead Region of Wisconsin, Iowa, and Illinois has failed to furnish a single specimen. Nor has a trace of fluor been observed in the great expanse of territory covered by the Niagara limestone in Illinois and Iowa.

Farther south, and higher up in the geological series, we find the only really considerable deposits of fluor-spar known to exist in the Northwest. These are in Gallatin county, Illinois, along the Ohio river, in rocks belonging to the carboniferous system:* veins occur here of considerable extent,

* See G. J. Brush in Silliman's Journal (2), xiv, 112.

in which calcite and fluor-spar form the gangue, and argentiferous galena, with zinc-blende, the ore. They are not worked, however, at present.

OXIDES.

Among the oxides, which follow next after the fluorides, chlorides, &c., we find very few species occurring in the unaltered rocks.

The anhydrous peroxide of iron—or hematite, as it is termed by mineralogists—and limonite, the hydrous oxide, are the only oxides found in any quantity in this class of rocks, with the exception of quartz, or silica, a compound of oxygen and silicon.

Hematite (Specular iron, Iron Glance, Red iron ore, Red ochre, and many other names). Under the term hematite are included all the varieties of the anhydrous peroxide of iron, which graduate down in purity and lustre, from the brilliant specular ores found only in the older crystalline and volcanic rocks, to the dull, earthy ones, like red chalk, or the dye-stone ore, as the blood-red powder or grain-ore is called. The peroxide of iron, when perfectly pure, contains 70 percent of iron and 30 of oxygen; but it is rarely found in this condition in any quantity, except in the oldest crystalline rocks. The only form of this ore which is of economical importance, in the unaltered rocks of the North-west, is the dye-stone or fossil ore, or lenticular clay iron ore, as it is also called. It consists usually of small flattened grains, which stain everything coming in contact with them of a deep blood-red. They consist of peroxide of iron, mixed with a variable amount of other substances, of which the most common is carbonate of lime, while clay and sand are also almost always present: these accidental impurities constituting, usually, from one-fourth to one-half of the mass.

The geological position of the only really important deposit of this ore in the Northwest is in the Clinton group. Two beds of it are found extending over a wide area in New York, and have been opened and worked at several localities, between Utica and the Genesee river. In Wisconsin, at the Iron Ridge, the same kind of ore occurs in the same geological position: that is to say, between the Hudson-river shales and the Niagara limestone; the Clinton group itself being hardly recognized beyond Green Bay. In the Lead Region, the exposures of this portion of the series are so few, and the rocks of its age cover so small a surface, that we should hardly expect to find any outcrop of this ore: it may exist around the base of the mounds, but not probably in workable quantity.

Limonite. The hydrous peroxide—commonly called brown iron ore, or bog ore—contains peroxide of iron 85.6 and water 14.4, or 59.9 percent of metallic iron; but it is rarely found in a pure state, being almost always mixed with clay and sand, or carbonate of lime, as also, smaller proportions of phosphoric and sulphuric acids, and oxide of manganese. It is the most common result of the decomposition of iron pyrites, and hence is found in rocks of all ages, where this widely diffused substance has previously existed. There is frequently a gradual passage from this ore to the one noticed above, the dye-stone ore, which often contains several percent of water.

There are heavy deposits of limonite in the State of Missouri, in rocks, however, more recent than any in the Lead Region, namely the Lower Helderberg. The same ore is also said to occur in southern Illinois in workable quantity. It is found also in Jackson county, Iowa, in the Niagara limestone, but not in any amount large enough to be of value, so far as has yet been ascertained. There are also numerous deposits of bog ore in Ohio and Michigan, both on the Upper and Lower Peninsula. It is very probable that beds of limonite will also be found in northern Wisconsin: but there are no indications of any deposits of value within the limits of the Lead Region.

Brown iron ore—very impure, however—is almost invariably found associated with the ores of lead and zinc in the Lead Region, and is called by the miners "ochre." It appears in such cases to have always resulted from the decomposition of iron pyrites, a process which goes on with rapidity, wherever the pyritiferous rock or veinstone is exposed to the air by mining. In connection with the detailed description of the mines, such facts as have been observed in regard to the distribution of this substance and its relations to the useful ores will be given.

Pyrolusite (wad). Oxide of manganese, containing 63.3 of manganese, to 36.7 of oxygen. The peroxide of manganese, and, indeed, every combination of this metal, seems to be quite rare in the unaltered rocks of the Northwest. No well-characterized specimens have been observed in the Lead Region, although small quantities are found occasionally, mixed with ochre, or forming thin incrustations in the seams of the limestone. On the whole, however, the absence of manganese, usually almost the invariable accompaniment of iron in its various combinations, is a noticeable fact in the mineralogy of the Northwest. The same scarcity of this element in the rocks and ores of Lake Superior has been noticed.

Quartz. This mineral, in the form of sandstone, frequently almost chemically pure silica, forms important portions of the stratified deposits of the Northwest. With this form of occurrence we have not to do at present, but will pass to the consideration of the accidental, or subordinate, occurrence of silicious matter, either as distinctly crystallized in the sandstone, or in any form in the calcareous and argillaceous strata.

The most eastern locality of crystallized quartz which is of importance is that of Herkimer county, New York, in the Calciferous sandstone, where the well-known, exquisitely-perfect, doubly-terminated, isolated crystals are found in such abundance. The Clinton group contains layers of hornstone, or flint, which sometimes passes into chalcedony, and occasionally presents cavities lined with delicate crystallizations of quartz. In the Niagara limestone, quartz seems entirely wanting in those remarkable geodes which characterize this rock, and which are filled with calc. spar, pearl-spar, celestine, selenite, and other minerals. The Oriskany sandstone exhibits a few nodules of flint, as does also the Onondaga limestone; and in the Corniferous limestone we have this kind of silicious material in such abundance as to give a name to the rock: it sometimes forms layers several inches thick, which alternate with the strata of limestone. It rarely passes into chalcedony, and almost never assumes the form of crystallized quartz. We know of no quartz in any of the sedimentary rocks of central and western New York, in any position above the Corniferous.

In the States west of New York, quartz continues to be of infrequent occurrence: indeed, it is almost unknown, except in the form of sandstone, and in that of flint or hornstone. In Wisconsin, the Lower sandstone, a silicious, and occasionally somewhat ferruginous, rock, is rarely, if ever, found to contain any distinct crystallizations of quartz: this is also true of the Upper sandstone. The Lower Magnesian limestone, the equivalent of the Calciferous sandstone of New York, presents occasional geodes lined with minute crystals of quartz: but by far the larger portion of this substance exists in the rock in the form of flint, sometimes passing into an imperfect jasper.

Throughout the Lead Region of the Upper Mississippi, the absence of crystalline quartz from the lead-bearing crevices, where it would naturally be looked for in connection with calcite, barytes, and other minerals accompanying the lead ore, is one of the most interesting facts in connection with the occurrence of this metal. The lead-bearing strata, however, contain a great abundance of silicious material in the

* Hall's Geology of 4th District, p. 67.

form of flint, which forms numerous and heavy layers all through the Galena limestone, and is especially abundant in its central and lower portions.

The Niagara limestone in the Lead Region, and the adjacent country in Illinois on the south, and Iowa on the west, is equally marked by the absence of crystallized quartz, and the presence of nodules and layers of flint. The summits of those most north-easterly outliers of this member of the series, the Blue mounds, are made up almost exclusively of this material; but, in the extension of the formation around the north side of Lake Michigan, the flint is almost entirely wanting, and the crystalline quartz has not been observed: the rock representing the Niagara being everywhere in the region a crystalline dolomite, remarkably free from silicious materials, as from all other impurities, whether in the form of clay or sand.

Although the lithological characters of the great dolomitic masses, known in the Lead Region as the Galena and Niagara limestones, are almost identical, and although they both contain an abundance of silica in the form of flint, there is a marked difference in the way in which their fossil contents have been preserved. In the Niagara, the numerous corals which characterize this member of the series are converted into silica; this is especially the case all through Iowa; while the brachiopods are chiefly preserved as casts, portions of the shells being, however, sometimes retained and silicified. In the Galena dolomite, on the other hand, there are no remains of corals or shells preserved in any other form than as casts, except where the original shell was composed of phosphate of lime, instead of carbonate—as is the case with the common *Lingula quadrata*, one of the most abundant and distinctive fossils of the Galena rock.

In the rocks of Devonian age, through the valley of the Upper Mississippi, silica is a substance almost entirely unknown, except in the form of silicate of alumina, which is sometimes intermixed with the usually very pure limestones of this period. There are some impure silicious beds, grit-stones and shales, in the upper part of the Devonian, along the Mississippi, but crystallized minerals are wanting in these rocks.

In the Carboniferous series we have, for the first time in the Northwest, well-crystallized silicious material, in the large and numerous geodes which characterize the so-called "geode-bed"—a stratum from 25 to 45 feet in thickness, made up of an impure argillaceous limestone, and lying between the Keokuk and Warsaw limestones. The geodes are of every size, up to 15 inches in diameter: and, among other interesting minerals, are sometimes lined with crystallizations of quartz: or, more commonly, with light-bluish chalcedony. I have never noticed any instances in which the six-sided prisms of the quartz were developed, but only the pyramidal terminations. The occurrence of geodes in the rocks below the Carboniferous series seems to be very rare; the irregular cavities in the Lower Magnesian, which are occasionally met with, never furnish handsome specimens, and can hardly be properly called by this name.

Silicates. Of the whole family of the anhydrous silicates, it is not known that a single species occurs in the unaltered sedimentary rocks of the Northwest: at least, so much may be said, that not one has ever fallen under my own observation in the five years that I have been engaged in exploring that region. The hydrous silicates are equally rare, with perhaps the single exception of the silicious oxide of zinc, or calamine, which may occur in small quantity, mixed with the carbonate, but of which no well-marked specimen has been observed. This absence of the silicates, as also the great rarity of crystallized quartz, indicates a very different condition of things from that which existed while the metamorphism of the rocks of the same geological age was going on at the East, since this class of minerals is that which predominates in, and forms almost the whole mass of, the metamorphosed strata. So, too, the lead deposits of the Northwest are distinguished from those in the altered rocks of the Atlantic States—and, in general, from all mineral veins in the metamorphic, crystalline, or igneous formations—by the same marked peculiarity. This absence of quartz from the lead-bearing crevices is one of the conditions which has led to the adoption of the theory in regard to their formation and the deposition of ore in them, which will be set forth in a succeeding chapter of this Report.

SULPHATES.

Barytes. This mineral, although not by any means abundant in the Northwest, is found in quite a number of localities. On Lake Superior, in connection with igneous rocks, it is quite common to find heavy-spar forming a considerable portion, or the whole, of powerful veins in both the trap and the accompanying sandstone. As soon as we come into the unaltered sandstones, we have no farther indication of this mineral; and, when found in the limestones, it is only in small quantity.

In New York, barytes occurs in the Lower Helderberg group, in Schoharie county, especially in the water-lime strata, associated with the carbonates of lime and strontian. In the Calciferous sandstone, in Herkimer county, there are small seams and geodes lined with crystallizations of this mineral.

Farther west, in the Clinton group, we have this mineral in geodes, as at Wolcott, in Wayne county; in the Hamilton group, in the septaria, which are so common in this geological position, and which have the cracks in them occasionally filled with barytes. The Portage and Chemung groups contain but a small amount of it, occurring in geodes, or in the cracks of the septaria.

In the Wisconsin Lead Region, heavy-spar is occasionally found, with calcite, in the lead-bearing crevices; but I have never seen a locality where there was more than a small quantity of this mineral, and there are comparatively few where it occurs at all. It does not appear in distinct crystals, but forms masses, which, when weathered, develop on the surface a peculiar wavy-fibrous structure. At one locality, near Scales Mound in Illinois, and at the very summit of the Galena limestone, in a position where no lead has been found, we have a thin bed of dolomite with numerous geodic cavities, in which, in connection with pyrites and brown spar, well-formed crystals of barytes are found. They are small, few of them being so much as an inch in length.

The localities noticed under "fluor," in southern Illinois, in the carboniferous limestone, afford a little heavy-spar: but this mineral appears to form no heavy deposits or veins, anywhere in the Northwest, in connection with unaltered rocks. It is not found in abundance anywhere south of the immediate shores of Lake Superior.

Celestine. There does not appear to be any instance on record, and none has ever fallen under my notice, of the occurrence of the sulphate of strontian in unaltered rocks of Lower Silurian age. In the State of New York, we find it in considerable abundance in the remarkable geodes of the Niagara limestone, and in small quantity in the Clinton group and the Onondaga salt group.

Celestine has not yet been recognized in any locality west of Ohio, so far as we have been able to ascertain. We have never met with that or any other combination of strontian in the rocks of the Lead Region, or in any part of the Lake Superior country.

Anhydrite. The only locality of this mineral in the West is that at Lockport, N. Y., in the Niagara limestone.

Anglesite. The sulphate of lead is frequently mentioned as occurring in the Upper Mississippi Lead Region: it is very likely that it has been found in small quantities; but few specimens of it have ever come under my notice. At Mineral Point some minute crystals of it were observed lining cavities in a mass of galena: they were not over a twentieth of an inch in length. A curious form of anglesite was noticed in a specimen from Durango, Iowa. A large crystal of galena is surrounded by a crust of the sulphate of lead about an inch thick, having the structure represented in the annexed figure (fig. 16), which beautifully shows how the sulphate has been formed from the sulphuret, at the same time developing the cubical structure of the latter, minute points of which (represented in the woodcut by the black portions) remain, in several instances, surrounded by parallel concentric layers of the sulphate, which has an earthy texture, and a greyish color. These specimens from Durango, and those above mentioned from Mineral Point, with some small crystals found in the Lower Magnesian limestone, at New Galena, Iowa, and noticed under "galena," are all that have been observed by me in the Northwest.

FIG. 16.—Anglesite with Galena.

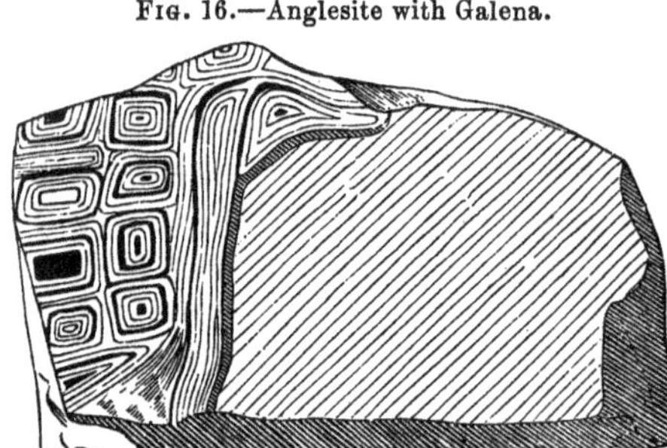

Gypsum. Next to calcite, gypsum may be put down as the most abundant and characteristic mineral of the unaltered palæozoic rocks. Although not entirely excluded from any part of the geological series, it is in the upper portion of the Upper Silurian that this mineral is collected in the largest quantity. We know of no locality in the Northwest where gypsum occurs in anything more than mere traces in rocks of Lower Silurian age. In New York, the first deposits of it make their appearance in the upper portion of the Clinton group, the same position which the limited beds of this mineral occupy on the eastern shore of Green Bay, in Wisconsin. The Niagara group, also, in western New York, furnishes handsome specimens of gypsum in small masses, but no deposits of economical value; neither do the Magnesian limestones equivalent to the Niagara in the Lake Superior region, or in Wisconsin, Illinois, or Iowa, contain anything more than traces of this mineral.

The Onondaga salt group, the next member of the palæozoic series above the Niagara, is throughout the Northwest the chief storehouse of this valuable mineral, which in New York is extensively quarried at numerous localities. For details of its mode of occurrence, reference may be made to the N. Y. State Geological Reports. To what age the heavy deposits of gypsum in Michigan, near Grand river, belong, we are unable to state: it is probable that they are in the same position, however, as those of New York. At all events, this is true of the gypsiferous beds of Canada West, as also of those, of much more limited extent, which are found on the islands and main-land of the Upper Peninsula of Michigan, near the island of Mackinac.

Gypsum is an almost constant associate of the coal of the Illinois and Iowa coal-fields, filling thin fissures, which run vertically through the beds, and usually associated with pyrites. It also occurs in distinct crystals in the fine clays of the coal formation, but no instance has come within my knowledge where it forms deposits of sufficient extent to be of economical value in the carboniferous rocks.

PHOSPHATES, ARSENATES, &c.

As regards the phosphates, arsenates, &c., we find no instance of any one occurring in the unaltered rocks, with the exception of pyromorphite, or the phosphate of lead, which is said to have been found in Pope county, Illinois; on what authority, cannot here be stated: but not a trace of phosphate or arsenate of lead has ever been noticed by me in the Lead Region.

CARBONATES.

The carbonates, or the combinations of carbonic acid with metallic or earthy bases, are, next to the sulphurets, the most important of the accidental minerals of the unaltered rocks, and, in the form of the carbonates of lime and magnesia, the larger portion of these rocks themselves are made up of this class of substances.

Calcite. Under this head we shall refer only to the crystallized forms of carbonate of lime, or such varieties as are distinct in form and structure from, and posterior in the time of their formation to, the mass of the stratified material, itself frequently carbonate of lime, in which they occur. The localities in which crystallized calcite is found are very numerous in the unaltered palæozoic rocks, and yet handsome cabinet specimens are almost unknown. One may search in vain among the lead crevices of the Northwest, where this material is abundantly diffused, for anything to compare with the magnificent crystallizations from the Saxon mines. The predominating forms are common calc. spar and the stalactitic; and it is only in rare instances that circumstances have favored the development of large and well-formed crystals. The famous geodes of the Niagara limestone, near Lockport, furnish almost the only noted specimens found in New York, at a distance from all signs of metamorphic action. These, however, are of but little interest, except from the other minerals with which they are associated. The uniformity of crystalline form in the specimens or deposits of calcite throughout the Northwest is remarkable, the scalenohedron — the form usually known as dog-tooth spar—being the one which largely predominates over all others. Calc. spar, or the variety in crystalline, broadly-foliated laminæ, is, however, the usual form in which the mineral occurs in connection with the lead crevi ces: well-formed crystals are among the rarities.

Geodes, lined with rhombohedral crystals of calcite, occur in the carboniferous limestones of the Mississippi valley; especially in the "geode-bed," referred to above under the head of "quartz."

Dolomite. The dolomitic masses of the Galena, Niagara

and Hamilton groups, in the Northwest, are almost pure; but large and distinctly crystallized specimens are not observed. The cavities in the Galena rock are not unfrequently lined with crystals of pearl-spar, but they are always minute. There are none equal in interest to those of the Niagara group in New York. The same may be said of the dolomitic formations along the shore of Lake Michigan, in Michigan and Wisconsin.

Chalybite. I have never seen a specimen of carbonate of iron in the unaltered rocks of the Northwest. Even the impure argillaceous carbonate is almost wholly wanting in connection with the coal-measures of Illinois, Iowa, and Missouri. In Ohio, the ore is already sufficiently uncommon, and becomes more and more so as we recede farther west.

Smithsonite. Next to the sulphuret of lead, the carbonate of zinc is perhaps the most characteristic accidental mineral of the unaltered rocks of the Northwest. The "dry-bone" of the miners—so called on account of the cellular, bone-like texture which it frequently exhibits—is the carbonate of zinc chiefly, more or less contaminated by various impurities, such as oxide of iron, carbonate of lime, clay, sand, sulphuret of zinc, &c. The appearance and associations of the dry-bone are such as to demonstrate that this was not the form in which the zinc was originally deposited in the Lead Region, but that it has been derived from the decomposition of the sulphuret. Among the proofs of this are: the occurrence of pseudomorphs of smithsonite after blende; the fact that the sulphuret often passes gradually into the carbonate, the latter retaining all the peculiarities of structure and aggregation of the former; and, finally, that masses of carbonate, when broken open, often show a nucleus of the sulphuret remaining in the interior—while the converse of all these facts has never been observed, The dry-bone occurs in the Lead Region of every degree of purity: some of the crystalline incrustations are quite free from all foreign substances; but the larger portion of the zinc ore raised with the lead contains a considerable percentage of impurities.

Three specimens of dry-bone were analysed by Prof. Chandler: these were selected as being earthy varieties, not representing the best and purest qualities, but still such as would be called dry-bone by the miners, and sent to the furnace as zinc ores.

The analysis of these specimens gave:

	i.	ii.	iii.
Insoluble................	53.50	31.71	35.08
Oxide of iron and alumina..	13.51	4.43	8.23
Carbonate of lime.........	14.55	10.37	12.69
Carbonate of magnesia....	10.79	5.37	9.54
Carbonate of zinc*........	4.73	47.00	32.51
	97.08	98.88	98.05
* Representing oxide of zinc.	3.07	30.49	21.09

The loss is probably water, not removed by drying at 212°.

No. i. was from the Gillam diggings at Centreville: it was an earthy, somewhat pulverulent mass, and is in fact a mixture of clay, disintegrated dolomite, and a little carbonate of zinc.

Nos. ii. and iii. were taken from the ore heaps at the zinc furnace at Mineral Point; they are probably below the average of the ore brought there, but a considerable portion is of this quality. They were selected as being thoroughly decomposed, and containing no visible particles of galena or blende.

Aragonite. This mineral is reported as occurring sparingly at Lockport, N. Y., coating gypsum in geodes. Farther west than this, I have never been able to detect it; although the fibrous stalactitic varieties of carbonate of lime are not entirely wanting, they are by no means common, and, when examined, have proved to be calcite, and not aragonite:

farther investigations, however, are required to decide this point, and of that minute kind which it was not easy to find time to make, however interesting the results might be with reference to the theory of the formation and deposition of some of the accidental minerals of the Northwest.

Strontianite. Not recognized, as yet, west of New York.

Cerusite (White lead ore, carbonate of lead). The carbonate of lead is very rarely found in the Lead Region of the Northwest, even in small quantity: handsome crystallized specimens have never been observed. An earthy stalactitic variety, of which specimens were given me at Brigham's diggings, near the Blue Mounds, as having formerly been obtained there in masses of considerable size, gave, on analysis by Prof. C. F. Chandler, the following composition:

Carbonate of lead	93.84
Carbonate of lime	0.58
Carbonate of magnesia	trace.
Peroxide of iron, &c	1.42
Insoluble (clay and sand)	3.43
	99.27

Malachite. This ore, which contains 19.9 percent of carbonic acid, 71.9 of protoxide of copper (equal to 57.22 percent of metallic copper), and 8.2 of water, is found in several localities in the Lead Region and its vicinity, but nowhere in large quantities. It occurs in delicately fibrous masses, with copper pyrites and azurite, at Bracken's copper mine, worked in 1859 and 1860, and it had been previously obtained in small quantities at the old workings for copper in that vicinity. The quantity obtained here is very minute. At a locality in Crawford county, six miles west of Wauzeka, where some attempts at mining have been made, the ore thrown out consists mainly of a sort of ferruginous mass, which would be called gossan by the Cornish miners, with small fibrous masses of malachite scattered through it, or occasionally forming botryoidal incrustations on the exterior; but always in small quantity, not making up, in the best specimens, more than six or eight percent of the whole. This material appears to have resulted from the decomposition of an ore composed of iron pyrites with a little copper pyrites intermixed with it: some of the latter has occasionally escaped decomposition. Exactly the same form of ore, with malachite, occurs at Mt. Sterling, about 15 miles due north of the locality at Wauzeka, on Sec. 27, T. 10, R. 5, W.

Azurite. Contains carbonic acid 25.6 percent, protoxide of copper 69.2, water 5.2. Quite handsome crystallizations of this beautiful and rather rare ore of copper were formerly obtained, although quite rarely, at the old copper diggings in the vicinity of Mineral Point. At the Bracken mine, now worked (1860), small but quite elegant specimens of azurite have been found, associated with malachite and chalcopyrite; the crystals, from $\frac{1}{20}$ to $\frac{1}{10}$ of an inch in diameter, occupying drusy cavities in the gossan. It has not been noticed, so far as I know, at any other localities than those about Mineral Point.

Zinc Bloom. The only locality where this mineral has been observed in the Lead Region is at Linden. Here, on the specimens collected, the hydrous carbonate (zinc bloom) forms an incrustation, about one-tenth of an inch thick, on the anhydrous mineral (Smithsonite). It is of a pure white color, concentrically aggregated, and delicately fibrous in its texture.

CHAPTER VI.

ECONOMICAL AND MINING GEOLOGY.

PLAN AND OBJECT OF THIS CHAPTER.—DIVISION INTO SECTIONS. *Section one:* GENERAL REMARKS ON THE OCCURRENCE OF THE METALLIC ORES.—NOTICE OF THE LEAD-MINING DISTRICTS THROUGHOUT THE WORLD.—STATISTICS, GENERAL AND COMPARATIVE. *Section two:* DESCRIPTION OF THE VARIOUS FORMS OF ORE DEPOSIT PECULIAR TO THE LEAD REGION OF THE UPPER MISSISSIPPI.—SHEETS.—OPENINGS.—FLAT SHEETS.—FLAT OPENINGS.—ARRANGEMENT OF THE ORE IN THE OPENINGS.—SECTION OF THE OPENINGS IN THE BLUE LIMESTONE. *Section three:* SPECIAL DESCRIPTION OF THE DIGGINGS IN WISCONSIN.—SPECIAL REMARKS ON COPPER MINING IN THE LEAD REGION:—ON ZINC MINING AND SMELTING. *Section four:* THEORETICAL CONSIDERATIONS ON THE MODE OF OCCURRENCE OF THE ORE IN THE LEAD REGION: SURFACE ARRANGEMENT OF THE CREVICES:—HOW FORMED:—HOW FILLED WITH ORE AND OTHER MATERIALS NOW FOUND IN THEM. *Section five:* PRACTICAL CONSIDERATIONS:—POSSIBILITY OF DEEP MINING IN THE LEAD REGION.—MINING IN THE LOWER MAGNESIAN.—HOW THE PRESENT SYSTEM MAY BE IMPROVED.

IN this chapter will be embraced all that relates to the mode of occurrence of the metalliferous ores and other economically valuable mineral substances which occur in the Lead Region. Having in the preceding divisions of this Report set forth with sufficient detail the character of the different stratified masses which underlie the district in question, and described the accidental minerals which occur in them from the strictly mineralogical point of view, we are now prepared to take up such of these minerals as exist in sufficient quantity and are of such a nature as to be, either actually or possibly, of practical importance, and to consider them as the objects of mining enterprise. In this connection, we shall endeavor to set forth all the facts necessary to enable the reader to form an opinion as to the probable extent and value of the mineral resources of the Lead Region, and to throw all the light possible on the difficult points which have presented themselves in the investigation of this interesting district.

In this attempt we shall follow this order of arrangement:

I. Some general ideas will be given with regard to the mode of occurrence of metalliferous ores, the different forms in which they are found, and the relations which these forms bear to the rocks in which they are enclosed: this is introductory to and necessary for an understanding of the real character of the mineral deposits of the Lead Region. As an appendix to this, a short account of the lead-mining districts of the North of England will be given, as convenient for reference and comparison, since it has been supposed by many that these were in most respects identical with those of the Upper Mississippi. A few words will also be added with regard to other important lead-producing districts in different countries, and especially those in the United States, for the purpose of comparison and reference. But little space will be required to exhibit the distinctive features of the different classes of metalliferous deposits, and they will probably not be considered out of place in this connection. A clear understanding of what is meant by some of the terms which must necessarily be employed in discussing the subject in hand will add much to the facility with which the reader will enter upon this difficult line of investigation.

II. The next step will be to present a general description of the various forms of ore deposits peculiar to the Lead Region of the Upper Mississippi, including definitions of the local and technical terms there employed, with figures and sections illustrative of the most striking peculiarities: this will be necessary in order to obtain a clear view of the complex phenomena presented by these deposits, and to prepare for succeeding divisions of the subject.

III. The third section will comprise a special description of the operations carried on up to the present time in the different mining districts of the Lead Region; showing the geographical position of the workings, and their peculiarities of arrangement and position: together with such historical and statistical details as could be obtained during the progress of the survey. In this division the various "diggings," as the lead-mining districts are usually termed, will be taken up and described, partly in a geographical and partly in a geological order; beginning with those which are highest in the series, and proceeding to localities worked in a lower geological position, until all which have been examined, or which are of any importance, shall have been noticed.

IV. We shall then be prepared to enter upon a discussion of some of the most interesting theoretical points which may have suggested themselves in connection with the lead deposits. The nature of the agencies, both mechanical and chemical, by which the crevices were formed, the openings developed on them, and the various metalliferous ores and mineral substances which are found in them deposited, will form an interesting subject for discussion; not only as being of great scientific interest, but as having an important bearing on the future development of the region, and as influencing the character of the mining operations which may be carried on there.

V. Some practical considerations will be presented at the close of this Report, and as naturally following after what has preceded. In this section we shall endeavor to show what application may be made of the facts and theories here advanced to actual mining operations in the Lead Region, and shall especially undertake to answer two questions which will be admitted by all to have an intimate connection with the future welfare of the district: the first of these is, whether deep mining is ever likely to prove profitable? and the second, what will be the most economical and judicious method of carrying on operations in future; or how can the deposits already known to exist be worked to the best advantage, and how can new ones be discovered with the smallest expenditure of time and money?

I. *General remarks on the occurrence of the metalliferous ores, and the nature of veins,* * *with a short notice of some of the principal lead-mining districts of the world.*

The forms assumed by the deposits of the economically valuable ores are various and complex, and the limits between them are not always capable of being drawn with such sharpness as to admit of their being satisfactorily classified. For convenience of description, however, it has been found best to arrange all the metalliferous deposits under two heads: the *stratified* and the *unstratified*. The first of these classes comprehends such masses of ore as are included within rocks of sedimentary origin, and which are in every way identical in their epoch and mode of formation with the strata in which they occur; this class of deposits may be illustrated by reference to the beds of iron ore in the coal-measures, which were deposited in the regular order of succession of the members of that series, one bed differing from another only in the chemical composition of the materials of which they are respectively made up.

The unstratified deposits, on the other hand—which class includes most of the forms of occurrence in which the metals other than iron and manganese are found—present a series of phenomena of a complex character, the real nature of which cannot always be easily made out. In the most general way, they may be divided into *irregular* and *regular*. The irregular, unstratified deposits include: igneous eruptive masses of ore, as, for instance, the iron mountains of Lake Superior and Missouri; stockwerk deposits, or bodies of rock impregnated over an irregular space with metalliferous particles; contact deposits, or accumulations of ore between the planes of contact of two different kinds of

* Extracted from the author's report on the economical geology of Iowa.

rock-masses. From this last class, we pass by gradual steps to that of the *regular* unstratified deposits, or mineral veins: the term by which this division may most properly be designated. A mineral vein may be defined as an aggregation of mineral matter, of indefinite length and depth, and comparatively small thickness, differing in character from, and posterior in formation to, the rocks in which it is enclosed. Veins may be divided into three classes: *segregated*, *gash*, and *true veins*. Segregated veins, which are peculiar to the altered crystalline, stratified, or metamorphic rocks, are usually parallel with the stratification, and not to be depended on in depth. Gash-veins may cross the formation at any angle, but are limited to one particular group of strata, and are peculiar to the unaltered sedimentary rocks. True veins are aggregations of mineral matter, accompanied by metalliferous ores, within a crevice or fissure, which had its origin in some deep-seated cause, and which may be presumed to extend for an indefinite distance downwards.

True veins are almost universally admitted by geologists to have originated in "faults," or dislocations caused by great dynamical agencies connected with extensive movements of the earth's crust; and for this reason they are believed to extend indefinitely downwards: an assumption which is supported by facts, since no well-defined vein has ever been found entirely terminating in depth, at any point which has yet been reached by mining industry. Gash-veins, on the other hand, are supposed to have originated in fissures produced by shrinkage, or some other cause confined in its action to a certain set of beds, and not extending into strata of a different character from those in which they originated. The principal distinction between true and gash-veins is, that the former may be worked to an indefinite depth; while the latter, however rich they may be for a certain distance, are sure to give out, or be cut off, on passing into another set of beds not suited to their development; so that no one vein can be made the seat of permanent mining operations, requiring a large amount of costly machinery, as is the case with true veins; some of which extend for miles in length, and have been worked downwards for centuries, without a permanent diminution of their metalliferous contents. Among the most striking characteristics of true veins, besides their persistence in depth, are: 1st. The presence of a peculiar gangue or veinstone, which consists most frequently of quartz, calcite, or heavy-spar, forming the bulk of the vein, and through which the metalliferous portions are disseminated. 2d. A peculiar, symmetrical arrangement of the contents of the vein, especially of the gangue, which is called the *comby structure* of the lode—lode being synonymous with vein—this consists in a disposition of the different mineral substances of which the vein is composed, in parallel layers on each of the walls, with their crystalline faces turned inwards towards the centre of the lode; so that, if the vein were divided longitudinally into two portions, each of these halves would correspond with the other in the nature and arrangement of the material of which it is composed. 3d. Well-defined walls, or sides of the vein, which are often grooved and polished, as if motion, accompanied by immense pressure, had taken place along their surfaces; and which are usually separated from the mineral substances forming the veinstone by thin bands of clayey matter called *selvages*, the clay itself being known as *flucan*. True veins are usually observed to traverse the rocks without being influenced by their stratification; sometimes coinciding in direction with the strike of the enclosing beds, but more frequently cutting them at a greater or less angle. On passing from one set of strata into another of a different nature, they often undergo changes in the character of the veinstone and the accompanying ore, but the fissure remains, even if quite barren of mineral matter; persistence in depth being the most marked feature of this class of veins.

Having thus noticed the most important characteristics of

the different forms of mineral deposits, we shall be able to proceed more intelligibly to a discussion of the varieties of forms under which the very remarkable deposits of ore in the Upper Mississippi valley present themselves. These deposits approach most nearly in character to what have been designated above as gash-veins; but they are, in some respects, peculiar in character, no mining region exactly resembling this in the mode of occurrence of its ores ever having been observed by me in any part of the world, unless it be in the Missouri mines, in which the conditions of the Upper Mississippi mines are closely imitated, although on a somewhat more limited scale.

Before entering on a minute description of the lead mines of the Upper Mississippi, and the mode of occurrence of the ore in that region, it will be proper to notice, in a few words, the principal districts in other parts of the world where this metal is obtained, and to consider with special attention those which have any considerable resemblance in their characteristic features to what is observed in the lead deposits of the Northwest.

The ores of lead have a wide distribution, both geographically and geologically, as there is hardly any important mining region where there is not more or less of this metal found in some of the veins; but the most productive deposits appear to occur in the carboniferous, or mountain limestone, and in limestones of Lower Silurian age. The great lead-mining districts of Spain and the United States are in Lower Silurian rocks; those of the North of England, in the mountain limestone; and these, together, furnish nearly 70 percent of the whole amount of that metal raised in the world.

There is one important fact to be noticed in connection with the mode of occurrence of lead ores, which is this: that they are found in heavy bodies, and extensively mined, in rocks which have not been metamorphosed, or rendered crystalline by those agencies to which the term "metamorphic" is usually applied by geologists, and among which heat and pressure were probably the most effective; differing in this respect materially from the metals gold, silver, tin, and copper, which are rarely found in workable veins except in the older and highly crystalline rocks. Zinc resembles lead in this respect; and these two metals are almost invariably associated with each other, and have many analogies in their mode of occurrence. They are especially the metals of limestones and dolomites: a class of rocks in which the other useful metals are much less frequently found occurring in such quantities as to be economically and profitably worked. Both lead and zinc are indeed found in considerable abundance, and are extensively mined, in the metamorphic rocks, but not in such quantity as in the unaltered strata; and in such cases it is usually the fact that their ores are associated with those of other metals, so that they are not themselves the exclusive, or even the predominant, objects of the miner's research. Thus, in the older crystalline rocks, a large amount of lead ore is mined, less on account of the lead that it contains than for the sake of the silver associated with it; and in such cases the lead itself could not be profitably raised were it not combined with the nobler metal. The ores of lead are found to contain almost always a trace, at least, of silver; and such are the refinements of modern metallurgical processes, that a quantity so small as seven or eight ounces to the ton may be profitably separated. It is chiefly, however, in the metamorphic rocks, that silver oocurs in large quantity associated with lead; and, as a general rule, the older and more highly crystalline the formation, the larger the amount of silver which is likely to be found in the lead ore raised from it.

Another important circumstance to be noticed in respect to ores of zinc and lead in the unaltered rocks is this: that they usually occur in irregular deposits, or in such forms as cannot with propriety be classed with true veins: hence they are liable to great and sudden fluctuations in their production, and lack that character of permanence which may be confidently looked for in mines wrought on well-developed veins. The irregular deposits in the unmetamorphosed strata are frequently worked for a time with great profit, but are liable to give out on reaching the bottom of the metalliferous formation, or of the particular stratum in which they are found to be productive: while, in the case of a true vein, it is taken for granted that mining may be carried on to an indefinite depth, without any serious and permanent exhaustion of its metalliferous contents.

ORES OF LEAD IN GREAT BRITAIN.

Aside from the fact that it is chiefly to England that we have to look to supply the deficiency of our own production of lead, there are some points connected with the mode of occurrence of its ores in the most productive lead districts of that country, which make the study of the English lead-mines, especially of those of the North of England, a subject of great interest in connection with the description of our own principal lead-producing region. The mines of Cumberland and Yorkshire are frequently referred to by those interested in the Wisconsin mineral district, and a brief review of the mode of occurrence of the lead ore, in those English localities most resembling our own, will be inserted here, for convenient reference when discussing the question of the persistency in depth of the latter.

The lead-mining district, of which Alston Moor is the centre, lies within the counties of Northumberland, Durham, and Cumberland, in the elevated region which occurs where they come together. The rock in which the lead ore is mined belongs to the Carboniferous limestone or Mountain limestone series, which lies next beneath the Mill-stone grit, the lowest member of the coal-measures, or the proper coal-bearing strata. The Mountain limestone series is made up of beds of limestone, which alternate with sandstones and shales, having a thickness, altogether, in the Allendale,

Alston, and Weardale districts, of about 2000 feet. There are about twenty beds of limestone, of each of which the thickness is known to the miners, and each having its local name. Thus, the main metalliferous stratum, which is about 60 feet thick, is called the "great limestone:" the veins in this bed have produced as much ore as all the others together. Owing to the dislocations of the strata, the depth beneath the surface at which this bed is found is very variable. Generally the veins are not worked below the "four-fathom limestone," which is 153 fathoms or 918 feet below the Mill-stone grit, and the vertical range of the mineral ground is about 600 feet; although some veins in the vicinity of Alston Moor have been worked as deep as the "tyne-bottom lime-stone," 1254 feet below the mill-stone grit, and immediately overlying the "whin-sill," a horizontal mass of trap-rock, of variable thickness, which is intercalated between the beds of limestone in an irregular manner, and appears to have been an igneous rock injected laterally between the strata; at least, this was the opinion of Prof. Sedgwick.

The miners distinguish three classes of deposits, namely "rake veins," "pipe veins," and "flat veins." Of these, the rake veins correspond nearly with what are commonly called true, or transverse veins, showing a comby structure, slickensides or polished walls, &c. They do not, however, always descend through the strata in a regular manner, but go down by a series of vertical and oblique portions, or by what the Wisconsin miners would call "flats and pitches," the change of inclination being coincident with a change in the character of the rock through which the vein passes. Thus, in the limestone or sandstone, the vein will be vertical, and, on passing into a shaly bed, will take an oblique direction. The thickness and productiveness of the veins is also greatly influenced by the character of the beds through which they pass. It is said, as an instance of this, that the vein of Hudgillburn, which is seventeen feet wide in the "great limestone," is only three feet wide in the underlying stratum of sandstone, which is known by the name of the "water-sill." In the shaly beds, the ore entirely disappears, and the vein becomes filled with an ochery clay, and even in the sandstone its productiveness is greatly diminished. Still, the fissure remains, and may be easily followed from one stratum to another.

Besides the "rake veins," or regular veins, there are the so-called "pipe veins" and "flat veins." The former are quite irregular deposits, of no great length, more like what have been designated as "gash veins:" they are sometimes quite productive, but soon give out. These pipe veins are evidently subordinate to the rake veins; and the same is the case with the flat veins, which are formed in exactly the same way as the others, and contain the same ore and vein-stone; which have, in this case, deposited themselves in the space between two adjacent beds, instead of in a fissure across them.

The lead region of Derbyshire is in some respects quite similar to that just described, but is more complicated in its details. The district, which is smaller in extent than the one last treated of, being only 25 miles long, is much more broken up by faults, which have deranged the continuity of the strata, and rendered their dip variable. Besides this, instead of one intercalated bed of trap, as in Cumberland—the whin-sill—there are three distinct belts of igneous rock associated with the limestone, the whole series of beds of both rocks having a thickness of over 1500 feet. There are four principal strata of limestone, the two uppermost being about 150 feet in thickness each, the others 200 and 350 feet; the three belts of trap which separate them have generally an amygdaloidal structure, the amygdules being filled with calc. spar and quartz. The local name of this rock is "toad-stone," which is a modification of the German *todt-stein*, 'barren rock,' so called because in this the veins are no longer productive.

The peculiarities of the veins in the Derbyshire lead

region have been the subject of much discussion among those interested in such matters, although we are not aware that any clear and satisfactory account of the phenomena which they present has ever been given to the world. The most striking fact with regard to these veins is, that they are cut off in the toad-stone, the fissure disappearing as soon as that rock is reached; this, however, is said not to be true in all instances, although it is so in much the larger number. It is said that, in some cases, the veins thus interrupted in the toad-stone are resumed again in the next succeeding stratum of limestone. The facts connected with the continuity in depth of the lead-bearing veins in the districts just noticed will be considered more minutely a little farther on, when discussing the question whether mining can be successfully carried on in the Lower Magnesian limestone.

Next to Great Britain, Spain is of the greatest importance as regards the amount of lead mined. The mines of the Sierras of Gador and Lujar were opened and worked most extensively about the time that the Wisconsin Lead Region first began to be settled. The production of this district was almost fabulous in quantity, amounting, in 1827, to 42,000 tons; so that the market became overstocked, a great fall in prices took place, and the miners were obliged to enter into a mutual agreement not to work the mines more than half the year. These deposits seem, from the description given of them by LePlay and other eminent mining engineers, to have a striking resemblance to those of the Mississippi valley. Like them, they are in the Lower Silurian formation, and in calcareous beds; which, however, are more metamorphosed than those at the West. In the richest districts of the Sierra de Gador, the lead-bearing rock is compared by LePlay to a calcareous amygdaloid, with its cavities filled with galena. The Loma del Sueño was said to look like a hill-side burrowed in by gigantic moles, and a shaft could hardly be sunk anywhere to a depth as great as 300 feet without striking ore. From the very nature of these deposits, it is evident that they could not have continued to produce so enormously for any great length of time; and, in fact, from 1827, when the amount raised attained its highest point, there was a rapid falling off, and the deposits are now comparatively exhausted. After these mines had been worked for some time, those of the Sierra de Almagrera were discovered, and a great mining excitement was the result. The deposits of lead in this district appear to be segregated veins in metamorphic slates of Lower Silurian age, containing intercalated beds of trap and porphyry. The ore is highly argentiferous, but the quantity of silver was found to decrease as the veins were worked in depth. The descriptions of the Spanish mining regions are, however, exceedingly meagre and imperfect, and but little reliable information can be obtained with regard to them.

Spain and Great Britain are the only lead-producing states which supply us with any considerable quantity of metallic lead. Prussia produces about the same quantity as the United States; Austria about one-half as much; the other German States about as much as Austria; France, Belgium, and Italy furnish much less than enough for their own consumption.

Aside from the lead-mining regions of the Mississippi valley, including both the Upper Mississippi and the Missouri mines, there is hardly anything doing in the United States in the way of the production of this metal. At various times within the last half century, a considerable number of lead mines have been opened in the Eastern States; but after more or less expenditure they have, with few exceptions, been abandoned, with considerable loss to those engaged in working them. Although the lead ores of New England are generally quite rich in silver, they occur in such hard rocks, and in so small quantities, that, although the veins are frequently large and well-defined, they have not thus far been found capable of being wrought with profit.

The most extensive workings for lead have been carried on at Eaton and Shelburne in New Hampshire; but these have been for some time abandoned. The mine at Warren, in the same State, which has been taken up several times within the last twenty years, is now working with a fair prospect of success. The ore here is chiefly argentiferous galena, containing 60 to 70 ounces of silver to the 2000 lbs. of lead, with blende and copper pyrites associated with it. There appears, from information obtained from the Superintendent, H. H. Sheldon, Esq., to be a large body of ore exposed in the mine, which can hardly fail to be got out and dressed with profit.

Several localities in Massachusetts and Connecticut have attracted capitalists at different times, especially those in Hampshire county, Massachusetts, and near Middletown and Plymouth in Connecticut; but they are all abandoned at present, and the Warren mine appears to be the only one now worked for lead in New England.

In New York, the mines of St. Lawrence county, near Rossie, were very productive at the surface, and, being on powerful veins, were thought by most mining engineers to promise well for deep mining. These expectations have been disappointed, however, and the mines are now all abandoned, the ore appearing to diminish rapidly in quantity as the veins were worked downwards. These veins, although in the oldest crystalline rocks, furnished a galena which contained only a trace of silver. The same results have attended the workings of the lead deposits in the Lower Silurian rocks of Ulster and Sullivan counties.

In Virginia, the Wythe county lead mines have been worked for many years, and are still in operation, but we have no reliable details as to the quantity of ore now raised.

There is but little or nothing doing at the Wheatley, Brookdale, and other mines near Phœnixville, Penn., which were supposed at one time to be of great value; and no mines of lead are known to be worked in any of the Southern

States, unless it be at the Silver Hill mine, Davidson county, N. C., where a mixture of argentiferous galena and blende has been mined to a limited extent for some years, producing a few hundred tons of lead annually.

The entire yield of lead in the States east of the Alleghanies will not exceed 1000 tons a year at present; hence the Eastern States are almost entirely dependent on foreign countries for this metal, as there is not more than enough raised at the West to supply the rapidly increasing demand of the interior States.

In Missouri, increased activity has been given to the lead business within the last two or three years, by the discovery of new deposits of ore in the southwest corner of the State. The Granby mines, in Newton county, which are in the Mountain limestone, have attracted numerous miners, and are producing, as I am informed, from 2000 to 2500 tons a year. Several other new discoveries have been made in this region, but no precise information is at hand in regard to them.

The old diggings in Franklin, Crawford, and Jefferson counties seem to be pretty much worked out: the whole amount of lead made in Franklin county in 1854 was only 206 tons.

II. *Description of the various forms of ore deposit peculiar to the Lead Region of the Upper Mississippi.*

Almost every mining region has some peculiarities in the mode of occurrence of its ores, and although certain general laws are found to govern each class of mineral deposits, yet every locality has some new fact to add to the common stock, and every district requires to be studied by itself; and even then, with the closest scrutiny, there will often be much that is uncertain and perplexing in the facts presented. No branch of applied geology is with so much difficulty reduced to fixed rules, and in hardly any department of science is there more to be done before we shall arrive at as clear ideas as in the study of mineral deposits. Yet this very circumstance undoubtedly lends a greatly increased interest to investigations in this department, while the highly practical character of the subject makes it one requiring a great amount of caution, and much experience. No one can be considered competent to pronounce on questions relating to the theory of veins and other metalliferous deposits who has not had large opportunities of comparison and investigation.

With these preliminary remarks, we commence the description of the peculiar mode of occurrence of the lead ores of the Northwest, necessarily including in our remarks much that relates to the ores of the other metals so generally associated with the lead, namely zinc and iron.

The simplest form of the lead deposits of the Northwest is the "sheet," and this we may consider first, as being the characteristic mode of occurrence of the lead ore in the Upper Mississippi Lead Region, and the one from which we may conceive all the others to have been derived by various modifications peculiar to certain limited areas.

By the term "sheet" is meant a solid mass of ore, filling a vertical, or nearly vertical, fissure in the rock, the whole remaining in the same condition in which it was when the deposition of metalliferous matter first took place; the rock not having undergone any decomposition since that time, so that the ore remains as it was originally deposited. It may here be remarked that, whatever changes in the chemical and mechanical character of the rocks and other ores associated with them may have taken place since the first filling of the crevices of this region with mineral matter, there is no reason to suppose that the galena, the only ore of lead occurring in any noticeable quantity, has itself been a sharer in those changes. The oxidized combinations of lead, or those products which are the usual results of the decomposition of the sulphuret of lead—such as the carbonate, the sulphate, the phosphate, the arsenate, &c.—are either altogether wanting, or else so exceedingly rare, in the region under consideration, as to prove conclusively that but little—hardly more than a mere trace, in fact—of the originally deposited sulphuret has changed its form since it was first deposited.

The sheet form of deposit, then, may be taken as the normal form, and made a standard of comparison for all others.

The annexed wood-cut (fig. 17), may be referred to as illustrating the nature of a sheet of ore in its simplest form, exhibited in a transverse section or at right-angles to its length. The dimensions of such sheets are very variable: in general, the thickness of the sheet of mineral will not be found to exceed three inches, and dwindles from that down to a mere seam, or film of ore no thicker than a knife-blade. Although there are cases where a solid sheet has been found much more than three inches thick, yet such instances are rare; for when the mass of ore is very thick, there has usually been decomposition in the adjacent rock, so as to give rise to what is called an "opening," as will be explained farther on.

FIG. 17.—Section of Sheets of Ore.

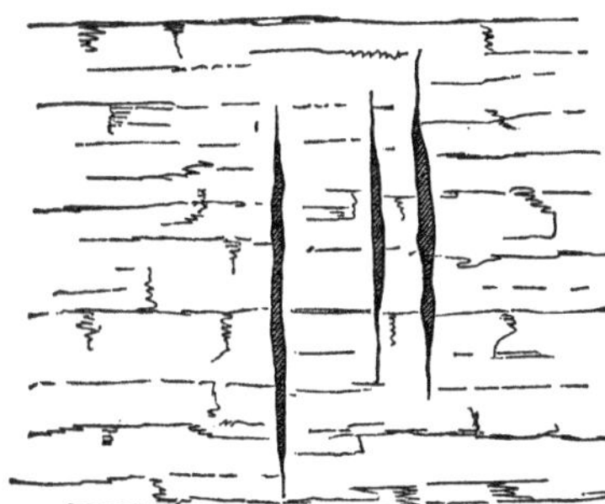

The longitudinal extension of a sheet of ore is not very great, usually varying from a few yards to a hundred: the greater the length and width of the sheet, the more likely it is to pass into some other form, and to lose its simple sheet character. The vertical height of the sheet is sometimes quite considerable, as compared with the usual vertical development of the ore deposits in the region in question. From twenty to forty feet may perhaps be considered the most usual limits of the sheet in vertical extension; but, in some instances, a much greater depth has been attained while following down an unbroken mass of ore. The deepest workings on a continuous sheet in the Lead Region are said to be those on the East Blackley range, which went down 140 feet on a continuous sheet of ore, as is said, the locality having been abandoned for some years.

The sheet of ore is characterized by the following conditions: it is usually regular in its form, as its walls maintain a pretty distinct parallelism for some distance, and then gradually close up as the ore thins out and disappears. In the sheet deposits there are rarely any of the usual accompaniments of a true vein, such as a gangue, or veinstone, and never smooth or striated walls; there is sometimes a little clay or ferruginous matter between the ore and the rock, a slight decomposition having, in such cases, taken place at the junction of the two; but more generally, the one is directly adherent to the other, without any separating substance. If the ore gives out, while the crevice continues, the latter becomes filled with clay, or ochre, or a mixture of the two. Sometimes calcareous spar takes the place of the ore, especially in the lower portions of the Galena limestone, while quartz is never present, and neither does the spar nor any other mineral substance in the crevice assume the comby structure characteristic of the true vein.

Vertical sheets, of the kind thus described, are rarely of great extent in any direction; but a number of them are frequently grouped together, so that they may be profitably mined in one excavation. Sometimes a large number of almost exactly parallel sheets will occur within a narrow space, forming what is called a "sheet-lot," or a "gang of sheets." The vicinity of the Hazle Green or Hardscrabble diggings furnishes some excellent examples of this mode of occurrence, which is almost exclusively confined to the upper portion of the Galena limestone.

The sheet of ore, as it occurs in the Lead Region, resembles the vein form of mineral deposit, in the fact that it is a mass of metalliferous material filling a pre-existing fissure in the rock; but differs from the true vein, on the other hand, in its limitation to a certain stratum, or set of strata, beyond which it cannot be traced; in the absence of veinstone, as a general thing, and, when it does occur, in lacking the arrangement in plates, or crystalline combs parallel with the course of the fissure; and finally, in the absence of smoothed and striated walls, which indicate motion of the sides of the vein, and are the necessary result of the formation of the fissure occupied by the mineral matters by the action of some deep-seated cause.

On the whole, however, but a small portion of the ore raised in the mineral region is obtained from the sheet deposits: in much the larger number of instances, the vertical crevice is connected with what is called an "opening," and forms then the "crevice opening," which is the characteristic and most general form in which the ore is found in the upper and middle portions of the Galena limestone, the flat sheet and the flat opening being equally charateristic of the lower part of that rock, and of the deposits in the Blue limestone.

The "opening" is the widening out of the crevice in a single stratum, or set of strata, in which the conditions were more favorable to the accumulation of ore, or where some chemical change has taken place in the vicinity of the fissure, so as to give rise to a softening or decomposition of the adjacent rock, which may still remain partly or wholly in its original position, or have been entirely removed, so as to leave a vacant space of considerable width. In either case, the expanded crevice, or softened material in its vicinity, is called the opening. The crevice, as followed down from the surface, will usually be a mere seam or fissure in the rock, with perhaps hardly a trace of ore in it: then, either suddenly or gradually, it opens out, and forms a kind of cave, in which the miner expects to find ore, since these expansions of the crevice do not generally take place except where the rock has been more or less mineralized, or subjected to some unusual chemical action. There are, however, instances where the opening occurs without any ore of lead accompanying it. The first and simplest modification of the sheet is the transition from the crevice filled with solid ore to the crevice opening, which term is generally applied to that modification of the crevice in which the ore is no longer in a solid sheet attached to the rock, but where, on the other hand, it lies in fragments, surrounded by, or embedded in, clay or decomposed rock; which materials, often with the addition of more or less ferruginous matter, generally almost or quite fill the fissure. The essential difference between the sheet and the crevice opening is, that in the latter case the rock has undergone decomposition, or become disaggregated in the vicinity of the crevice, so that the ore lies disseminated through a mass of loose materials which do not require blasting, but which frequently can be shovelled out like loose dirt. The width of such crevice openings is very variable, but this name would hardly be given to the metalliferous fissure unless it were a foot or more in width: less than this, it would more generally be called simply a crevice. When the dimensions are very irregular, the fissure contracting and expanding suddenly and frequently, so as to give rise to numerous isolated cavities of different shapes and sizes, connected by the general line of fissure, the whole is called a crevice with *pocket openings*. These two forms of occurrence may be understood, perhaps, by referring to the annexed wood-cut (fig. 18) in which they are represented in cross-sections. In this figure, *a* represents a crevice opening, or expanded fissure, filled with the opening material, which may be ferruginous clay, or disintegrated dolomite, and which is usually called "dirt" by the miners. If rich

FIG. 18.—Cross Section of Crevices.

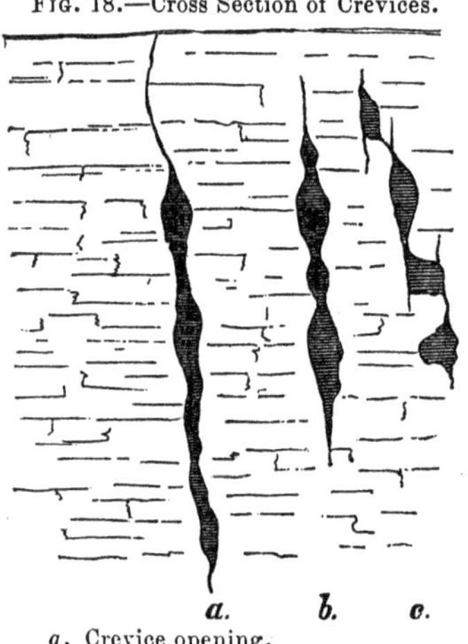

a. Crevice opening.
b, *c*. Crevices with pocket openings.

enough in disseminated particles or masses of ore to pay for taking out and washing, it is called "pay dirt." The pockety form of the crevice, shown in cross-section at *b* and *c*, in fig. 18, is better illustrated in the annexed longitudinal section (fig. 19), as the horizontal extension of these

FIG. 19.

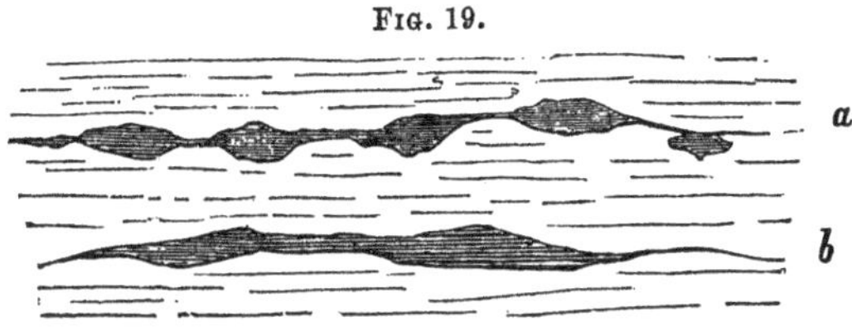

a. Crevice with pocket openings. *b.* Crevice opening.

crevices is much greater than their vertical range, and the variations in dimensions are more marked in following the length of the fissure. It is evident that these two forms of occurrence are closely allied to each other, the essential differences being irregularity of dimensions produced by unequal decomposition, arising from original unequal impregnation of the rock with mineral matter.

There are frequently great irregularities in the vertical height of the openings, which sometimes rise up in conical or cylindrical cavities, irregularly tapering to a considerable height above the average level of the opening: these are called "chimneys," and their form may be illustrated by the annexed longitudinal section (fig. 20) of a crevice forming chimneys, such as are occasionally met with in this region. These sometimes extend up twenty to thirty feet above the

FIG. 20.—Crevice with chimneys (longitudinal section)

opening, terminating in a fine point, and are often lined with stalactitic incrustations of carbonate of lime, or worn beautifully round and smooth by the slow chemical action of the water trickling down through them, and sometimes with a layer of galena and another of stalactites, as represented in the figure annexed (fig. 21). The "cave opening" is but a highly magnified form of the crevice opening, where its dimensions are so expanded that the opening becomes what may properly be called a cave; in such cases it is usually only partly filled with detritus, an empty space of greater or less extent being left above the materials at the bottom. Some of the caves in the vicinity of Dubuque, where this form of opening is found on the most extensive scale, are from fifteen to thirty feet wide, and nearly or quite as high. Thus the cave-like expansion of Levin's lode was one hundred and thirty feet long or more, forty to forty-five high, and from twenty to thirty feet wide, and when first opened was found to be about half filled with detritus, &c.

FIG. 21.—Chimney, lined with Ore and Stalactites.

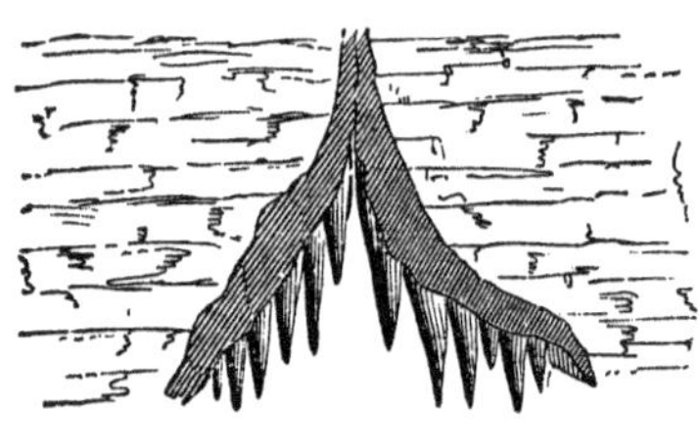

The crevice openings and cave openings are almost exclusively confined to the upper portion of the Galena limestone. In the lower portions of that rock we have the "flat sheet" and "flat opening" as characteristic forms of deposit, while the latter is the only form of deposit which is found to any extent in the Blue limestone.

The difference between the vertical and flat sheet form of deposit is one chiefly of position, but there are peculiarities connected with the latter which are of importance. The flat sheets rarely consist of simple layers or masses of galena, without other accompanying mineral substances or ores, as is usually the case in the vertical ones. Much more frequently, the flat sheets are made up of blende, calamine, and pyrites, associated with galena, which latter may be present only in small quantity, as compared with the mass of the other ores. The mineral substances which are of common occurrence in other mining regions as veinstones are also found, in some cases, in connection with the flat sheet deposits. Calcareous spar, called "tiff" by the miners, is the only one which is at all abundant, although heavy-spar is occasionally met with; while crystallized quartz, the most common of all gangue minerals in most mining districts, is here wholly wanting. The different ores and minerals associated together in the flat sheets are not unfrequently arranged in something like the same symmetrical manner which they exhibit in true veins. Thus, at Mineral Point, at Bracken & Allen's mine, a flat sheet was observed in 1853, which had nearly the form and arrangement represented in the annexed figure (fig. 22):

Fig. 22.—Flat sheet with Galena, at Bracken & Allen's Mine, Mineral Point.

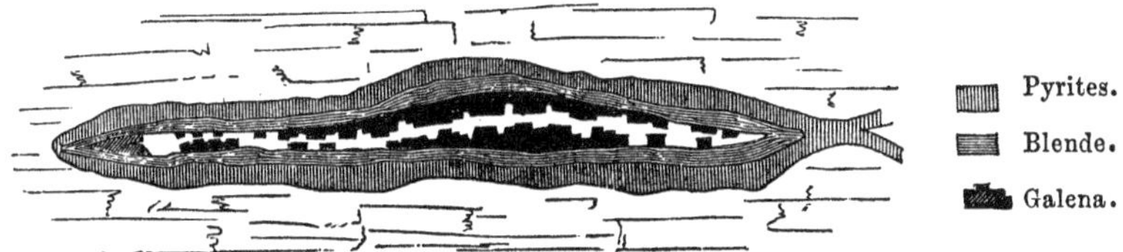

the crystals of lead ore lining the interior of large cavities in blende and pyrites, which sometimes formed separate sheets, as in the figure, but more generally were mixed together, while the galena appeared always to have been the last mineral deposited. The sheet of ore was about eighteen inches thick. Sometimes the different ores are arranged in parallel layers on one side—which is always the upper one, so far as observed—of the opening, there being a shallow cavity below, at the bottom of which is a mass of decomposed pyritiferous rock, with fragments of ore: an arrangement of this kind observed at the Marsden lode,

Fig. 23.—Section of Marsden Lode.

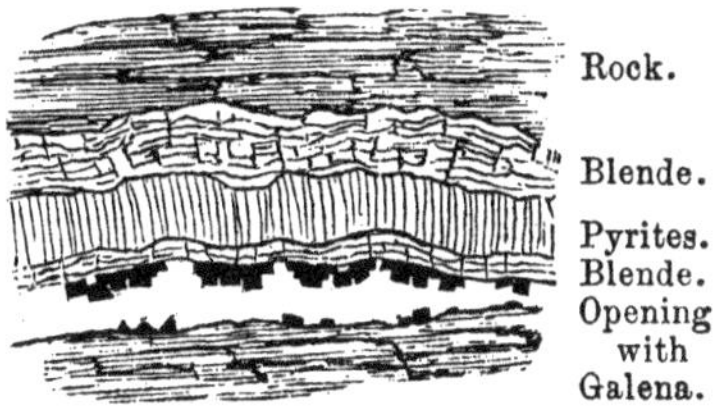

Rock.
Blende.
Pyrites.
Blende.
Opening with Galena.

near Galena, is represented in the accompanying wood-cut (fig. 23): here there were two distinct layers of blende, with one of pyrites between them; but such symmetry as this is quite uncommon.

In the flat openings, the galena may occur without any trace of gangue associated with it, the pure ore being attached to the solid rock in groups or sheets of crystals. The irregular openings at Shullsburg, which are often intermediate between crevices and flat sheets, and which present many curious peculiarities, are frequently of this kind, and have some analogy with the mode of occurrence of the lead at the Sierra de Gador in Spain, as described by LePlay, and which he compares to an amygdaloid, with enormous cavities filled with galena.

The annexed figure (fig. 24) represents the position of the

FIG. 24.—Flat Opening with Galena, near Shullsburg.

galena in a flat opening observed at Shullsburg, in 1855: the cap rock was seen fractured above, and encrusted with heavy masses of crystals of ore: beneath was a deposit of the usual opening material, with fragments of ore scattered through it. Another instance of this irregular form of deposit may be illustrated by a wood-cut (fig. 25). This was a cavity three or four feet in diameter, studded with large crystals of galena, firmly attached to its walls. One of these single crystals was seven inches in length across its face, and weighed between sixty and seventy pounds.

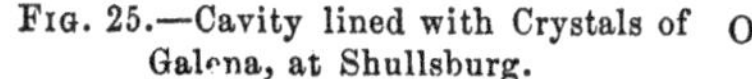
FIG. 25.—Cavity lined with Crystals of Galena, at Shullsburg.

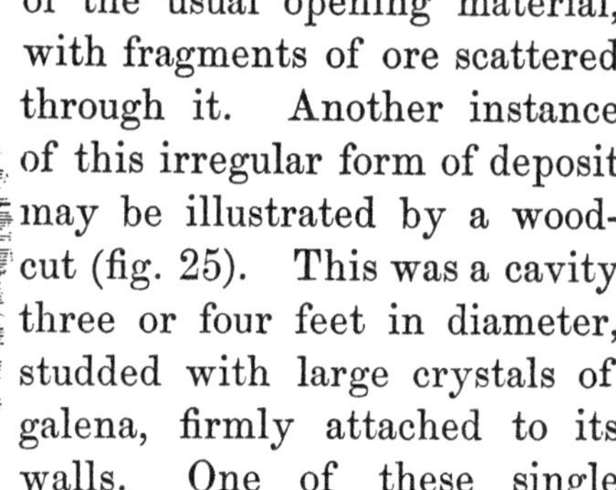

The general shape of these flat sheet deposits is very irregular, as seen above; but they are sometimes circular in their general outline, the metalliferous mass gradually thinning out in all directions from the centre. At the Marsden lode, for instance, the deposit of ore has something like the form represented in the annexed wood-cut (fig. 26), the sheets descending by steps from the interior towards the limits of the mass in each direction, and the diameter of the whole being about 100 feet. On the summit of the dome-shaped deposit, galena was the predominating ore, but the quantity of blende and pyrites appeared to increase considerably as the workings were carried down. More recent explorations have shown that there are one or more other deposits of the same general form in the immediate vicinity of this.

FIG. 26.—Section of Marsden Lode.

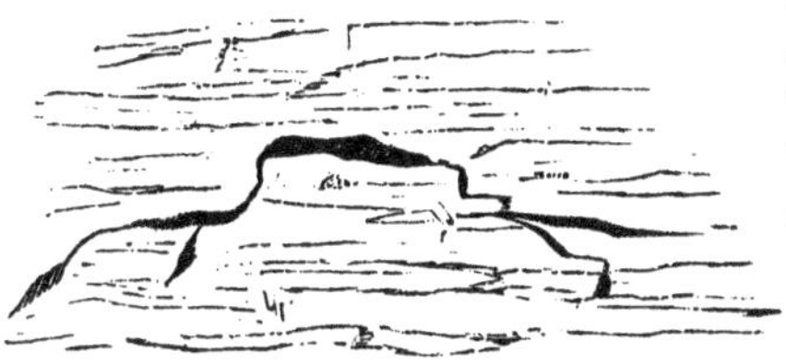

What may be called the saddle form of deposit, or a double flat and pitching sheet, is sometimes noticed, as in the very interesting locality called Mills's lode, near Hazle Green; which, when examined in 1857, had this form, the main body of ore on the top of the saddle-shaped mass being three and a-half feet thick, and composed of pure, solid galena. At Stewart & Bartlett's lode, near Dubuque, an opening was observed of this shape; but, instead of being filled with a solid sheet of galena, it was only partially occupied by crevice "dirt," with a little ore in small fragments scattered through it.

From what has been said above, the nature and form of the crevices may probably be understood, as also the passage of the vertical sheet into the flat one, and their connection with each other by the flat and pitching sheet, which may be considered as a combination of the two simpler forms. Some additional remarks may be appended with regard to the form of the openings on the vertical crevices, and the manner in which they are filled with the materials which they contain.

Although the crevice and cave openings are quite frequent in some parts of the Lead Region, the more usual form of opening connected with the crevices is that in which one or more sudden expansions of the latter take place in the fissure, on its entering into the productive stratum, as may be illustrated by the annexed figure (fig. 27), which represents the cross-section of a crevice with two openings, of a form exceedingly common in the Lead Region. The difference between the crevice opening and the crevice with openings is but very slight, and consists merely in the fact that, in one case, the rock in the vicinity of the crevice has been equally and regularly favorable to its development into an opening, while in the other, only certain strata have allowed the fissure to expand in them, so that the productive openings, if there are more than one, are separated by intermediate beds of rock, in which the crevice may remain tightly closed, or even disappear altogether. Frequently the rock above the opening is firm and solid, and covers it like a cap; hence the usual term of the miners for the stratum overlying the expanded crevice, which is called the "cap-rock." If the crevice extends up to the surface of the rock, it is called an open one; but if covered by a stratum into which it does not penetrate, it is said to be "capped." In some localities the crevices are all open to the surface: that is to say, only covered by clay and soil or superficial detritus. In other districts there are no signs of fissures to be detected until the cap-rock has been sunk through.

FIG. 27.—Section of Crevice with two Openings.

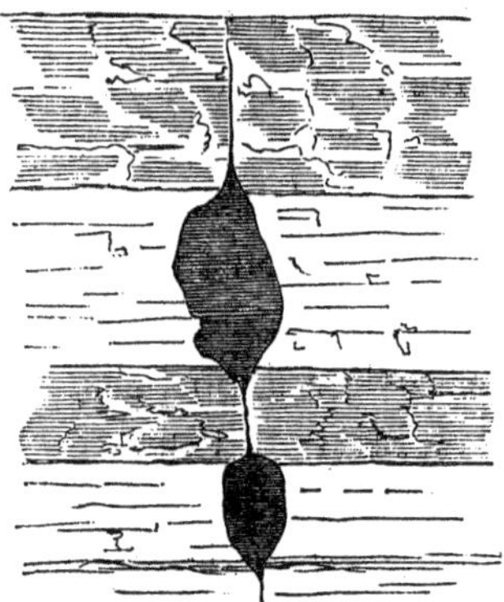

In regard to the nature of the "opening," it must be borne in mind that this term is applied by the miners not only to those cavities connected with the fissures in which there is an actual vacant space, or a cavity partly or wholly filled with materials introduced from above, as is frequently the case, but also in all instances in which there have been such changes in the character of the rock as usually take place when it has been more or less impregnated with mineral matter.

The arrangement of the ore and accompanying materials in the openings is very simple. In some cases the expanded crevice or opening is wholly or partly filled with substances brought in after the expansion was formed: in others, the rock, ore, &c., forming the opening material, are in the position in which they were originally deposited, but have undergone certain chemical changes, which will be described farther on. Where the fissure was originally an open one, we may conceive that the deposition of the lead ore took place on the walls, not completely filling the cavity, as may be represented by the accompanying ideal section (fig. 28); where the crevice was entirely filled up with ore, a sheet

Fig. 28.

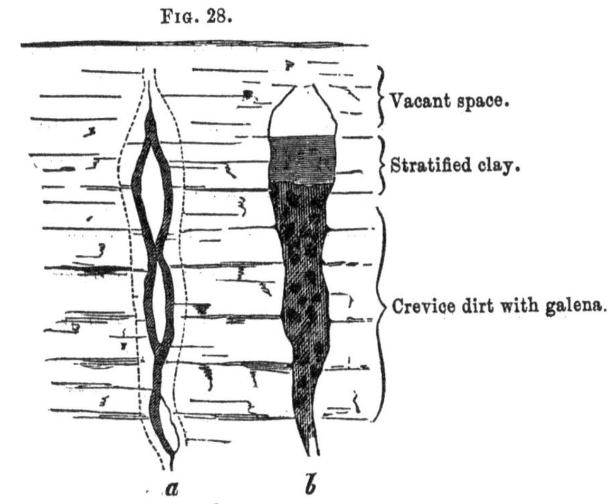

a. Crevice as originally filled.
b. Crevice after decomposition of the mineralized rock.

of mineral was produced which would be likely usually to remain in its original position, unless very extensive decomposition took place around it.

In the case illustrated above, the usual condition of things seems to have been that a portion of the rock adjacent to the fissure—as, for instance, that enclosed within the dotted lines on the figure—was thoroughly permeated with sulphuret of iron, which seems hardly ever to have been absent from the solutions containing lead. In a very few instances, the ore and cavity have remained as thus originally deposited, showing a cave lined with a hollow shell of galena. A remarkable case of this kind is described by Dr. Owen: according to him, a mass of ore was discovered at the Vinegar Hill diggings in 1828, occupying a crevice which was thirty-five feet in length, and expanded in the centre to a width of six or eight feet; the ore was deposited on the walls of the crevice so as to form a hollow shell of solid galena about a foot in thickness. Generally, however, the whole of the mass adjacent to the fissure, which had been impregnated with pyritiferous matter, has undergone decomposition more or less completely, and the resulting condition of things, when the crevice was a wide one, may be illustrated by referring to the crevice marked *b*, on the right-hand side of the last figure. Air and water acting from above, access having perhaps been allowed to meteoric influences by the partial denudation of the rock overlying the fissure, the pyrites underwent decomposition, the crystalline grains of the dolomite lost their coherence and were partially dissolved, and the result was a disintegrated material, made up of the carbonates of lime and magnesia, with a large proportion of the oxide of iron, and some sand and clay intermixed. As this decomposition took place, the mass of ore was loosened from its place, broken into fragments, and dropped to the lower part of the crevice, where it gradually accumulated, and became mingled with the decomposed rock. When the dolomite was unequally impregnated with the sulphuret, unequal decomposition was the result, and large masses of hard rock are frequently found in the openings, with the disintegrated portions: these undecomposed fragments are called "tumblers," or "tumbling rock," by the miners, while the softer loose materials are known as "dirt," or "ochre," according as they are more or less ferruginous. The presence of more ferruginous matter in the rock in the vicinity of the crevices, or in the detrital materials lying over them, is a fact everywhere recognized by the miner, who frequently forms his opinion of the probable yield of his diggings from the color of the crevice dirt.

Some chemical examinations made to ascertain the composition of the "crevice dirt," by Messrs. Chandler & Kimball, gave the following results.

A decomposing dolomite from Bracken's copper mine, near Mineral Point, contained:

Carbonate of lime	59.95	
Carbonate of magnesia	34.65	(by loss.)
Oxide of iron and alumina	2.14	
Insoluble, clay and sand	3.00	
Soluble in water, sulphate of lime, chloride of magnesium, &c.	.26	
	100.00	

This rock is not materially different in composition from the usual dolomite of the region, except that it contains a small excess of carbonate of lime above that required to form the double carbonate of lime and magnesia. On examination with the microscope, it is seen to be made up of loosely-cohering crystalline grains, with thin coatings of oxide of iron, the washing out of which allows the crystals of dolomite to fall apart.

Another specimen of thoroughly disintegrated crevice dirt, from a flat opening near Mineral Point, which was taken as a fair sample of such material, as associated with this class of deposits in the lower beds of the Galena limestone, gave on analysis the annexed results:

Insoluble, clay and sand..........................	6.18
Oxide of iron, soluble in acid, with a little alumina....	15.53
Carbonates of lime and magnesia (by loss)...........	78.29
	100.00

The substance of which the analsysis was given above, when dry, has nearly the color and appearance of Scotch snuff. Examined with the microscope, it is found to be made up of minute crystals of dolomite, thickly coated with pulverulent oxide of iron, of which the analysis shows an amount present equal to fifteen percent. Here there would seem to be no doubt that the disintegration of the opening material was caused by the oxidation of the sulphuret of iron originally contained in it.

Where the opening was not entirely filled with the disintegrated material, and a communication was opened to the surface of the rock, more or less clay from the superficial detritus has commonly worked its way into the crevice, and been deposited over the regular opening material in stratified layers. This clay may either wholly or partially fill the cavity, according as the crack through which it was introduced was large or small, or according to other circumstances connected with it.

In the flat openings frequently, and sometimes, although much more rarely, in the vertical crevices, the opening material consists of disintegrated rock, with fragments of ore disseminated through it, neither having been removed at all from its original position since its deposition. Of course, this would be the case when there was not originally a vacant space left after the mineralizing influence had ceased to act, or when there had not been considerable material removed from the opening by solution. Sometimes the opening material is quite hard until brought to the surface, when it soon decomposes and becomes a heap of detritus. This is the case with the flat openings in the Blue limestone, which are extremely pyritiferous, and which furnish a more argillaceous material on decomposing than is usually found in the vertical crevices of the Galena limestone.

Sometimes the opening is traversed continuously in length by a mass of undecomposed rock rising from the floor, and forming what is called a "key-rock." This arrangement is frequent in the wide vertical openings, and resembles the splitting of veins so as to include large masses of rock, which are called by the Cornish miners "horses," and are common in other mining regions. The persistency of the key-rock through a long crevice, from one end of it to the other, is sometimes not very easy of explanation. The annexed section of a crevice, showing this arrangement, is one obtained in Kerrick & Jones's lode, near Dubuque. What the shape of the bottom of the opening is, or how the key-rock is connected with it, could not be ascertained. That such masses, however, originate in the splitting of the crevice into two branches around a central mass, which afterwards forms the key-rock, seems hardly to be doubted.

Fig. 29.—Section of Crevice with Key-rock.

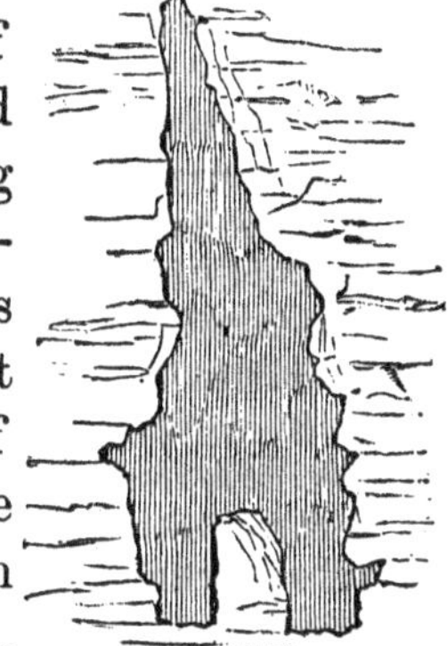

The number of openings which may occur, one above another, on a vertical crevice, is quite varying. Two or three are not at all uncommon, and as many as five have been observed. It is very rare indeed that all are equally productive; in much the larger number of instances, there is one which carries the larger part of the ore, and this is usually the largest one. In general it appears to be the fact that the upper opening is the most productive; certainly there are exceedingly few cases where the lower ones contain a larger amount of ore than the upper ones.

The openings on vertical crevices in the Galena limestone may occur at any stage in that rock, and there are no fixed names for the different ones over any particular district. In the Blue limestone, however, the flat openings are somewhat regular in their position at certain geological horizons, with reference to the subdivisions of that group.

The diagram (plate VI) will show the position of all the openings recognized in the Blue limestone and the subdivisions of the Galena limestone next above it, as far up in the series as the lower flint beds. This is not an actual section, as there is no one locality where all the openings have been found together, so far as I have observed; but it will be convenient for reference, as exhibiting, at one glance, the different subdivisions of the Blue limestone, with the accompanying mineral deposits, which may or may not be present, according to circumstances: it most nearly represents the condition of things near Mineral Point.

The middle and lower portion of the Galena limestone abounds in flints, although they are very unequally distributed in different parts of the Lead Region. The openings in the flint beds are usually flat ones, although sometimes combined with crevices. Some of these flat openings are very wide; they are usually filled with ochery decomposed rock, numerous flints, and masses of galena, although the latter are generally so small that the crevice dirt requires to be washed in order to separate them.

Next below the flint beds is the "green rock," so called, or, in some localities, the "calico rock:" the former is the usual designation. In some parts of the Lead Region, the green rock is a well-marked subdivision, and easily to be separated from the flint beds above; in others, the two are more or less united. Sometimes the green rock is very thin, and only exists as a subordinate layer, in connection with, and intercalated in, the flint beds. In the Mineral Point diggings, the distinction between the two is well-marked; but the thickness of the former seems to be very variable in the different sub-districts; that given on the section may be taken as the maximum. The green color is not very distinctly marked, but is rather a faint greenish stain on some of the layers, which disappears after exposure. It seems to be caused by organic matter, decomposing slowly in connection with pyritiferous substances. I have generally considered the green rock as forming the base of the Galena limestone, although perhaps it would be more satisfactory to take this and the underlying brown rock as beds of passage from the Galena to the Blue limestone.

The "brown rock" is a dolomite, stained of a quite dark brownish-red color by peroxide of iron, and lying between the green rock and the upper pipe-clay opening; its thickness is quite variable.

An analysis of the brown rock from Mineral Point gave the following results:

Carbonate of lime	69.79
Carbonate of magnesia	4.02
Peroxide of iron	7 02
Insoluble, sand &c	6.75
	97.58

The fact that this rock contains so little magnesia, as shown by the analysis, seems to be a reason for putting it with the Blue limestone rather than with the Galena dolomite. So far as observed, it contains no fossils. It is sometimes as much as fifteen or twenty feet thick, but usually much less, perhaps three or four feet on an average, only a portion of the layers having the peculiar brown stain. The chief characteristic of the opening in the brown rock is the quantity of calcareous spar which occurs in connection with it. Zinc ores are also rather more abundant in this position than in any other. This opening, however, is usually quite subordinate in importance to the pipe-clay opening below it, at the bottom of the brown rock.

The upper pipe-clay opening lies either directly on the glass-rock, or a short distance beneath its upper surface.

Very commonly the brown rock and pipe-clay openings are merged together, and cannot be distinguished; and sometimes the brown rock lies beneath a considerable thickness of the glass-rock, as is the case at the Holyhead diggings. The term "pipe-clay opening" is derived from the fact that the rock adjacent to the opening, and which has become mineralized, was of a very argillaceous character, so as to leave on decomposition a clayey mass, in layers alternating with shale and limestone; the metalliferous ores are distributed through the more or less decomposed materials of which the opening is composed, usually in small masses and isolated crystals; or, occasionally, in sheets. These openings are frequently very wide, sometimes as much as 100 feet; but occasionally they extend only a few feet on each side of the vertical crevice coming down from above. The vertical height of the pipe-clay opening varies from one foot or less to five or six feet; but it is not often as much as six. One of the most interesting points connected with this opening is the immense quantity of fossils which occur in connection with it, and which are frequently converted into pyrites. The pipe-clay opening may be recognized in many places where it is not worth working, as an argillaceous or shelly stratum on the glass-rock; in some of the sections given under the head of the Blue limestone, this circumstance will be found noticed, although they were made at points considerably removed from any locality at which the opening is recognized as metalliferous.

At a varying distance below the pipe-clay opening is the "glass-rock," or "dry-bone" opening, as it is sometimes called. In the vicinity of Mineral Point it is about ten feet from one to the other. I have had but little opportunity of seeing it worked, but it seems to be in every respect much less important than the pipe-clay opening. Its contents are frequently largely made up of zinc ores in many localities, and in its other general features it resembles that opening.

The "lower pipe-clay opening" is in the Buff limestone,

near the bottom; in its characters it is said to resemble the upper opening of the same name. In only one or two instances has ore been found in as low a position as this, and I have never had an opportunity of inspecting the opening.

Having thus given a general account of the mode of occurrence of the ore deposits in the Lead Region, and explained the terms there made use of, we will proceed to the third section of this chapter, which will embrace a detailed description of the different diggings within the limits of Wisconsin.

III. *Special Description of the Diggings in Wisconsin.*

As there are many particulars relating to the various mining districts of the Lead Region which are of both scientific and practical importance, and which can only be properly brought forward under a geographical arrangement, the following section of the Report will be devoted to this subject, namely:

The detailed mode of occurrence of the various ores in the principal mining districts of the Lead Region embraced within the limits of Wisconsin, with such historical and other particulars in regard to the workings as have been collected during the progress of the Survey.

But before entering upon this division of the Report, a caution must be inserted with reference to the absolute accuracy of some of the information contained in it, especially that relating to the amount of ore raised from the different crevices, and also, in some degree, to the depth and extent of the workings on ranges no longer worked, and of course inaccessible, or those which were temporarily suspended when visited for the purpose of procuring information. It is almost an unheard-of thing that any written record should be kept of the particulars mentioned above, or, indeed, of any facts relating to the mining operations carried on in the region in question; thus we are obliged to give up any hope of absolute accuracy, and to rely chiefly on the traditions current among the miners, or on the memory of some one who has felt an interest in such subjects, and who can give an approximate statement on matters connected with former mining operations in his own immediate vicinity.

Some persons may indeed think that it would have been better to omit altogether such information as was not based on personal observation of the geologist or some one of his corps; but we are confident that, in this case, imperfect data are better than none, and that, in the larger number of instances, the statements in regard to yield, extent, and time of working are pretty near the truth. Besides, the publication of imperfect materials is the best method of calling out more reliable information, as attention is directed to points in which the greatest deficiencies occur, and an effort will be made by those interested to have the errors corrected. It were much to be desired that such considerations as are presented above should lead to the formation of a society or combination of some kind among the miners, which should have for its object the careful investigation and record of all the facts connected with the lead-mining interest, for the benefit of future generations, as well as of those now employed in this business. When one considers how small a sum annually expended, if conscientiously and judiciously applied, would effect all that is required, it seems hardly possible that there should not be intelligence and public spirit enough to bring about so desirable a result. In European states, such work is always a matter of governmental supervision, and a mining bureau or office, for the collection and preservation of facts connected with the mining interest, forms an essential feature of the state policy. In every large and well-ordered country of Europe, the establishment of national mining schools, and the collection of mining statistics, has proved the importance which is attached to information of the kind here called for. In the United States, on the other hand, this subject has remained uncared for by either State or United States authorities, and it is due almost wholly to private exertions and expenditures that we have any general idea of our mining resources, or approximate knowledge of our yield in metallic products. The little that our census bureau has effected in this direction has been so badly done that it has amounted to less than nothing. Grossly inaccurate as our census returns have usually been, there is no department in which they have been so entirely at variance with the truth as in what they have indicated with reference to mining and smelting.

With these preliminary remarks, we pass to the consideration of the different mining districts of Wisconsin, within the limits of the Lead Region, preserving as nearly as possible a geological order in their arrangement: that is to say, beginning with those districts where the workings are highest up in the rocks in reference to their geological position, and proceeding to those where the mining ground is lower—as will be seen on referring to the succeeding pages. At the same time, reference may be made to the *Section showing the amount of denudation and the position of the mining ground in the different districts of the Lead Region* (plate No. VII), which has been compiled for the purpose of representing at one view some of the more important facts connected with the mining interests, and in reference to which a few words of explanation will here be inserted, for the purpose of making it more intelligible.

Whatever theories may be held in reference to the possible existence of lead ore in the lower rocks, no one will deny the fact that, at present, within the limits of the productive Lead Region, the mining is confined exclusively to the Galena limestone (or Upper Magnesian) and the Blue limestone: or, in other words, that the mining ground, as a whole, is comprised between the Blue shales (Hudson-river shales), which lie at the base of the Mounds, above, and the Upper sandstone below, making a vertical thickness of from 325 to 350 feet. But it is only over a very limited portion of the Lead Region that this whole thickness of lead-bearing rocks exists: and that is in the vicinity of the Mounds, and, in general, near the line of outcrop of the Niagara limestone, as explained in the preceding pages (see page 191). The denudation of the region, which has been discussed under the head of "Surface Geology," has removed more or less of the Galena limestone everywhere except near the Mounds; and this circumstance, together with the general southerly and southwesterly dip of the strata, with occasional undulations, brings about the result that very different thicknesses of the lead-bearing rocks are exposed in the different mining districts, and that sometimes the streams have cut their channels deep down into the underlying sandstone and the still lower rock, the Lower Magnesian, so that these formations are exposed to view in the midst of the mining region. As a general rule, the thinning out of the productive rocks takes place towards the north, so that their greatest thickness is found on the southern edge of the State; but the irregularities of denudation, and the effect of the varying dip of the strata, are such, that a considerable portion of the Galena limestone is preserved in the extreme northeastern corner of the Lead Region, near the Blue Mounds, while the very rapid falling off of the ground beyond that point, to the north or east, brings us, within a very short distance, on to the lower unproductive rocks.

The section in question, therefore, is of course only an ideal one, and does not represent any exact line drawn through the region, but only indicates at any given point the amount of denudation—or, in other words, the thickness of the productive strata or rock in which lead *may be* found—at the particular locality noted in the line standing above it. The same colors being used as on the geological map, the whole thickness of the Blue shales (Hudson-river group) is represented as remaining on the right-hand side of the section, and, proceeding towards the left, the ground is supposed to fall off until we reach the top of the Blue limestone. The vertical scale of heights on the left shows the thickness of rock at any particular locality, the distances being reckoned from the top of each group of rocks downwards. The amount of denudation is to be taken as referring to the general level of the district to which reference is made, and not to exposures in the vallies of the streams. Thus, under "crevice-opening, Galena" on the diagram, it will be seen that the general level of the workings near Galena is where about thirty or forty feet of the Galena limestone has been denuded, and that the main body of ore has been taken out at from 50 to 120 feet below the upper surface of that rock.

After this explanatory notice, we proceed to the detailed description of the different mining districts, commencing in the southwestern corner of the State, at the Fairplay diggings, which are high up in the Galena limestone.

FAIRPLAY DIGGINGS.

The Fairplay district forms a well-marked group of diggings, situated in the southwestern corner of the State, a little west of Sinsinnewa Mound, and surrounding the village of Fairplay. This mining district is closely allied in the nature of its crevices and its geological position to that of the vicinity of Dubuque, from which it is separated by about four miles of unproductive space; it occupies about three square miles of area. There is a large vacant space where no lead has been found, to the south of the Fairplay diggings; but they are connected with the Menomonee diggings, to the north, by a few isolated groups of crevices, as may be seen by referring to the crevice map.

The Fairplay diggings were first struck in June, 1841,* and the news of their discovery made a great excitement in the region, several hundred miners flocking to the place, and a village growing up almost in a day. Up to July, 1843, the crevices which had been discovered had produced as follows, on the authority of H. A. Wiltse, Esq.:

* Mr. Wiltse, in Grant County Herald for July 15, 1843.

	Pounds.
Fairplay range	1,800,000
Purdy	500,000
Sweeny	105,000
Gilbert	1,820,000
Utt	650,000
Ten-strike	600,000
Goda	250,000
Stone & Walker	60,000
Wood	150,000
Goodwin	610,000
Gilbert & Goza	200,000
Bruce & Demint	1,100,000
Bradwell	801,000
Bunches	600,000
	9,246,000

The following information respecting the Fairplay diggings was obtained by Mr. Kimball and myself in 1859 and 1860, with the aid of Mr. John R. Gray, by whom the surveys were made, and of Mr. Hugins of that place.

Section 36, South Half.

Smith & Galbraith's ranges: several parallel crevices near each other: course S. 85½° E.; have yielded 850,000 lbs.

Hugins r., 2.28 chs. N. of Smith & Galbraith's: course S. 85½° E.; produce 100,000 lbs.

Penberthy & Ralph r., 3.90 chs. N. of last named crevice: course N. 88° E.; yield 800,000 lbs.

Sheridan r., N. of Penberthy 1.80 chs., S. 82½° E., yield 100,000 lbs.

Elson r., N. of Sheridan 5.00 chs., N. 89½° E., yield 250,000 lbs.

Whitaker r., N. of Elson 4.75 chs., N. 89½° E., 50,000 lbs.

Clary r., north of Whitaker 5.00 chs., N. 82° E., 80,000 lbs.

Brady & Brennan r., N. of Clary 4.10 chs., N. 87° E., yield 250,000 lbs.

Section 36, North Half.

Beginning at quarter post on north line of section 36:

* The figures indicating the product or yield of the mines express the number of pounds of ore.

Distance between the ranges. Chains.	Links.	Name.	Direction.	Yield.
0	0	Shadel range,	N. 89° E.	200,000
4	80	Engine range,	S. 86½° E.	500,000
(60 links north of Engine range).		Buel side range,	N. 87½° E.	
7	15	Obischon range,	N. 89½° E.	
2	77	Elson range,	N. 85½° E.	
2	18	Thomas range,	N. 79½° E.	400,000
3	30	Doherty range,	N. 84¾° E.	10,000
		Gray range,	N. 87¾° E.	

The above ranges are included in Colburn & Buel's diggings. At the east end of these ranges, where the ground is highest, about forty feet of the "pipe-clay," or Blue shale, must be passed through before reaching the lead-bearing rock. Then about twenty-five feet of cap-rock covers the first opening, below which the shafts do not usually penetrate, on account of the water. The deeper shafts reach a second opening, three or four feet below the upper one, and the engine shaft on the Engine range reached a third opening; this was, however, quite small, being about one foot wide and three and one-half feet high.

The engine referred to here was placed on this range by the American Exploring Company. When first visited by me, October, 1855, the work had been in progress about two years, and a shaft had been sunk at the intersection of several crevices, one of which had an east and west and the other a north and south direction. The shaft was located at this spot by Dr. Percival, afterwards State Geologist, and was intended to prove the region in depth: it was then down 138 feet; and the hardness of the rock, a greyish-blue compact dolomite, may be inferred from the fact that progress was made in it, at that time, at the rate of only one foot per week, working night and day. The engine was of about fifty horse power, with four feet stroke and eighteen inches diameter, and was discharging, through twenty-one inch lifts, about thirty barrels of water per minute. The work on this shaft was stopped in October, 1856, the depth attained having been one hundred and fifty-six feet, which was twenty-two feet below the lowest opening, and only about eight hundred lbs. of ore had been taken out in the sinking.

Of the sum expended here I am not informed, but it was undoubtedly very large; and that the whole amount thus invested was literally thrown away need hardly be stated. The office of the company was in New York city.*

SECTION 35, NORTH HALF.

Southwest Fairplay diggings.

Several of the ranges on this section are supposed to be identical with, or continuations of, those on section 36; others have not been traced across. They are as follows:

Goodwin r., supposed to be the same as the Obischon r.: has produced 2,500,000.

Sink-hole r., 2.65 chs. S. of Goodwin: course S. 88½ E.

Goza r., 5.48 S. of Sink-hole r., supposed to be the continuation of the Doherty r., but not certain: course S. 88½° E.; has produced 75,000.

Sam Lemon r., 8 chs. S. of the Goza r., proved to be the continuation of the Engine or Bradwell r.

French r., on line between sections 35 and 36.

Gruce r., 4 chs. S. of Sam Lemon r.: course S. 80° E.

SECTION 25, SOUTH HALF.

Fairplay diggings.

The starting point for the survey of the ranges on this section was 300 feet east of the quarter-post on south line

* Since writing the above, I learn through the kindness of J. R. Gray, Esq., that about $30,000 was expended here. Mr. Gray remarks that, when the shaft had reached the depth of 150 feet, a marked change took place, the rock becoming concretionary, containing nodules of silicious matter, with abundance of carbonate of lime, and numerous pockets filled with sand, ochre, and small cubes of galena. He infers that the work was abandoned just at the time when a new opening was about to be reached. It does indeed seem unfortunate, that when so much had been expended, a little more should not have been done to settle this question.

of section, and the distances, going north from range to range, are given in the table:

Name of range.	Distance.	Course of crevice.	Yield.
Burns range	5.35	S. 89° E.	150,000
Wilkinson No. 1 range	2.50	S. 85° E.	10,000
Wilkinson No. 2 range	1.00	S. 85° E.	
Soward range	1.66	S. 87½° E.	200,000
Nolan range	1.90	S. 89° E.	100,000
Cave range	7.70	N. 89½° E.	100,000
Engine range	4.65	S. 89° E.	450,000
Carr range	3.65	S. 89° E.	150,000
Kinian range	4.95	N. 88½° E.	200,000
Dupee range	5.65	N. 85½° E.	

These are mostly pretty heavy and regular ranges, of considerable length, some of them running over on to the next section west, as seen on the crevice map.

The *Burns range* is a regular crevice, with openings below a cap-rock varying in places from twelve to twenty-five feet in thickness; above the cap-rock is a variable thickness of the pipe-clay and shales, according to the elevation of the surface. At the depth of about ninety feet, water is struck, the openings still continuing below, but closing up gradually; the crevice is only shown in the pipe-clay and shale by a ferruginous stain, but is plainly indicated as soon as the Galena limestone is struck.

These observations apply equally to all the ranges on this section.

The *Wilkinson ranges* are very well-marked crevices, widening out in some places in the openings to from forty to sixty feet, but not productive in ore.

The Soward range. In this range, six smaller crevices unite going east, and form two larger ones, separated by a key-rock six feet wide; at the point of junction the opening is thirty feet in width. This range intersects the Nolan range going west.

Nolan range. This range has been worked across on to section 26, nearly a mile in length.

Cave range. An opening, at the usual random, 300 feet long and from fifteen to thirty feet in width, partially empty; the ore all lying at the bottom, and left going down in the water. The Cave range is supposed to be the same as the Bruce, on section 26, west.

Engine range. Formerly worked with an engine; the shaft being 100 feet deep, and passing through three openings, of which the first is at the usual random, and the second twelve feet below the first and six feet wide; the third six feet below the second. Ore was found in each opening. This range has been worked about a mile in length, at intervals.

Carr range. This range is an opening indistinctly capped, which is not usually the case in this vicinity.

Kinian range. Very slightly capped, owing to its position on the brow of an elevation.

SECTION 26, SOUTH HALF.

The *Engine range* extends over on to this section, as before noticed.

Seeley range, 6 chains S. of Engine range: course N. 87½° E.

Bruce range, 71 feet S. of Seeley range: course S. 87½° E.; supposed to be the continuation of the Cave range on sec. 25.

Baird range; continuation of Nolan range: 8.15 chains S. of Bruce range; course N. 87° E.

Smalpage range, 3.50 chains S. of the Baird range; course S. 87° E.

The *Williams range* is nearly on the line between sections 26 and 35, and is supposed to be the continuation of the Shadel range.

SECTION 25, NORTH HALF.

North Fairplay diggings.

Sparks range, 10 chains N. of south boundary of this half-section; course S. 78° E. Branch of Sparks range, going off on the north side, with a course of N. 84½° E.

Engine range (Carey), 4.90 chs. S. of Slater range; course E. and W.; shaft 70 feet deep; yield 50,000.

Slater range, 6.70 chs. S. of Barnes r.; course N. 87° E.; yield 250,000.

Barnes range, 2.23 chs. S. of Gregoire r.; course N. 85° E.

Gregoire range, 9.20 chs. S. of north line of section 25; course S. 88½° E.; 150,000.

Sweeney range, in the village of Fairplay, 5.92 chs. S. of Turnbull r., E. and W.; 150,000.

Turnbull range, 3.18 chs. S. of Fairplay r.; course N. 81° E.; yield 300,000; open to the surface.

Fairplay range, 7.67 chs. S. of Penn Stone range. A heavy range, carrying a 24 inch sheet of ore in many places, and in bunches, nearly continuous; course S. 87° E., near line between sections 24 and 25; has produced 2,000,000.

Section 24, South Half.

Continuation of North Fairplay diggings.

Penn Stone range, 5.24 chains S. of Godey r.; course S. 87° E.; crevice open to the surface, and has not been followed to the high ground, where it would probably be found capped; yield 600,000.

Godey range, 4.15 chains S. of Ten Strike r.; course S. 84¾° E.; yield 250,000; sometimes capped and sometimes open, according to the elevation of the ground.

Ten Strike range, 8 chains S. of Jerney range; course S. 87° E.; open crevice; yield 600,000.

Jerney range, 7.90 chs. S. of Carnes & Co's r.; course S. 85½° E; open crevice throughout, except at eastern end; gradually widening towards its central part, where it is 15 feet wide: large fragments of tumbling rock in it, but no regular key-rock; yield 200,000.

Carnes, Sweeney & Hutt range. A long and heavy range, sometimes capped on the higher ground: 11.40 chains S. of line dividing the section E. and W.; course S. 86½° E.

There are two small crevices on the southeast quarter of section 24; one, the *Gregoire range*, is 5 chains N. of S. line of section; course S. 85½° E.: the other, the *Menson & Merrick range*, 3.35 chains N. of the Gregoire r., course N. 85½° E. The Gregoire is a regular opening beneath 14 to 18 feet of cap-rock. The Menson & Merrick is an open crevice, making in chimneys and pockets; yield 70,000.

From the above notices of the Fairplay diggings, it will be seen that they are on long and well-defined crevices, which have in some instances been worked for a mile in length. Their parallelism is remarkable, agreeing in this respect with the Dubuque crevices: hardly any one of those to the south of Fairplay varies more than one or two degrees from a true east and west line. There are very few quartering ranges, and no productive norths and souths. In character, the Fairplay crevices are crevice openings, or crevices expanding into openings in the regular random, which is very high up in the Galena limestone, for the first opening. Three openings have been observed in some of the deepest shafts; but the upper one is the largest and the most productive. The second and third can only be reached by the aid of pumps and a steam engine, and the employment of these does not appear to have been profitable. In the case of the Colburn engine range (on sec. 36), the experiment was a very disastrous one, as mentioned above. It would appear that no shaft in these diggings has gone down as low as the middle of the Galena limestone. As the lower beds are not exposed in the immediate vicinity of Fairplay, it is, of course, not impossible that they should be found productive on sinking to them. The extreme hardness of the unproductive bars of ground is a great obstacle to the proving of the lower openings.

HUNSACKER DIGGINGS.

The Fairplay diggings are connected to the north with the Lower and Upper Menomonee mining districts by the Hunsacker diggings, which are situated about one and one-half miles N. N. E. of the village of Fairplay, at the corner of sections 18, 19, 24, and 13.

The principal Hunsacker range consists of one principal or master crevice, and two smaller parallel ones: course S. 89° E. In October, 1859, an engine of ten horse power was pumping on this range, and the shaft was sunk seventy-seven feet deep. There were two openings, at a vertical distance of fifteen feet apart, with a small seam connecting them. The upper opening was eighteen feet wide, and worked for a length of three hundred and fifty feet; the lower opening six feet wide, as far as then worked. Water was reached at twenty-five feet in depth. At that time the produce of these diggings was given me by Mr. Carnes as 2,100,000 lbs.

There is another crevice, about 750 feet south of the Hunsacker, worked by Harney & Co., where a shaft has been sunk, but not much ore raised.

There are several ranges on section 18, about one-fourth of a mile north of the Hunsacker: the principal one was called the *Carnes & Tomlinson* range; this is made up of two crevices, six feet apart, of which the southern is much the larger: course S. 85° E.; worked, in October, 1859, forty-five feet deep, by the aid of a horse pump: yield in a very small space, up to the above-mentioned time, 450,000 lbs.

Carnes range, 70 yds. N. of Tomlinson; crevice not much worked up to 1859, on account of water; yield 12,000.

Taylor range, 100 feet N. of Tomlinson; worked in 1849 and 50: course N. 89° E.; yield 100,000: this crevice runs under Mr. Carnes's house.

The *Obischon range* is a short one in the northeast corner of section 24, which has produced 200,000.

SHAWNEETOWN DIGGINGS.

SECTION 20.—(*Town.* 1, *Range* 1 W.)

A group of heavy diggings is found on the north half of section 20; the principal ranges are the following:

Van Vleck's range. Nine chs. south of quarter-section corner, on N. line of section 20: bears N. 88½° W. In October, 1859, a horse pump was in operation here, and the shaft down fifty-two feet; in 1860, an engine of sixty-five horse power was being placed on the range. One opening only has been proved to exist here; but another one is believed to exist, sixteen feet below the upper one, which is thirty feet in width. Several norths and souths cross the easts and wests here, and at the intersections very productive chimneys of ore are found: at other points the norths and souths are entirely barren. The cap-rock at Van Vleck's is about twenty-five feet thick, and contains some ore disseminated through it, though chiefly in a leading seam extending continuously with the vertical sheet of the crevice: yield 1,500,000.

Turner's range. A heavy lode, 5.50 chains south of Van Vleck's: course N. 88° W.: the heaviest diggings are on a length of four hundred feet: not worked at present. It has produced 600,000.

FINITY LOT.

There are five or more short ranges, which have produced considerable ore, on what is called the Finity lot, of which the names and the amount produced were given as follows in October, 1859:

Charles Hueston range, worked in 1852: course E. and W.: yield 500,000.

Carnes & Butterfield range, 50 feet south of Hueston r.: E. and W.: yield 60,000.

Thorson range, 150 feet S. of Carnes r.: course S. 86° E.

Carnes South range, 90 feet S. of Thorson r.: course S. 88° E.; yield 200,000.

Driscoll & Butterfield range, 120 feet S. of Carnes South r.: course S. 88° E.; worked in 1856; yield 450,000.

MENOMONEE DIGGINGS.

(A.) *Lower Menomonee, or Kilbourn diggings.*

The Lower Menomonee diggings are situated chiefly on the east half of Sec. 12, Town. 1, Range 2, west; but they extend east on to Section 7 (T. 1, R. 1, W.), for a short distance, and also on to Section 13. They form quite a distinct, isolated, and well-marked group of crevices, nearly parallel with each other, and connected with the Upper Menomonee diggings, two miles north, by the Clinkor and Williams ranges, which are about half-way between the Upper and Lower Menomonee districts. The village of Jamestown lies between these diggings, which are fourteen miles north of Galena.

The following ranges were known and worked up to 1843, as appears by Mr. Van Vleck's account, in the Grant County Herald of August 12th of that year:

Thos. M'Knight's Lode and Patch	1,200,000
May	1,000,000
James Boice	1,150,000
Ramsay Patch	175,000
Brooks & M'Allister	75,000
Scane & Kilby	140,000

The following ranges are the principal ones worked up to this time:

Commencing at the quarter post on the E. side of section 12 (T. 1, R. 2, W.), and going south, we have:

M'Knight's range. 30.00 chains long, course N. 82° W.

Two chains north of a point nine chains west of east end of M'Knight's, the *Konkey & Kilby range*, 35 chains long: course N. 78½° W.

South on section line 15.00 chains, thence N. 82° W. 10.00 chains, to the west end of *Morgan range:* 30.00 chains long: course N. 83° W.

Nineteen chains south on line, to the *May range:* 37.00 chs. long on the west side of the line, and 18.00 chains on the east: course N. 87½° W.

The Ramsay Patch, 3 chs. north of a point on the May range 20 chains west of its east end, 5 chs. long: course N. 83° W.

Marlow range. South 20.00 chains on line, length 10.00 chains: course N. 85° W.

Hall range. South 25.50 chains on line, then N. 80° W. 20 chains, to the E. end of this range, which is 10.00 chains long.

At 35.00 chains south on line, a crevice (no name), 4.00 chains long: course N. 87° W.

South from section corner between sections 12 and 13, 14.00 chs., thence N. 85° W. 5.00 chs. to east end of *M'Knight & Ewing's range:* 20.00 chains long: course N. 87° W.

From the E. end of the above named crevice, N. 87° W. 13.00 chains, to the intersection of a *quartering sheet crevice:* course N. 55° W.: length 10.00 chains.

Peyton range. The east end of this range is 18.00 chains W. of section line, and 4.00 chains south of N. line of section 13: course N. 82½° W.: length 6.00 chains.

Quartering crevice, on section 12: commencing 20.00 chains W. of S. E. corner of section: course N. 64° W.: length 20.00 chains.

Pinch crevice, 1.25 chains south of Marlow range; it commences 20.00 chains W. of section line, and bears N. 80° W.: length 15.00 chs.

Reed & Van Houten range: one chain N. of quarter post, centre of section 12, and its W. end is 5.00 chs. E. of N. & S. quarter-section line; course S. 83½° E.: length 4.00 chains.

The following information was obtained from Mr. Kilbourn in regard to the Lower Menomonee diggings.

Between the May and the Marlow ranges, and crossing the May range to the north, are four or five small norths and souths, from twelve to fifteen feet apart, which intersect the easts and wests, and form chimneys at the intersections. The norths and souths themselves carry ore, in sheets from one-half inch to one inch thick. The whole ground is cut up by these norths and souths; but only in a few instances have they been found worth working.

All the easts and wests have about the same course and character of occurrence. The crevices are pretty open, and when the rock closes up, it is quite soft and friable. When they are open, they are filled with clay, or clay intermixed with tumbling rock.

Pocket openings are found within the depth of seventy feet on the highest ground, and in the lowest twenty to thirty feet, at which the cap-rock is reached. This cap has only been worked through in three places, and those on the May range, where it is found to be from ten to fourteen feet thick: the presence of water is the cause of this. No regular opening has ever been struck above this, only pockets being met with; and the dimensions or yield of this have never been proved. In the case of the May range, the opening below the cap was not worked to any extent, as it contained but little ore, and the water was very troublesome. The pocket openings are entirely irregular in number and position.

But little mining has been done at these diggings of late years, and the account of them must necessarily be meagre.

(B.) *Upper Menomonee Diggings.*

The first discovery in this district is said to have been made by James Boice* in 1827, and up to 1843, according to Mr. Van Vleck, 15,000,000 lbs. of ore had been mined. The following list is given of the principal ranges worked, and their yield to that time, when about 100 miners were at work:

* Grant County Herald, August 12th, 1843.

	Pounds.		Pounds.
Christy range..........	2,000,000	Gilmore & Whittiker....	300,000
Bunn..................	1,700,000	Morrow & Taylor.......	150,000
A. M'Cormick lot........	1,000,000	Brock & Crocker lot.....	500,000
Van Vickle range.......	900,000	Ford & Whittiker.......	100,000
Brooks & M'Adams......	700,000	Taylor & M'Cormick.....	350,000
Donaldson & French patch	500,000	Jackson or Four crevices,	600,000
Scofield lode...........	300,000	Jackson or Bunn lot.....	50,000
Rigsby & Gilmore.......	300,000	Kilbourn lode..........	150,000
Gilmore & Bowmer......	300,000	Ford..................	250,000
Gilmore & Paul.........	200,000	M'Collough	100,000
Gilmore & Arnat........	160,000	Trespass lot............	300,000
Williams & Hutchinson..	100,000	Hard times range.......	250,000
Taylor & Phipps........	150,000	Cave lot................	500,000
Morgan	50,000	Smith lot..............	150,000
Vosburgh..............	50,000	Patches, in all..........	100,000

The following are the notes of Mr. Wilson's surveys, with the names of the crevices, as given by B. Kilbourn, Esq.:

Commencing at the centre of section 31, T. 2, R. 1 W.

South 13.20 chs. to *M'Cumber range:* course S. 58½° E.; length 10.00 chains. Thence 26.20 chs. to

Long range; course S. 55° E.; length 85.00 chains. Thence 30.70 chs. to

Hopkin's range; S. 65° E. 3.00 chs. and N. 65° W. 16.00 chains; thence N. 49½° W. 10.00 chs.; entire length 29.00 chains.

Van Vickle range, one chain south of Hopkin's r.; course N. 58° W.; length 48 chains.

Commencing at the center of the S. W. quarter of sec. 31, T. 2, R. 1 W.; thence N. 2.00 chains; thence N. 52° W. 2.00 chs., to the Short Kilbourn range; course N. 52° W., length 5.00 chs.

Gilmore range, commences 10 chs. E. of quarter post on W. side sec. 31; course S. 52½° E.; length 6.00 chs.

Scofield range, commences 13.00 chains N. of sec. line and 15.00 chs. E. of W. line of sec. 31; course N. 60½° W.; length 48.00 chains.

Gilmore & Bowmer range. 20.00 chs. N. of S. W. corner

of sec. 31; course N. 62½° W.; length 15.00 chs. (5 chs. E. of line and 10. chs. W.),

Gilmore & Whittiker range, commences at a point 12.00 chs. N., and 5.00 chs. W. of the S. E. corner of sec. 36, T. 2, R. 2 W.; it bears N. 58° W. for a distance of 18.00 chs.; then it "jumps" 50 feet, thence N. 58° W. for a distance of 23.00 chs.

Christie range, commences 4.00 chains S. of the E. end of the above crevice; course N. 60° W.; length 70 chains.

Morrow lode, commences 25.00 chains N. of quarter post on S. side sec. 36; course S. 60° E. for 12.00 chs.; then lost for 5.00 chs.; thence 12.00 chs., with former bearing.

Commencing at quarter post on S. side sec. 36 (T. 2, R. 2 W.), thence N. 8.00 chs.; thence E. 5.00 chs.; thence N. 4.00 chs., to the *Four crevices;* S. 59° E.; 10.00 chs. At the point where thus intersected, two crevices stop, the other two are as follows: the north one bears N. 51½° W.; length 15.00 chains; this is called the *Paul & Robinson range;* the other is called the *Bunn range;* course N. 60° W.; length 40.00 chains.

Going north from the point of starting as above, 8.25 chs.:

Taylor range; course N. 58½° W; length 11.00 chs. (8.00 on the W. side of line, and 3.00 on the E. side). Thence 9.00 chs. to

Morgan range; course N. 55½° W.; length 12.00 chs., 10.00 on W. side and 2.00 on E. side of line. Thence 13.20 chs. to

May range, east end 20.00 chs. W. of sec. line; course N. 62° W.; length 20.00 chs. Thence 19.20 chs. to

Morrow range, previously located. Thence 23.70 chs. to

Gilmore & Whittiker range, located before; bears at this point N. 54° W. One chain N. of Scofield r. is a small crevice, and 3.00 chs. N. of this another short one.

Commencing at a point 15.00 chs. W. of quarter post on S. side sec. 36; N. 16° E. 12.00 chs. to *Gilmore Patch ;* course S. 54° E.; length 5.00 chs.; yield, 600,000 lbs.

Commencing at a point 20.00 chs. E. of quarter post on line between sections 35 and 36; thence south 24.00 chains to

Shields range; course N. 60° W.; length 4.00 chains. Thence 25.00 chs. to

Shields range; course N. 59° W.; length 23. chs. (15.00 chs. W. of line, and 8.00 chs. E). Thence 26.50 chs. to

Shields range; N. 55° W.; length 5.00 chs.

The last three are Shields's diggings; they have produced 400,000 lbs.

Commencing at a point 10.00 chs. E. of S. W. corner of sec. 36, T. 2, R. 2 W.; thence north 12.00 chains to

Trespass crevices; these commence 4.00 chs. E. of this point; their W. end is 5.00 chs. W. of section line; course N. 53° W.; amount of ore raised 1,000,000 lbs.; average depth 50 feet. Thence 24 chs., and N. 48° W. 14.00 chs., to the E. end of *Morrow range;* course N. 50° W.; length 10.00 chains; amount of ore raised, 50,000 lbs; depth 30 feet; no cap-rock.

From the E. end of Morrow range, S. 30° W., 10.00 chs. to *Williams crevice;* course, S. 54° E.; length 8.00 chains; ore raised 100.000 lbs.; greatest depth worked 70 feet. There are two openings, one at 40 and one at 70 feet; 20 feet of cap rock.

From the point of intersection with the Williams crevice, as above, S. 30° W., and at a distance of 11.00 chs., the *Penn & Spencer range;* course S. 49° E.; length 8.00 chs.; yield 150.000 lbs.

The *Sciota range* is an east and west, crossing the above and several smaller crevices; yield of ore 100,000 lbs.

From the point of intersection with the Penn & Spencer range, as above, running S. 74½° W., we have at 3.00 chs. *Ford crevice;* bearing S. 52½° E.; length 4 chs.: at 4.00 chs. *Williams crevice;* course S. 52½° E.: at 5.00 chs. *Long crevice;* course same as above: at 10.00 chs., *Wornic crevice;* course N. 52° W.; length 6.00 chains; yield of ore, 20,000 lbs: at 14 chs., *Lane range:* course N. 53½° W.; length 6.00 chs; yield 15,000 lbs.

N. 53½° W., at a distance of 4.00 chs., is a crevice.

At 8.00 chs. from the other end of crevice, left it at right angles; thence one chain to *Finley range*; course N. 29° W.; length 7.00 chains: yield of mineral 150,000 lbs.

From intersection with Finley crevice, S. 68½° W., 4.00 chains to *Sheet range;* course N. 54° W.; length 8.00 chs. (5.00 to E., and 3.00 to W. of line); depth of workings 25 feet; the sheet averaged 1 inch thick and 12 feet in vertical height: yield of ore 70,000 lbs.

On the same course (S. 68½° W.) 5.50 chs. to *Cave diggings;* depth 40 feet to the cap rock, then 70 feet to the cave, which is 10 feet wide; course N. 57° W.; length 4.00 chs., the intersection of the line being nearly in the middle of the range. There are three side crevices on the S. W. side, all coming together to the S. E.; yield of mineral 1,200,000 lbs.

Commencing at the S. W. corner of Sec. 1 (T. 1, R. 2, W.), thence N. 8.00 chs. thence S. 63° E., 2.50 chs., to *Williams range;* length 10.00 chs.; yield of ore 200,000 lbs.

Commencing at a point 20.00 chs. E. of the S. W. corner of Sec. 1 (T. 1, R. 2, W.): thence N. 23.00 chs. to *Clinkor range;* bearing N. 70° W.; length 15.00 chs. There are two or three small crevices on the north side, at about half the distance from one end to the other of the range; yield of ore 400,000 lbs.

The above are the principal ranges of the Upper Menomonee diggings, forming a marked group, both by the uniformity of the general direction of the crevices, and their isolated position in regard to the circumjacent mining districts. There is an extensive area to the north, northeast, and northwest, where but little lead has ever been raised. The crevices in the district in question are remarkably straight and well-defined, although not penetrating very deep; or, at least, not carrying mineral to any great depth. The average depth of the diggings is given by Mr. Kilbourn at thirty-five feet, although in some instances seventy feet has been attained. The geological position of the crevices is in upper beds of the Galena limestone, but not quite so high up as the Fairplay. The denudation is estimated at about fifty feet, leaving from

150 to 175 feet of the lead-bearing rock remaining. The crevices of the Upper Menomonee district do not open out into wide caves, or form under a well-marked cap-rock: the ore is found chiefly in sheets, of very irregular dimensions, sometimes forming bunches.

Towards the western end of this group of diggings, however, there appears to be a tendency to form regular openings under a cap-rock. On the Williams range a chimney was struck forty feet from the surface, and thirty below this, sinking through hard rock, an opening was reached of considerable size, and well filled with ore.

These crevices seem to have been pretty thoroughly worked out at an early day, as in several visits to the district I have found little or nothing doing in the way of mining, and hence am able to give but little information derived from personal inspection beneath the surface. The agricultural capacity of the surface in the vicinity is so great that the inhabitants undoubtedly find their operations above ground more profitable than those below. For a time, however, the working out of these crevices must have been very profitable, as the ore lay so near the surface.

BIG PATCH DIGGINGS.

This is the name given to a group of diggings on sections 2, 3, 10, and 11, T. 2, R. 1, W. They cover about one square mile of area, the larger portion of them by far being on section 10. The Big Patch is about half-way between the Upper Menomonee and the Platteville diggings. These diggings derived their name from the uncommon size and singular position of the largest discovery ever made at this place. The ore of this lode, or patch, lay entirely upon the top of the rock, averaging eighteen feet in width and three in thickness. Pieces of mineral raised from this 'patch' weighed as high as 25,000 lbs., and such was the extraordinary facility with which it was obtained, that four men raised in one day 45,000 lbs.* (worth about $1500, at the present value of the ore).

From the same authority quoted above, we learn that these diggings were discovered in June, 1828, and that up to 1843 4,226,000 lbs. of ore had been raised; the "Big Patch" having furnished about half this amount.

The following are the notes of Mr. Wilson's survey of the principal ranges at these diggings:

Commencing at the centre of Section 10, T. 2, R. 1 W., thence N. 6 feet to *Atwell & Cobin's range:* course S. 63° E.; length 10.00 chains. Thence 4.00 chains to

Scofield range: course N. 62½° W.; length 35.00 chs. (20.00 chs. W. and 15.00 chs. E. of line). Thence 6.00 chs., then S. 70° E. 5.00 chs., to

Last range: course S. 70° E.; length 5.00 chs.

From quarter-section line, S. 70° E., by side of Last range, distance 7.00 chs. to

Big Patch: course N. 67° W.; east end, 10.00 chs. W. of section line; length, 45.00 chs.

Commencing at center of section 10 again, and going S. 15½° W. 10.00 chains, to

Hancock range: it commences 2.00 chs. E. of quarter-section line; bears N. 65½° W. for 5.00 chs.; then lost for 5.00 chs.; then commences again, and runs 10.00 chs. farther in the same direction.

The crevices of the above diggings are worked in three openings, which occur at a uniform random, and are all capped except the upper one, which is frequently open to the surface of the rock. On the higher ground the shafts are from 40 to 60 feet deep. Only the two upper openings can be worked to advantage, owing to the water in the lower one. The first and second openings are separated by 14 feet of rock, of which three feet make up a solid cap.

The diggings in the ravines are worked to the same randoms as those on the higher ground, and no lower,

* Grant County Herald, October 14th, 1843.

although Campbell's branch is at least forty feet lower than the lowest opening in the vicinity. The following is the best estimate which could be procured of the yield of some of the principal crevices up to this time:

	Pounds.
Big Patch	3 to 4,000,000
Scofield range	2,000,000
Hancock range	400,000
Last range	40,000
Cabanis range	15,000

These diggings have been almost entirely abandoned for some years, so that any information in regard to them could be with difficulty procured.

HAZLE GREEN, OR HARD SCRABBLE DIGGINGS.

The Hazle Green diggings form a well-marked and important district, which lies about the branches of Fever river called Hard Scrabble and Bull branches. They are on sections 18, 19, and 30 of T. 1, R. 1 E. and 13, 24, 25, 26, 35, and 36 of T. 1, R. 1 W. They occupy a space about four miles long from northeast to southwest, the principal ranges being concentrated in the N. W. corner of sections 30, 19, and 25. The village of Hazle Green is situated in the midst of these diggings, and has grown up with their development. They are among the first mines opened in Wisconsin, and were extensively worked at an early day. Up to 1843, the Hard Scrabble district was estimated to have turned out 27,300,000 lbs. of lead ore, from the following ranges, or lots:

Durley & Coates	1,000,000 lbs.	Binninger	600,000 lbs.
Tesant & Ojan	800,000 "	Bruse	3,000,000 "
Phelps	1,800,000 "	Adney	1,500,000 "
Wetherbee	900,000 "	M'Coy Upper	700,000 "
M'Coy or Thompson	700,000 "	Lower Water lode	1,300,000 "
Edwards	800,000 "	Upper "	700,000 "
Craw	1,000,000 "	Bull	1,300,000 "
Wolcott & Billings	1,200,000 "	Dry Bone	500,000 "
Pearce	2,300,000 "	Scattering	6,000,000 "
Badger	600,000 "		

Very careful surveys have been made of a large part of the ranges in the Hazle Green district by Messrs. Burrill and Scheller, at the expense of Jefferson Crawford, Esq., by whom they were kindly furnished for reduction and transference to the crevice map. The original survey was platted on a scale of seventeen inches to the mile, which is hardly larger than would be desirable to show the complicated systems of crevices which exist in the district; but which requires a sheet four and one-half feet by three to contain the vicinity of Hazle Green, and which is, therefore, larger than can be conveniently published. The main ranges, and almost all the smaller crevices, are shown, however, on the two inch scale, except on the N. E. quarter of the S. E. quarter of section twenty-five, where they are so numerous that only the more conspicuous ones could be exhibited.

There are in the Hazle Green district, as will be seen by referring to the map, two pretty well marked sets of crevices; namely, one set bearing approximately east and west, and forming the heaviest ranges, while these are crossed by a great number of smaller crevices with a nearly north and south bearing. The deflections from a due east and west line in the first set are not very considerable, but their general bearing is a few degrees to the north of east and south of west; the average would perhaps be about five degrees in that direction. The norths and souths vary more from the true meridian: N. 15° E. is pretty nearly the direction of several of the best marked crevices, and the range of the heaviest body of ore, taking the whole district together, is about in this line. The parallelism of the crevices in their minor groupings, and their assemblage in sub-districts, or "lots," are marked features of these diggings.

Beginning at the southwest extremity of the district, and noticing some of the details of the principal ranges and crevices, we have the following:

Henderson range (N.W. quarter of S. E. quarter of section 35): three parallel crevices, of which the western one is much the largest; course N. 10° E.; worked about 300 yards in length, and chiefly in 1838; has yielded probably about 300,000 lbs.

Keeno range and lot. A range on the west with this name has a course N. 72° W., and has been worked 300 yards in length: it has produced 50,000 lbs. To the east, a series of parallel N. and S. crevices, crossed by easts and wests, bearing S. 86° W.: the whole lot has produced 150,000 lbs.

East of the Keeno range, on the W. side of the S. W. quarter of N. W. quarter of section 36, is a N. and S. range, bearing N. 2° E., and worked 300 yards in length.

Allen Rand range: on the E. side of N. W. quarter of N. W. quarter of section 36; several parallel crevices; direction N. 15° E.; length worked 320 yards; amount raised not large.

Tallow Clay lot: N. half of N. E. quarter of N. W. quarter of section 36: a group of easts and wests; direction N. 74° E., with several heavy norths and souths on the west side of the lot, having a direction of N. 16° E.

Stevens range and lot. The Stevens range bears N. 60° E. at its south end, then bends around at its northern extremity to N. 14° E.; the lot is crossed by two sets of crevices parallel with the above directions; yield of the lot 1½ million lbs.

Tindall range: E. and W. exactly; worked 150 yards in length; yield 300,000 lbs. Several parallel crevices to the north.

Criger range: direction S. 70° E., cutting off on the south a number of N. and S. crevices.

The Tindall, Stevens and Criger, together, occupy the S. E. quarter of the S. W. quarter of section 25, and the whole forty acre lot is estimated to have produced five million lbs.

Ailsworth range: worked about 100 yards in length; course N. 30° E.; yield 200,000 lbs.

Kendall range: cut off on the S. by the White range; course N. 20° E.; worked 150 yards in length; yield 150,000 lbs. This and the Ailsworth are on the N. W. quarter of S. E. quarter of section 25.

Purdy range and lot. This lot occupies the N. half of the S.

E. quarter of section 26: the main range runs N. 87° E.; this has yielded 400,000 lbs.; the whole lot about a million.

Hitchcock lot: N. E. quarter of N. W. quarter of section 25; a group of norths and souths; course about N. 15° E.; yield 2,000,000 lbs.

White range: a heavy range on N. half of S. W. quarter of S. E. quarter of section 25: course N. 87° E.; worked over a fourth of a mile in length; cuts off the N. and S. ranges of the

Durly lot, which lies just north of the White range, and consists of a group of norths and souths, having a direction of about N. 15° E. The whole of these forty acres, the N. E. quarter of S. E. quarter of section 25, is filled with a perfect net-work of crevices, of which the north part is called the

Tesant lot. The main body of the ranges crossing this have a course of from N. 16° E. to N. 21° E., the *Gribble range*, which is the longest, running N. 16½° E. These norths and souths are traversed by an east and west, the *Rowland Madison range*, course N. 89° E., and beyond this to the north is a complicated series of easts and wests, all deflected to the south at their extremities, both east and west.

Phelps lot: on the E. side of N. E. quarter of section 25; has one heavy range, the *Phelps range*, bearing N. 15° E.: the other smaller ones nearly parallel, and traversed on the south side by three easts and wests, of which the *Kittoe range*, with a course of N. 70° E., is the most important. North of this, in the N. E. corner of the same fraction, is the *Sulphur lot*, consisting of five or six parallel easts and wests: course N. 75° E.

On the N. W. quarter of section 30, through which Hard Scrabble branch runs diagonally, there are several long and heavy easts and wests, with parallel side crevices, forming lots.

Rock Point lot: at the centre of section 30; a series of small norths and souths; course N. 9° E.; cut off to the north by an east and west, which is on the south side of the

Craw lot. This is traversed by the *Craw range*, of which

the general direction is about S. 70° W., with many short parallel crevices on the north and south.

The *Whiteside lot* occupies the N. E. corner of this quarter-section: it has one principal east and west, called the *Hardy Waters range*, with several short, or parallel ones. All along the east side of this quarter-section are long norths and souths: course N. 15° to 18° E.

Pearce lot: on the N. W. corner of N. E. quarter of section 30; principal E. and W. ranges, the *Vandyke* and the *Young range*, which vary from 3° to 10° south of west, and are accompanied by several smaller parallel crevices, and crossed by smaller norths and souths, having a course about N. 15° E. The *John Tyra range* crosses these again obliquely from southeast to northwest.

The *Badger lot* is northeast of, and a continuation of, the Pearce lot: it is on the line between sections 19 and 30. The *Old Badger range*, with a course of N. 87° E., is the main range, to which the others are nearly parallel.

Binninger lot. The main range on this lot is an east and west, more than a third of a mile in length, called the Binninger range: its course is N. 85° E. This is crossed at its west end by numerous short norths and souths. Near the centre of section 19 are three lots called the

Adney, Bruse, and Yount lots, which form one group of broken concentric crevices, arranged as if following three of the sides of an octagon. In the Adney lot, at its south end, the crevices run north and south; farther north they are deflected to the east, and have a course about N. 35° E. The Bruse lot exhibits another set, with a course a little more inclined to the east, and in the Yount lot they are nearly east and west—an interesting illustration of the passage of the norths and souths into the easts and wests.

The Hard Scrabble branch, as it passes across the N. E. corner of section 24, is crossed by several easts and wests, of which the *Ned Williams*, *Dry Bone*, and *Pawning* ranges are the most conspicuous. Along the north side of this quarter section runs the *Adolphus Howland range*, which has a course of N. 83½° E., and has been worked more than half a mile in length. There are several lots on the west side of the east half of section 24, made up of parallel east and west crevices, but not heavy ones.

On the S. E. quarter of section thirteen, near Jefferson, or the "Twelve-mile House," there are several heavy east and west ranges, which only vary a degree or two from an exact E. and W. course, and which have been traced nearly across the whole quarter section. Of these, the *Engine* and *South ranges* are the most important. They run closely parallel with each other.

The Harvey lot is on the south side of this quarter section, and consists of a group of norths and souths, varying but little from the true meridian in their direction.

The *Sheet lot* is on the adjacent quarter section east, namely the S. W. quarter of section eighteen. It is traversed by a large number of due east and west crevices, closely parallel with each other, and cut off at the west end by a quartering crevice, running N. 33° E. at its south end, and on the east side of which are several shorter parallel crevices.

Farther south and east, along Bull branch, are several ranges, some of which have been very productive. On the east side of the N. W. quarter of section thirty-two are the *Sabbath* and *Bull* ranges. The former has been traced nearly half a mile in length, and has a course of N. 8° E. at its southern end, and is deflected about as much to the west of north at its northern extremity, with which the *Bull range* also is parallel. There are several short ranges on the west side of section thirty, and a group of norths and souths, crossing Chapel Hollow Branch on and near the line between twenty-nine and thirty, about one-eighth of a mile north of the quarter post.

These are the principal ranges and lots in the vicinity of

Hazle Green. But few of them are worked now, and consequently the diggings are almost entirely inaccessible.

The characteristic mode of occurrence of the lead ore at the Hazle Green diggings is the sheet: not only do the norths and souths make in sheets, as is so frequently the case in other districts, but even the easts and wests assume chiefly this form, differing materially from the crevices with this direction at Fairplay, and at Dubuque and vicinity, where they make almost exclusively in crevice openings. Sometimes, at Hazle Green, the east and west sheets are connected with crevice openings, but this seems to be rather exceptional. The diggings in this district are usually quite shallow. According to Mr. Crawford, the average depth of the workings is about forty feet; a few shafts are sunk as deep as ninety-five. No regular openings are recognized, and no well-marked cap-rock.

These diggings are quite high up in their geological position, as we find traces of the Hudson-river shales (the pipe-clay with small shells), not far south of Hazle Green, which indicates that in that vicinity the whole thickness of the lead-bearing strata is preserved. According to Mr. Scheller's surveys, the elevation of the village of Hazle Green is 283 feet above Fever river at the junction of Hard Scrabble branch, which is not far from the level of the top of the Blue limestone. Thus it will be seen that the diggings in this vicinity cannot have gone below the upper division of the Galena limestone; they probably do not, in general, reach within 150 feet of the bottom of that rock. Whether the sheets make into regular openings at greater depths than have been thus far proved, as is supposed by some, remains to be demonstrated. Water being very troublesome here, the workings have usually been abandoned at a very shallow depth, and although efforts have been made, and a good deal of money expended, to drain portions of the ground by machinery, the result has been far from satisfactory. A water-wheel, above fifty feet in diameter, was put up on

Hard Scrabble branch, and connected by a flat rod with the crevices in the vicinity of the east end of the Madison range. The power, however, was not sufficient to overcome the water so as to admit of proving the ground to any considerable depth. Other attempts of a similar kind in this neighborhood have been equally fruitless, so far as proving the profitableness of deeper mining was concerned.

A negotiation was opened, some time since, for the conveyance to an English company of all the mining rights in the vicinity of Hazle Green, with the expectation that, in case the arrangement was effected, powerful steam engines would be erected, the region drained by an adit-level running down to Fever river, and the systematic proving of the ranges in depth undertaken. The plan proposed was, not only to mine in the lead-bearing rock, but to sink to the Lower Magnesian limestone, under the idea that this rock would also be found productive. Whether the arrangement has been, or will be, carried through, we have not been informed. Our own ideas with regard to the probable success of an undertaking like this will be found given at length in another part of this Report.

The whole amount of ore raised in the Hazle Green diggings, from the beginning of working, is estimated by Mr. Crawford at 127,000,000 lbs. The smelters' books show that 63,000,000 lbs. have been delivered from this vicinity since 1845. At present, they are said to be producing about two millions a year, mostly in small lots, and in working over old ground, without sinking much, or making new discoveries. At one locality, however, I have been able in former years to see a very fine show of ore, namely at the Mills lode, on Bull branch. I first visited it in May, 1857, when it presented the following appearance. A mass of ore was exhibited in the workings, of a saddle-shape from east to west, as shown in the annexed figure (fig. 30), which represents a cross-section of it in that direction, the flat part being above twenty feet across, and varying from two to three and a half

FIG. 30.—Section of Mills Lode.

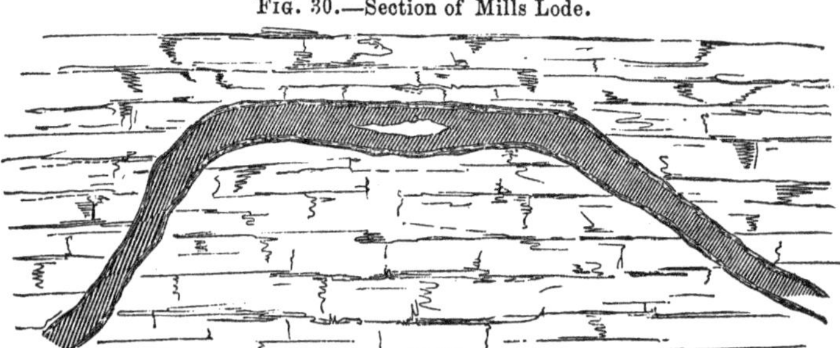

feet in thickness of solid galena, which was separated from the rock by thin selvages of a decomposed ferruginous substance, called "dry-bone" by the miners; in each direction, as observed in the east and west cross-section, this mass falls off at a steep angle, varying from 30° to 45°; and it had been worked on one side to the depth of twenty, and on the other of fifteen feet, the ore slightly diminishing in thickness in its descent, but still exceeding one foot on each side. In a north and south direction the mass had been removed for a length of a hundred and twenty-five feet, the last forty towards the north rising gradually. Thus it will be seen that a face of nearly one hundred square feet of solid ore was exposed in one section of the workings, presenting, truly, a beautiful sight—one of the great prizes which are occasionally drawn in the lead-mining lottery. About 1,200,000 lbs. of galena had been taken out from this place previous to May, 1857, and since that between two and three millions more, the expense being very small, of course, especially at first, as the deposit in its richest part was only thirty to forty feet below the surface, and entirely free from water.

In 1860 the workings were found to have been carried down one hundred feet on a flat and pitching sheet, with some ochre and a little dry-bone. Considerable pyrites is also mixed with the ore, and the appearances would indicate that the bottom of the deposit would soon be reached; or, at least, the point beyond which workings could not be profitably carried; the yield is still very large, however, it is said.

HORSE DIGGINGS.

This is a small group of crevices, about two miles north of Hazle Green, on the S. W. quarter of section 12, T. 1, R. 1 W. The diggings run obliquely across the north half of this quarter section, along a ridge which has the same general direction with the ranges of mineral, namely N. 55° E. The heaviest lode is on the south of the diggings, and is called the *Big range:* it runs N. 51½° E., and has been worked for one hundred and twenty-five yards in length. The crevices are constantly cut off, and the ore carried north, by quartering northeast and southwest crevices, coming in on the south.

DIGGINGS IN BENTON TOWNSHIP.

This whole township is so cut up with diggings, that it is difficult to subdivide them into groups, or to follow any other than a geographical order in describing them. Probably no other township in the Lead Region has produced so much ore, and it is supposed that portions of it have never been equalled in the amount raised on the same area.

For convenience, we will describe these diggings in the following order: 1st. Diggings northwest of Benton village, on sections 4, 5, 6, 7, 8, and 9, including Swindler's Ridge, which is one of the most marked sub-groups in this vicinity. 2d. Diggings south of Benton, on sections 20, 21, 28, 29, 32, and 33. 3d. New Diggings and its vicinity, including all south of Shullsburg branch, in Benton township. 4th. The northeast corner of Benton, and Buzzard's Roost, including sections 1, 2, 3, 10, 11, 12, 13, 14, and 15, in T. 1 N., R. 1 E., and sections 21 and 28, T. 2 N., R. 1 E.

Diggings northwest of Benton.

In sections 5, 6, 7, and 8 (T. 1, R. 1, E.), we have a considerable number of isolated ranges scattered over the surface, and a large and complicated group of crevices on the N.W. quarter of section 4, called the *Swindler's Ridge diggings.*

Beginning at the northwest corner of the township, we have in section 6 the

Pitner diggings; worked in 1838–1840; now plowed over; did not produce much.

Reed diggings (N. E. quarter, near the east line of section). An E. and W. crevice, not well defined; course about N. 80° W.; crossed by numerous small N. and S. crevices, coming up from the south.

Hicks & Co.'s diggings (S. E. quarter of section six, near S. line of section); recently discovered; had produced 100,000 lbs. in the first year after discovery: course S. 71° E.

Dickinson range (N. E. quarter of N. E. quarter of section seven); course N. 70° W.; worked 150 yds. in length, and 48 feet to water; ore left going down; produced 165.000 lbs.

Pole lode (N. W. quarter of N. E. quarter of section seven); course N. 70° W.; worked in 1840, and now abandoned; water near the surface; ore left going down in considerable quantity, as is reported; it is believed to be a good place for putting up an engine; the heavy workings are quite limited in length; produced 700,000 lbs.

Dodge & Co.'s diggings (S. W. quarter of N. E. quarter of section seven); new discovery, worked since winter of 1858-9, and has yielded heavily; shaft, in fall of 1859, 75 feet deep, sunk at the crossing of an east and west and north and south; crevice 3 to 12 feet wide and 10 to 12 feet high, filled with "dirt," and heavy chunks of ore. This was still producing ore in the spring of 1860.

Nine-strike range (S. W. quarter of N. W. quarter of section eight); course N. 62° W.; has produced heavily, but is not now worked, on account of the water, which is near the surface; said to promise well for putting up pumping machinery; has yielded about 300,000; traced for about a quarter of a mile in length. South of this a few rods are large patch diggings, not now worked. There are several other ranges and patch lots on these sections, but they are not important. The general direction of the ranges in this vicinity is about N. 70° W., and the crevices make regular openings, but the workings are soon interrupted by water. The probability is, that it is a rich mineral region, which will be more extensively opened at some future time.

Swindler's ridge. This is a very extensive group of ranges, which has turned out a large amount of ore. The principal diggings are on the N. half of the N. W. quarter of section nine, which is crossed by a great number of nearly parallel ranges, broken into two groups by a north and south ravine running nearly through the middle of the half quarter section. Going south on W. line of section nine; from the N. W. corner of the same, we have the following as the most conspicuous crevices of which the course can be traced at present: it must be remarked, however, that the whole ridge is so "cut up with diggings," that it is difficult to make out the crevices.

South (from N. W. corner of section nine):

50 yds. to *Dane r.;* 400 yds. long; thence
24 yds. to *Dormer r.;* 400 yds. long: course S. 79° E.; thence
26 yds. to *Murphy & Davis r.;* thence
40 yds. to *Foley & Sheridan r.;* 350 yds. long: course S. 78° E.; thence
24 yds. to *Barker r.;* 250 yds. long: course S. 72½° E.; thence
20 yds. to *Roundtree & Robeson r.;* 300 yds. long: course S. 74½° E.; thence
27 yds. to *Harker & Metcalf r.:* course S. 76½° E.; thence
35 yds. to *Knox r.:* course S. 79° E.

On the east side of this fraction, the ranges converge towards the east, and the north side of the ridge is entirely dug over in "patch-work."

After crossing the line between sections nine and eight, the above ranges are slightly deflected to the north for a short distance, and then completely cut off by a group of three parallel north and south crevices, extending for 400 yards in length, with a course of N. 3½° W. A long quartering range also commences at about the middle of the line bounding the N. E. quarter of section eight on the east, and extends N. 39½° W. for 500 yds. to the south line of section five, where it leads into another "patch-work diggings"—called the Sebastopol, from the fighting character of the miners of those parts—in which but little can be made out, except that the ranges have a bearing not far from N. W. and S. E. The parallel ranges on the north side are called the *Ellis* and the *Gear lodes;* they run N. 51° W., and are worked about 500 yards in length. The above data are from Mr. Burrill's surveys.

The following section (fig. 31) represents the number and character of the openings, as intersected in the diggings on the most elevated part of the ridge, according to information obtained from the miners. Here it is about fifty feet to the cap-rock, under which is the first opening, which is

FIG. 31.—Section of Openings at Swindler's Ridge.

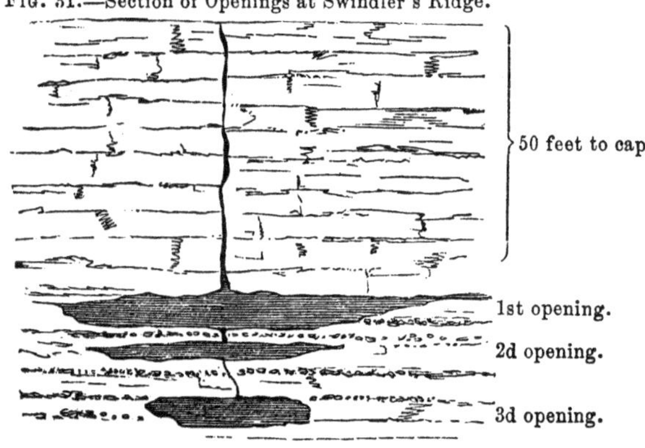

usually five or six feet high; two to three feet below is the second opening, three and one-half to four feet high; thence six or seven feet to third opening, which is usually under the water level, and but little worked, especially as it is sometimes barred up very hard. The openings are frequently worked quite wide; in one place, a space one hundred feet square was excavated, and left without support, so firm was the cap. The ore is found in the openings in "sand," with flints, small fragments of "tumbling rock," and a little ochre.

Thus the vertical height of the mining ground is seen to be from sixteen to twenty feet, not including the lowest opening. The crevices are frequently connected together by crossings, and the facilities thus given for getting on to another person's range in advance of him, and taking the ore from his opening, and the swindling practices thus occasioned, gave rise to the very appropriate name of "Swindler's ridge." These diggings have been worked since 1844, and have produced from fifteen to twenty million pounds of ore; at present they are not yielding much; but it is thought by some that it would be a paying undertaking to run a level into the ridge from the south or north, so as to unwater the lower opening. It may be added, that the geological position of these diggings is about in the middle of the Galena limestone.

Diggings south of Benton.

Proceeding from Benton towards the South, we find almost every quarter section covered more or less with diggings; they are, however, not usually on well-defined crevices, but rather in patches, not worked deep or for any considerable length of time, and but little is doing on them at present; hence the amount of information which can be given is but small.

Directly south of Benton village is the *Sallee lot*, on the S. half of section 9, of which the principal ranges run a little south of east: this lot has been worked since 1827, and has turned out a large amount of ore, but no clue to the quantity could be obtained.

On the east of the Sallee lot is the *Thomas lot*, on the S. W. quarter of the S. E. quarter of section 9: a patch.

On section 16, next south of Benton, there are scattered diggings all over its surface, but no heavy bodies of ore. Of section 21 the same may be said. The *Langworthy Ridge diggings*, on sections 20 and 21, extending along for nearly a mile on the E. and W. line dividing the section in the middle, and one-eighth of a mile wide, have produced a large amount of ore, but are now entirely abandoned. All along Coon branch, through sections 21 and 28, are diggings of the same character, on "patches" and "sheet lots," as a general thing, not much worked at present, and which it is not worth while to specify: their position may be seen on the map.

On section 15, southeast of Benton, are the *Democrat diggings*, occupying a large part of the northeast quarter of the section, which were once extensively worked, and supported a miners village, called Democrat, situated in the N. E. corner of section 14. These diggings were in flat openings on east and west ranges, and they seem to have been pretty much worked out, as the town has entirely disappeared. On the north half of the N. W. quarter of section 22 are several ranges which have turned out large amounts of ore; they have an almost exact E. and W. course. The *Crossman range*, on the north, produced 500,000 lbs. The *Crossman Well range*, 50 yds. south, course from E. to S. 87½° E.; 115 yds. farther south three ranges close together, called the *Parish*, *Ross*, and *Grieves ranges:* course S. 87½° E.; then 100 yds. farther south the *Martin range*, with the same course. On the north half of the N. E. quarter of the same section (22) is the *Hull & M'Gee range*, worked since 1831, in the green-rock, or "black-rock," as it is here called: has yielded 1,000,000 lbs.

New Diggings and vicinity.

The principal portion of the New Diggings ranges are situated on the north half of section 26, and the village itself of that name is near the north line of the fraction, on what is called the New Diggings branch of Fever river. These diggings have been worked for a long time, and have turned out a vast amount of ore, considering the limited area to which they are confined, and they are still productive.

The principal range of the New Diggings is the *Wiley range*, one of the longest and best defined in the whole of the Lead Region. It starts near the centre of section 26, and keeps a general east and west course, passes one and a half chains N. of the quarter-post on line between sections 25 and 26, and is believed to extend at least to the line between sections 25 and 30, which would make a length of one and a half miles. A steam engine was formerly in operation on this range, near the centre of section 26; but nothing is doing on it at present. From this range north, over nearly the whole of the half section, the ground is so intersected with short, irregular, but very heavy ranges, more like bunches than crevices, that it is difficult to lay them down upon a map. Starting at the centre of section 26, and going north 11.00 chains, we intersect the *South range;* then, 18 feet farther north, the *South Whim range;* 31 feet farther, the *North Whim range;* 16 feet, the *East Whim range;* 100 feet, the *Main Champion range:* course E. and W.; has produced, in a length of 100 yards, 2½ million lbs. of ore: 114 feet, the *Dodge range;* 81 feet, a heavy range, without a name; 160 feet, another; and finally, at 100 feet, the *Hawthorne range:* course S. 84° W.—making nine heavy ranges on the space of 620 feet. The *M'Clintock range* is another extensive range, 321 feet north of the Hawthorne. To the west, these ranges are with difficulty to be traced, but a large portion of the N. W. quarter of section 26 has been dug over, and much ore raised. To the east, the New Diggings ranges make heavy on to the N. W. quarter of section 25, on which the *Blackstone range* has been worked since 1827, yielding three million lbs. of ore. The ranges become less productive on the adjacent quarter section to the east, the N. E. quarter of section 25, and are finally entirely cut off on the N. W. quarter of section 30 by a series of N. and S. ranges, on the Catchall lot.

To the south of the Wiley range, on the S. W. quarter of section 25, are two groups of N. and S. crevices, which are intersected, however, by a great number of small easts and wests and quartering crevices. The *Craig* or *Dutch lot* is on the W. half of the S. E. quarter of section 25. Here is one main range on the west, running, at its south end, N. 17° E.; and, near the Wiley range, N. 9° E.: to the east the ground is intersected by easts and wests every five to twenty feet, with quartering northeast and southwest ranges, so that no regularity in the workings can be made out. This lot has been worked since 1827, and is said to have produced ten million lbs. of ore. The other group of norths and souths runs on and near the centre line of section 25, with a direction N. 13° E., and crosses the Wiley, where the ranges are deflected to the west, and have a course of N. 22° W., and are worked 350 yards in length on that side, forming sheets.

The productive opening at the New Diggings is in the flint bed of the Galena limestone, and no mineral has been obtained here at any lower level. A level is driving across the ranges, to unwater the ground on the ridge south of the village, by Samuel Scales, Esq.; here it is seventy-six feet to water, as the water level stood in May, 1860, and the level will drain to the depth of 100 feet. If it had been carried in on the random of the pipe-clay opening, it could probably have been done at a much less expense, and would have proved the ground at so much greater depth, say about fifty feet. The cap-rock at the New Diggings is about four feet thick, and is overlaid by what is called the "grey shale," a bed of reddish-gray impure dolomite, with a large amount of organic matter in it, apparently the remains of marine plants. An analysis of this material, by Messrs. Chandler & Kimball, gave the following results:

Insoluble in acid.	Clay and sand	11.88
	Carbon	13.80
	Hydrogen	1.40
	Oxygen	7.25
Soluble.	Carbonate of lime	35.25
	Carbonate of magnesia	27.70
	Alumina and peroxide of iron	1.57
		98.85

This substance is so impregnated with bituminous matter as to take fire and burn with a bright flame when heated.

North of New Diggings, on the S. W. quarter of section twenty-four, and the W. half of the S. E. quarter of section twenty-three, are the Crossman diggings, on land of Geo. Leakley; these have produced large amounts of ore; they run nearly east and west, but the ground is so broken, besides being covered with a thick growth of small trees, that it is difficult to make an accurate survey of them. They are limited on the east by a series of parallel crevices, running N. 20° E. which have been worked since 1836, and, according to Mr. Leakley, have produced three and one-half millions.

On section thirteen, in the S. W. quarter, are some ranges which have formerly produced heavily. The *Ellis sheet range* starts from the quarter-post on the south side of section thirteen, and has been worked about half a mile in length; its course is not regular, but averages N. 19° E.; at its south end it runs N. 23° E., and, at its north end, N. 29° E. This has been a productive sheet of ore, ranging from three to five inches in thickness, tightly wedged in the rock, but in some places widening out to eighteen inches. A few traces of copper pyrites were observed here in the rubbish thrown out, associated with heavy-spar. Before 1847, and chiefly before 1840, 750,000 lbs. of ore had been obtained from the Ellis sheet. The "Western Wisconsin Mining Co." put up a little rickety engine, of five or six horse power, on the north end of this sheet; but it has not been running for the past year or two.

The *Bobineau* and the *Dowd & M'Ginnis* are two very heavy ranges, worked in former years, but now abandoned. The latter produced over a million pounds, it is said. No particulars could be obtained with regard to them.

Appleby's diggings. On the N. E. quarter of the N. E. quarter of section eleven. A drift has been run in on the course of the range, for a distance of 1700 feet (Oct. 1859), on Abram Looney's land, and known as "Looney's level." It was commenced in June, 1848, and has been worked almost uninterruptedly since that time. It is in the lower flint beds of the Galena limestone, about twenty feet above the Blue limestone, which is exposed at the bottom of the bluff where the level starts in. There is one main crevice, having a course of N. 23½° W., and some smaller side-crevices, occasionally running parallel with it for a little distance, and communicating with it by flat openings connecting them. The main crevice is of varying width, usually from three to five feet, and is filled with ochrey earth and galena, in small pieces ("small mineral"), which is found pretty uniformly disseminated in it, from one end of the opening to the other. There is a large amount of pyrites mixed with the rock in the vicinity of the opening, with some black-jack and a little dry-bone. In many places the dolomite is, as it were, eaten out in irregular cavities, so as to give it almost a brecciated appearance; these cavities are filled with calcareous spar, wholly or partly, or lined with incrustations of pyrites, with occasional crystals of galena. The spar is sometimes crystallized in rhombohedra, forming irregular geodes, and furnishing tolerably pretty cabinet specimens.

At the end of the level, as it was when visited in October, 1859, a hard bar of ground had been passed through for a distance of 100 feet. This bar was made up of alternate layers of flint and dolomite, the latter very hard and of a bluish-gray color, with a large amount of pyrites disseminated through it, in irregular seams, and occasionally a little galena in patches. Whether this bar has ever been cut through, and the crevice found continuing on the other side, I have not learned. The whole amount of ore raised here up to 1859 was about 1,000,000 lbs.

A number of crevices have been opened and worked recently, to the north and northwest of Appleby's diggings, on sections two and three. They all appear to have nearly the same course, which is from 15° to 20° west of north, and they are also about in the same geological position, namely in the lower beds of the Galena limestone, only a few feet above the Blue. They make chiefly in the flat openings characteristic of this position, the pieces of ore being usually small, and more or less mixed with dry-bone and ochre. The following ranges may be mentioned:

Dean & Pedelty: N. E. quarter of S. E. quarter of section 3, T. 1, R. 1 E.; course about N. 20° W.; worked in a wide opening; ore in small pieces, in ochre and dry-bone; opened in 1850; amount raised, about 1,200,000 lbs.

Merritt diggings: nearly in a line with the Dean & Pedelty, to the south, on the adjacent forty-acre lot: course about N. 12° W.; worked only since last year, and has produced 400,000 lbs.

Robinson diggings: N. W. quarter of N. E. quarter of section 2.

Besides the above, there are several ranges, with the same character, on the N. E. quarter of the N. W. quarter, and on the N. W. quarter of the N. E. quarter of section 2, most of which are recent discoveries, and were producing a good deal of ore last year.

Following up the Peaslee branch of Fever river—which empties into Shullsburg branch on section 12, coming down diagonally through the east half of section 1—we find several diggings of importance, which connect the Benton diggings with Earnest's, and thus with the Shullsburg district, in which order a description of them will be given.

On the south side of Peaslee's branch, on the south half of section 12, are a few small ranges. The *Dormer* and the *Quimby ranges* are near the centre of the S. W. quarter of section 12: they run N. 15° E., and have been worked from 300 to 400 yards in length.

The *Van Hook diggings* are on a patch, worked 60 yards in length, in a direction approximating N. 60° W., on the N. W. quarter of the S. E. quarter of section 12: the ore is much mixed with dry-bone.

Peaslee's diggings. The "Peaslee Big Lode" is on the N. W. quarter of the N. E. quarter of section 12, on the north of the branch, on two ranges nearly at right-angles with each other, of which one runs S. 20° E., and has been worked 200 yards in length; and the other S. 59° W., 100 yards in length: opened in 1838, and has produced probably two and a half million lbs. There are other diggings of the same name on the S. W. quarter of the S. W. quarter of section 6 (T. 1, R. 2 E). Here are two ranges 94 yards apart, the north one of which runs N. 45° W., and has been worked 200 yards in length; the other N. 47½° W.; length opened, 160 yards; these have been worked since 1840, and have yielded about 300,000 lbs. of ore.

M'Coy diggings. These are on the W. half of the N. W. quarter of section 7. The M'Coy Dry-Bone range consists of two or three parallel crevices, running N. 35° E., and worked 150 yards in length; the Stonebreaker range, an eighth of a mile farther north, has a course of N. 30° E., and has been worked 150 yards in length.

Old French diggings: on the N. W. quarter of the S. E. quarter of section 6 (T. 1, R. 2 E.); course from southeast end, N. 54° W. for 200 yards, then N. 61½° W. for 200 yards farther: principal amount of ore taken out within 250 feet in length; goes down in a series of flats and pitches at an angle of about 45°: has been worked for the last seventeen years, and has produced 1,200,000 lbs. of ore.

Earnest & Myers's diggings: on the S.W. quarter of section 5. These diggings are chiefly on two ranges which run N. 78° W., intersected or connected by a quartering range which runs N. 33½° E. for a length of 400 yards: the range on the west side of the quartering one is worked 15 chains in length.

Mr. Kimball's notes on the above diggings give some additional particulars, especially in regard to the geological position, which is interesting, since this is the farthest point to the south and west in the mining region, where ore has been obtained in the Blue limestone. All these diggings are along the ridge between the Peaslee and the Shullsburg branches of Fever river. On the higher ground, the workings are in the lower beds of the Galena limestone; but, at each of the diggings, shafts have been carried down into the Blue limestone. Drainage has also been had, both at the Peaslee, the M'Coy, and the Earnest ranges, by levels carried in a little below or on the level of the pipe-clay opening, which is on the top of the Blue limestone. At M'Coy's and Peaslee's, shafts communicate with the levels; at Earnest's, the level is not sufficiently advanced to effect drainage as yet: the length required for that purpose is 2300 feet, and in October, 1859, 1500 feet had been driven; at the end of the level as laid out, under the summit of the ridge, the vertical height to the surface will be 166 feet. At M'Coy's and Peaslee's three openings are recognizable. The uppermost is in the lower, heavy-bedded Galena limestone, with interstratified masses of flint: the second and most important is four feet below the first, and on the top of the Blue limestone: the third, the pipe-clay opening, on the glass-rock, about twenty feet below the second. The shafts are sunk about 150 feet from the highest ground to reach the level of the pipe-clay opening.

The pipe-clay opening is characterized at each of these diggings by the brown rock, and at Peaslee's diggings there is a brecciated mass of rock, fourteen feet thick, the fragments composing which are of various sizes, and sometimes quite large; they are also quite angular, as if they had suffered no attrition after the original mass which they composed had been broken up. The material of which the fragments consist is the usual dolomite of the enclosing strata, and the substance filling the interstices is the same, except that it is a little more friable and sandy, resembling the "sand" of the mineral openings, except that it is more consolidated. This brecciated rock is very pyritiferous, and has also some galena disseminated through it. It should be noticed, in connection with the fact of the occurrence of this breccia, that there is, according to Mr. Kimball's observations, a synclinal axis along this ridge, the strata on each side dipping towards the centre, at an angle of 4°. The inference would be, that the brecciated stratum was formed by the crushing force exerted on the material by irregular sinking of the ground, although it is possible that chemical changes may have had something to do with it: at any rate, there is no appearance of its having been originated by currents of water. The annexed section (fig. 32,) represents,

Fig.—32.

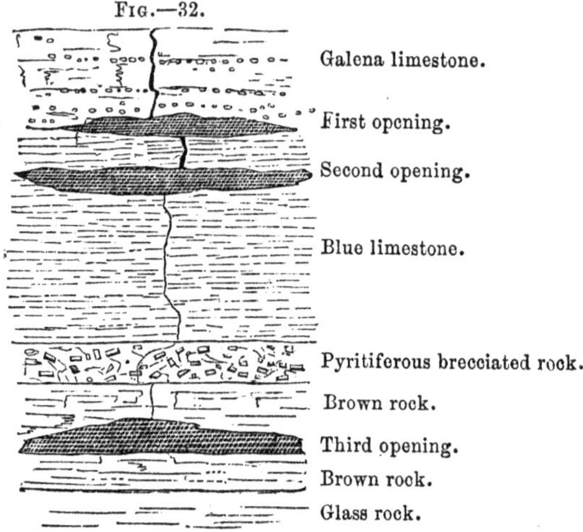

on a scale of about twenty-five feet to one inch, the position of the openings, and the lithological character of the associated beds, at the Peaslee diggings.

The lead ore from these openings is always associated with blende and calamine, and frequently with iron pyrites. The crevices leading to the openings are numerous, and, although small, have a uniform course. The ore sheets are all of the kind called "flat and pitching." At Earnest's diggings, one of these pitching sheets, carrying the usual ores of zinc and lead, follows for some distance the stratification of the Galena limestone, of which the beds dip here at an angle of about 10° to the northeast; then suddenly drops down, following an oblique line, and carrying ore all the way, a distance of from four to six feet, to another stratum below, where it again follows the planes of stratification for some distance, and then goes down again, and so on. There is no regular opening recognized at Earnest's, where the ore obtained is exclusively from the Galena limestone. Geodes in the dolomite are occasionally met with here, which are lined with pyrites, and this again with crystals of galena, forming the handsomest cabinet specimens which have been found in the Lead Region: these geodes are not filled with ochre or sand; hence the beauty of the crystals, which retain their sharp edges, although not brilliant on their faces. The pipe-clay opening does not seem likely to be as productive in this region as it is farther north, in the Mineral Point district.

Dry Bone diggings. On the south half of the south half of section four, and chiefly on the S. W. quarter of the S. E. quarter and the S. E. quarter of the S. W. quarter.

There are several ranges on this lot, running about 5° north of west, so far as can be made out; but the whole tract is so intersected by short crevices, and covered by confused workings, that their direction and position cannot be accurately given. The workings appear all to be very shallow, and are in the lower beds of the Galena limestone. The amount of calamine occurring here is more considerable than at any other locality this side of Mineral Point, so far as we could ascertain; and some excavations were being made here, and the old rubbish picked over, a year ago, for the purpose of obtaining zinc ore to be sent to La Salle, Ill., to be smelted by Messrs. Matthiessen & Hegeler. The appearance of things did not, however, impress us favorably as to the ore being sufficiently abundant at this locality to supply extensive zinc-works for any length of time.

Townsend's diggings. They are situated on the E. half of the S. W. quarter of section nine, two miles west of Shullsburg. These diggings are on a group of norths and souths, with a course N. 8° E. They have been worked since 1827; but not much ore is raised here at present. The depth worked is from fifty to eighty feet, which is forty feet below the water-level. These diggings have yielded from two to three million pounds of ore.

Half a mile east of the Townsend diggings, on the E. half of the S. E. quarter of section nine, and occupying nearly the whole of that fraction, there are extensive diggings entirely in the clay: the whole surface is literally riddled with pits; depth to water thirty to thirty-two feet. There are several main N. and S. ranges running through this lot. Yield from the whole, probably from three to four million pounds. Hardly anything is doing on this tract at present, and the deposits of ore seem to have been very superficial.

SHULLSBURG DIGGINGS.

No portion of the Lead Region has produced more ore on an equal extent of ground, with perhaps the exception of a limited area near New Diggings, than the vicinity of Shullsburg. And at the present time, mining operations appear to be more successfully and judiciously carried on here than at any other point. The principal Shullsburg diggings are on the south half of section ten, connecting on the west with the diggings last described, and being cut off on the east by an extensive series of norths and souths, which begins on the south in section fourteen, and extends for about four miles in a northeasterly direction, limiting the really important and productive diggings of the Lead Region on the east. The same irregularity of the ranges, and want of well developed crevices making up to the surface of the rock, is perceptible at Shullsburg, which was noticed in regard to New Diggings, and even in a still higher degree; so that any attempt to represent on a map the real position of the masses of ore by their surface arrangement could hardly be attempted. There are, however, two important ranges, or channels of ore, exhibited in the workings as at present carried on, having a course nearly S. 68° E., which is the general direction of the Shullsburg diggings, most of the shorter ranges being nearly parallel to these.

The most persistent horizon or random in these diggings is the so-called "green-bed," a stratum of dolomite, occasionally and irregularly stained with greenish argillaceous spots, which has a thickness in the various diggings of from three to twelve inches. Below this is the main opening, called here the "wash-dirt opening," as it contains the ore usually in small fragments, which have to be separated by washing from the sand, ochre, &c., or "dirt," in which they are imbedded. In some instances there appears to be a thickness of three or four feet below the "green-bed" before coming to the opening beneath. Below the "wash-dirt opening" is a stratum of hard rock, averaging two feet in thickness, succeeded by a thin argillaceous band, called the "white clay," below which ore appears never to have been obtained, except in a few exceptional instances, if at all, and over a limited area. Above the "green-bed" is the "flint-run," which is a dolomitic stratum, varying in thickness from five to eight feet, and containing numerous layers and irregularly interspersed masses of flint; and again, above this, the Galena limestone with its usual characters. A section of the strata at Major Davenport's diggings (fig. 33) will serve to exhibit the condition of things in this vicinity.

FIG. 33.—Section at Major Davenport's Diggings.

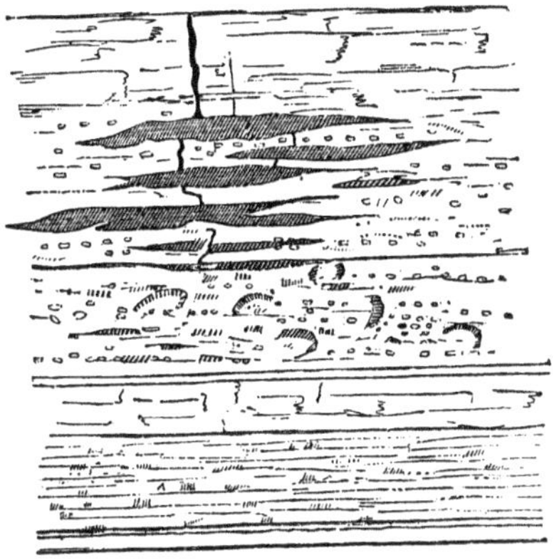

In this case, as in some others at Shullsburg, the ore makes in heavy masses above the green-bed, forming irregular flat layers, which, when the locality was visited by me in the spring of 1860, had been proved to extend upwards for a vertical height of fifteen or sixteen feet, and which might continue up to the surface of the rock some thirty feet higher, in a sort of chimney, or series of layers one above the other. Below the green-bed the ore was found in the usual wash-dirt opening, which has here a thickness of six to eight feet, and is separated from it by a thickness of three or four feet, of a hard barren rock.

The "Mississippi Mining & Manufacturing Company" worked the ranges on the west side of the N. W. quarter of section 14, a little southeast of the town of Shullsburg. The direction of the principal range is about N. 7° E., and there seem to be two principal crevices, running nearly a quarter of a mile in length, with several smaller ones, at distances of 150 to 200 feet apart, on the east side and towards the northern extremity of the main range. An engine was erected about midway of the principal crevice, and a shaft was sunk 110 feet deep, on a vertical sheet of ore, which is said to have continued all the way down, and to have been two or three inches in thickness. The bottom of the shaft is said to be just down to the level of the top of the principal productive opening in the Shullsburg mines: why it was discontinued at this depth, I have not been able to ascertain. Extravagant and foolish expenditures seem to have characterized the operations of this company; as, in both the localities where they commenced mining, the work was discontinued just before the point was reached at which something might have been proved with regard to the value of the property. It is currently reported that some $40,000 was sunk by the concern, in this way, at Shullsburg and Mineral Point; but I have no authentic information as to their expenditures, although it is evident from what can still be seen at the surface that they must have been large.

IRISH DIGGINGS.

These are chiefly on section 2, T. 2, R. 2 E., a mile to a mile and a half northeast of Shullsburg. Although formerly quite productive, they have not been worked much of late years. The principal ranges and lots are the following:

M'Farren ranges: on the S. E. quarter of the N. E. quarter of section 2; general direction N. 25½° E. There are several parallel crevices here, which seem to be interrupted for a short distance, and then resumed again on the northwest corner of section 1, at the Estey diggings, and again on the south half of the S. W. quarter of section 36, at the Hawthorne diggings, so called; these have been worked at intervals since 1828, on several crevices having nearly the same course as the M'Farren ranges; the shafts are from thirty to eighty feet deep, and ore was left going down in them when stopped on account of water. These diggings are said to have yielded about 2,000,000 lbs.

A little northwest of the M'Farren ranges a bull pump was erected, but never put in operation; the ranges are said to be rich in ore, but the water is near the surface, and too abundant to be kept under without expensive machinery. The bearing of the range here is N. 40¼° E. These ranges appear to be continued south on to the N. W. quarter of the S. E. quarter of the section, on the *Hardy lot,* now owned by M. Slavin, on which a shaft was sunk thirty-eight feet deep last year, and a horse pump put in operation; direction of the workings at this point, N. 33½° E. The principal range here is called the *Dougherty range,* and it runs so as to connect pretty nearly with the M'Farren and other ranges to the northeast. Considerable ore was raising here in 1859.

There are several short parallel ranges a little to the N. W. of the pump shaft on the Dougherty range, having a course N. 23¼° E. These have been worked to a depth of about thirty feet only, but have been very productive.

The *Doyle lot* is on the N. E. quarter of the S. W. quarter of section 2. The principal range is an east and west, running about S. 75° E., on which is a pump-shaft; this range cuts off the norths and souths coming in from the south, and appearing to converge at the pump-shaft. Of the norths and souths, the Doyle range on the east bears N. 18¼° E. The *Boner lot* is a little southwest of the Doyle; the ranges run about N. 25° E. The *Lynch lot* is on the west half of the S. W. quarter of section 2; the ranges have about the same course as those in the vicinity. The *Brazier range* is west of the Lynch, and almost exactly on the line between sections 2 and 3; it runs about N. 5° E.; there were formerly heavy workings on this range. West of this, on the E. half of the S. E. quarter of section 3, are the *Indian* and *M'Cuskey ranges,* also nearly north and south in direction, and not now worked.

Most of the diggings in this vicinity are shallow, but have been quite productive; the water is struck so near the surface that the shafts have usually been abandoned, it is said, before all the ore was taken out. It is thought by many that there is a good chance to make valuable discoveries, by draining the ground by means of a level, which could be done without great expense.

WHITE OAK SPRINGS DIGGINGS.

The village of White Oak Springs is situated on the N. half of section 32, T. 1, R. 3 E., and the diggings are on that section chiefly. The most important are the *Blackleg diggings,* in the southeast corner of section 32, and on the W. half of section 33. These are not at present worked, but have been very productive in former times. According to information obtained from Judge Blackstone, there were five main north and south crevices, and several smaller ones; the principal crevices were worked for a distance of 1200 yards.

DIGGINGS IN ELK GROVE TOWNSHIP.

Elk Grove is on the S. E. quarter of section five, T. 2, R. 1 E., and the principal diggings in the vicinity are the Strawberry, and Ballad & Deming's.

The *Strawberry diggings* are on the south half of section one, over which they are scattered. The excavations are very shallow, being sunk only about twenty feet, through ferruginous beds with many flints for ten feet, and below this a series of soft argillaceous beds, without flints, also ten feet in thickness. The range of the float mineral, as near as can be ascertained, is N. W. and S. E. Indications of crevice openings have been frequently detected; but these have not been followed, owing to water at this depth. A good deal of float mineral has, however, been taken out.

Ballad & Deming's diggings. On the S. E. corner of the S. E. quarter of section eight. Two drifts have been run in from the base of a bluff; they are about 100 feet apart, aud were about 40 feet long when examined. There is a cap-rock of four feet in thickness, of hard Galena limestone, with intercalated layers of flint. Below this is the opening, of soft ferruginous material, filled with flints, in which some ore has been found, but not a large amount. The course of the range is about N. W. and S. E.

There are many "prospecting-holes" over this township, and indications of crevices are observed; but, on the whole, the appearances are not sufficiently favorable to lead to any extensive expenditures in proving the ground.

DIGGINGS NEAR MONROE.

Monroe is situated on the north half of section thirty-five, T. 2, R. 7 E., and is connected with Janesville by a railroad, which is intended to be continued west to the Mississippi at Menomonee City, or else to unite with the Ill. Central at

Warren, Ill. Its situation is quite elevated, being about 500 feet above Lake Michigan. Hence, although the streams on each side, Sugar river on the east and the Peccatonica on the west, have cut their beds down into the sandstone, a very considerable thickness of the Galena limestone is probably remaining at Monroe. As there is a difference of level of 306 feet between Monroe and Sugar river at the crossing of the railroad, where the sandstone has a thickness of perhaps thirty or forty feet above the river, this would indicate that over 150 feet of the Galena limestone was still left. The diggings in this region, however, are sparsely scattered, but little wrought at present, and seem never to have been productive. So little attention is now paid to mining, that it was difficult to procure any information in regard to the position of the diggings. The only point in the vicinity where anything was doing in the way of mining last year, so far as I could ascertain, was near the corner of sections two, three, ten, and eleven (T. 2, R. 7 E.), called the *Skinner diggings*. These are on the ridge of ground between two parallel branches forming the head-waters of Skinner's creek. The ranges run about N. 68° E., and are worked, apparently, in the lower beds of the Galena limestone. They have been worked more or less for the last thirty years, but what amount of ore they have turned out we are unable to say.

SUGAR RIVER DIGGINGS.

The Sugar River diggings are in the vicinity of Exeter, which is situated on section 36, T. 4, R. 8 E. They are principally in section 27; but are also scattered over sections 28, 33, 34, and 35. The diggings are chiefly on the high rolling prairie, where a thin stratum of the Galena limestone remains undenuded. The surface is usually thickly covered with flints, derived from the decomposing beds of this rock. Most of the ore raised here is from vertical crevices in this rock, although there are some workings on flat openings in the underlying Blue limestone. The first mining in the vicinity of Exeter dates back as far as 1828, and here was the first settlement made in the county of Green. Twenty years ago, two furnaces were kept running on the ore raised here; but, at present, there is little doing. Some fifteen miners were employed in the winter of 1858–9, mostly in working over the old rubbish on the surface. One of the richest lodes discovered was Deville's, which is said to have produced 2,000,000 lbs. of ore, but it was soon worked out. The deepest shaft in this region was down 102 feet: this was nearly twenty years ago: it appears to have been a trial shaft, for the purpose of proving the ground in depth, and did not probably lead to any satisfactory results, the deposits of ore being apparently quite shallow all through the eastern part of the Lead Region. No diggings are known to have produced anything of consequence to the east of Sugar river, and none of those in Green county seem at present to be worked with any continuous success.

BLUE MOUND, OR BRIGHAM'S DIGGINGS.

This once important group of diggings, now almost entirely abandoned, lies on the extreme outskirts of the mining district, to the northeast; beyond them, in that direction, we pass immediately on to rocks lower in the series, which have not been found to contain any valuable deposits of ore. The principal ranges are on sections 7, 8, 17, 18, 19, and 30 of T. 6, R. 6 E., and sections 14, 24, and 25 of T. 6, R. 5 E., distributed over a space about three miles square. The most important single crevices are the Brigham north and the Brigham south lodes, of which the southern one is the heavier. It commences near the S. E. corner of section 7, and has been worked nearly across the section, running a few degrees N. of W. At the west end of the crevice its bearing is S. 76½° E.; at the eastern extremity S. 67° E., the shafts being distributed over a length of about 1800 feet. The north crevice is nearly parallel with the southern one, but is much less important.

On the south lode the distance to the cap-rock is between eighty and ninety feet: then below is the opening, which is very large, being twenty-six feet wide in its widest part, and thirty-six feet high: it was filled with tumbling rock and clay, intermixed with fragments of galena, some of which were of very large size. The annexed wood-cut (fig. 34)

FIG. 34.—Section of Opening at Brigham's South Lode.

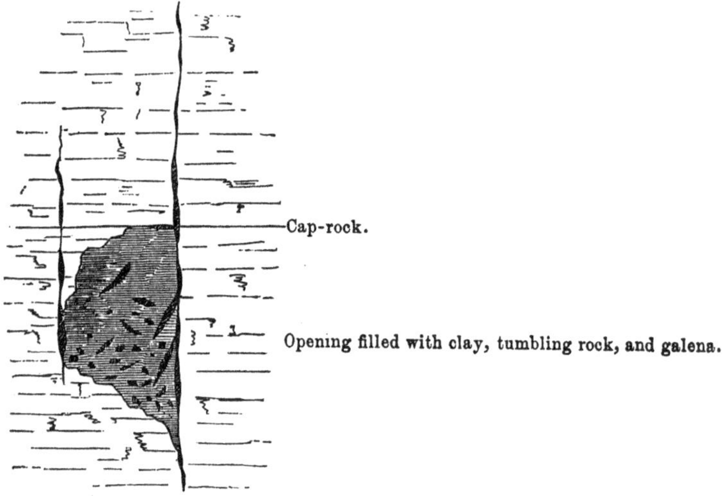

will serve to convey an idea of the form and position of the opening, and its relations to the crevice. A pretty heavy sheet kept along on the side of the opening, sometimes two or three feet in width, of solid ore. Below the opening but little ore was found in the crevice, which was followed down to the depth of 120 feet below the surface. When visited by me in 1857, this lode was worked by a New York company, which had been engaged in mining on it for three years, having carried the engine shaft down from a depth of 80 to 120 feet, by the aid of a steam engine, and taken out about 200,000 lbs. of ore, the operation on the whole having been decidedly an unprofitable one. This is one of the places where, among other curious experiments in mining, the Worthington pump was used for draining, it being placed at the bottom of the shaft, and steam carried down from the surface: it need hardly be added that the operation was attended with much loss and inconvenience.

The diggings in question were discovered by Ebenezer Brigham, Esq., one of the pioneer settlers of the Lead Region, and worked by him at an early day with profit, having been very productive above the water-level: the yield of the south lode is estimated at 4,000,000 lbs.

The *Hawthorne diggings* are on the S. E. quarter of section 18, and were worked on several parallel crevices running nearly E. and W., and occupying a space a few rods in width.

Hyde diggings: a series of rather shallow excavations, running obliquely through the S. E. corner of section 24 (T. 6, R. 5 E.), on to section 30 of the adjoining township.

Dudley diggings: W. half of N. E. quarter, and E. half of N. W. quarter of section 14, T. 6, R. 5 E.; worked for one quarter of a mile in length on two or three parallel crevices closely adjoining each other, running S. 76° E.; worked several years since, and about 3,000,000 lbs. of ore raised, as is estimated.

There are several other patches of shallow diggings in this vicinity, but none worthy of especial notice. *Shaw's diggings*, on the S. E. quarter of section 27, are the most easterly in the region, but have never been productive.

All the diggings above noticed are in the lower portion of the Galena limestone, and have very much the same character: the ore makes in wide openings, with clay and decomposed and tumbling rock. In the ravines, where the cap-rock has been denuded, the ore lies in patches in clay at the surface. At West Blue Mound village, or Pokerville, two or three years since, an interesting deposit of bones was found in a crevice at a depth of about forty or fifty feet, as will be seen by referring to the chapter on Surface Geology.

Porter's Grove diggings, on the W. half of S. W. quarter

of section 12, T. 6, R. 4; N. E. quarter of section 28; W. half of N. W. quarter and W. half of S. W. quarter of section 23. The principal range is on the so-called *Brush lot*, on which are three main crevices running N. 28½° E.; workings chiefly within a length of 500 feet in the lower beds of the Galena limestone. According to Dr. Percival, the Brush range has been traced for about two miles to the north, where it terminates in a flat opening, with "dice mineral," in the upper bed of the Blue limestone.

Pump crevice: bears N. 31° E.

Cooper range: three crevices, twenty feet apart, parallel with each other, and having a course of N. 28½° E.

Most of the norths and souths in the Porter's Grove diggings make sheets of ore, but the Brush range is a wide, open crevice, with large fragments of ore. On the south, these norths and souths are limited by a heavy east and west, called the Wakefield range.

There are a number of patches of diggings along the elevated ground between the Porter's Grove and the Blue Mound diggings, but none of them are of any importance. There was no mining going on at the Grove at the time of my visit, except on the part of a few persons engaged in stealing ore, and hence no reliable information could be obtained in regard to its mode of occurrence, &c.

MESSERSMITH'S DIGGINGS.

These diggings are situated in the vicinity of George Messersmith's house, which is on the S. E. quarter of the N. E. quarter of section 24, T. 6, R. 3 E., about three miles E. N. E. of Dodgeville. The following are the principal groups:

Messersmith's diggings, on the E. half of the S. E. quarter, W. half of the N. E. quarter, and W. half of the S. W. quarter of section 24; also on the S. E. quarter of section 13. On the last-named tract the ranges run north and south nearly; they are in the lower beds of the Galena limestone

On section 24 the ranges bear about N. 20° E. on the N. E. quarter, and about as much to the west of north on the S. E. quarter. On this section the ore makes in vertical sheets down to the cap-rock, and below it in flat openings, which are in the lower beds of the Galena.

Holyhead diggings: these are on the N. E. quarter of section 25. On this tract the ore makes in flat openings in the Blue limestone, connected with large amounts of dry-bone. The following section of the strata was given by Mr. Messersmith, as the usual order of succession at the Holyhead diggings:

Common mineral-bearing rock, or Galena limestone	35 to 45 feet.
Glass-rock, a hard brittle limestone	6 to 9 feet.
Brown rock	18 inches to 2 feet.
Mineral opening, ferruginous mass, with galena in sheets and bunches, and a large quantity of dry-bone	2 feet.

Below the opening is found the brown rock, of which the thickness has not been determined.

The galena appears to occur in sheets, between sheets of cellular and earthy dry-bone, derived from the decomposition of the sulphuret of zinc, the carbonate of zinc forming the exterior of the sheet, as if this were the first metal deposited. These sheets are occasionally a foot in thickness. A larger amount of zinc ore has been raised here, in proportion to the extent of ground dug, than in any other part of the Lead Region, at least so far as could be judged by the eye.

Norway diggings: these are situated on the S. E. quarter of section 36. They are on vertical crevices, in the lower beds of the Galena limestone; their course is nearly east and west: these crevices are open to the surface of the rock, and are not capped over.

Garrison diggings: on the N. W. quarter and S. E. quarter of section 32, T. 6, R. 3 E. These diggings are on crevices running a few degrees east of north, one principal range running N. 4° E. Nothing was doing here when this locality was visited, and no information was obtained in regard to the names of the crevices or their yield. They appear to be in the lower beds of the Galena limestone.

DIGGINGS ON SECTION 35, NEAR DODGEVILLE.

On section 35, T. 6, R. 3 E., next west of the Norway diggings, are several ranges, some of which are now worked, and are quite productive.

W. Watkins's range: N. E. quarter of N. E. quarter of section 35. There are several parallel crevices, forming a range, running very irregularly, hence called sometimes the Ram's-horn range; general course a little north of east; worked chiefly in the glass-rock, where the lead ore occurs much mixed with dry-bone.

On the S. W. quarter of the N. E. quarter of the same section, in the high ground between the Welch Hollow and the Furnace branches of the Dodgeville branch, there are a number of diggings, not regular in their course. *Arthur & Co.'s* and *Glanville & Co.'s* and the *Old Clayton range* are among the prominent ones; they are productive chiefly in the glass-rock, and yield a large amount of dry-bone associated with the galena.

There are very numerous excavations on the N. W. quarter of the same section (35). The *Welch Hollow diggings* are on the sides of the bluffs along the branch, and have been recently turning out considerable ore. On the S. E. quarter of the N. W. quarter, along the ridge between the two branches, are the *Kelly, Robinson, & Co.'s diggings*, which, like all the others about here, carry much zinc ore with the lead. All these ranges seem to be chiefly productive in the glass-rock openings.

On the Furnace ridge, south of the Furnace branch, on the S. W. quarter of section 35, are various ranges, of which the M'Donald is the heaviest.

South of this range is a sort of cave called Sowden's cave, which is an opening seventy feet square, and one or two feet high, with a flat roof, and a floor covered with irregular blocks of rock: this appears to have originated in the sinking down of the strata, caused by the washing out from below of a portion of the softer decomposed material, such as usually fills the openings. Traces of copper ore are reported to have been found in some of the diggings on the Furnace ridge.

DODGEVILLE DIGGINGS.

The town of Dodgeville is situated on the N. W. corner of section 34 and the S. W. corner of section 27, and there are several ranges in the immediate vicinity, which have formerly produced a large amount of ore, although not at present worked to any considerable extent. The most important diggings are on the S. W. quarter of section 27 and the W. half of section 28.

The most extensive range near Dodgeville seems to be the *Lamb lode*, which extends from the town in a direction N. 17° W., to the north line of section 28, nearly a mile in length. There are five or six main parallel crevices, apparently, and a number of other shorter ones, maintaining the same general direction. Towards the town, at the south end, this range is either deflected to the east, or is crossed by quartering N. W. and S. E. crevices, throwing the range in that direction. There are two or three small groups of north and south ranges in the S. E. corner of the section (28), just west of the town, and a large E. and W., called the *Prideaux range*, coming in to meet them from the west; there seeming to be a sort of concentration of the crevices towards the corner of sections 27, 28, 33, and 34, where the ground is almost entirely dug over.

In the S. W. corner of section 27, the most important range is the *Lathrop*, which, starting on the south from near the court-house, runs N. 10° W., a little west of Washburne & Woodman's engine shaft, to the ravine, a distance of about

300 feet, in which space a large amount of ore has been mined. The Lathrop range has been sunk on to the depth of seventy feet, in the lower beds of the Galena limestone, in open crevices with tumbling rock, going off on each side of an unproductive bar of ground, in a series of flats and pitches. At its northern extremity the Lathrop either intersects, or passes a little to the west of, the *Penborthy range*, which comes in from the east with a course of S. 78° W. This latter is crossed by a counter, running S. 22° E., near its western extremity.

The engine shaft of Washburne & Woodman, above referred to, situated in the angle made by the approximation of the Lathrop and Penborthy ranges, coming together at almost an exact right angle, appears to have been sunk with a view to drain the ground in that vicinity, so as to allow of the probable intersection of these two ranges being proved. At all events, it was an unfortunate undertaking, having had no other result whatever than the expenditure of $20,000 or $30,000. The shaft was carried to the depth of ninety-five feet, and is supposed to have entered the glass-rock. The stuff thrown out from the excavation, which is now filled with water and abandoned, is a very hard, brittle, bluish-gray rock, with numerous seams and bunches of pyrites ramifying through it, forming one of the most difficult substances possible to blast, as may be gathered from the fact that $100 per foot was paid for sinking in it; the company bearing the very heavy expense, in addition, of pumping out the water. It would seem as if, by some fatality, these attempts to sink deep shafts in the Lead Region were always made exactly at those points where the work would be most expensive, and the results least satisfactory.

The geological position of the Dodgeville diggings seems to be in the middle and lower beds of the Galena, reaching pretty near the bottom of that rock in the work done on the Lathrop range. It was found impossible to procure any reliable estimates of the yield of the different ranges.

YELLOWSTONE DIGGINGS.

These diggings are situated around the head-waters of the Yellowstone branch of the East fork of the Peccatonica river, and on the divide between those two streams: they are in T. 4, R. 4 E., and R. 5 E. In the lower portions of the vallies in this vicinity, the Upper sandstone appears, and is overlaid by the Blue limestone, which rises to a considerable height in the bluffs, while the general higher level of the region is occupied by the lower beds of the Galena limestone. The principal diggings are in the vicinity of Scott's, or Yellowstone, situated at the corner of sections 23, 24, 25, and 26, T. 4, R. 4 E. It is to Mr. Scott that I am chiefly indebted for information in regard to what has been done in the way of mining in his neighborhood.

Beginning with the most eastern diggings, we have the

Fretwell diggings: on the S. W. quarter of the S. W. quarter of section 27, T. 4, R. 5 E. These consist of three patches, worked quite shallow, usually; the deepest shaft sunk was ninety-three feet below the surface, intersecting the glass-rock at about fifty feet, and the pipe-clay opening being five feet in thickness upon it, but apparently not productive enough to justify sinking to it. Most of the ore was taken out in the brown rock opening. On the most eastern patch of diggings, the course of the range is about N. 80° W. Workings have been carried on here since 1827; yield estimated at three million pounds.

Glass lot: south and a little west of the Fretwell; on the N. E. quarter of the N. W. quarter, and the N. W. quarter of the N. E. quarter of section 33; the main diggings on the last named fraction; worked in several small patches, and very shallow, in decomposed rock; the deepest sinking not over thirty feet, it is said; the main workings on a space fifty to seventy-five feet wide and about eighty rods long: general direction of the ranges nearly E. and W.

Frame's diggings: E. half of N. W. quarter of section 30 (T. 4, R. 5 E.); patch diggings, in clay, worked sixty feet deep; the main run of ore is nearly N. and S. in direction, and about one-quarter mile in length; several short easts and wests on the north side of the patch. The workings indicate a heavy but shallow range. Discovered in 1847, and chiefly worked in 1850: has produced probably about one million pounds.

Hall diggings: W. half of N. W. quarter of section 30; worked on a patch of north and south crevices, making in tumbling openings; depth about seventy feet; yield 15,000 pounds.

Martin diggings: E. half of S.W. quarter of section 30: working in 1859, on several small east and west crevices; depth not exceeding thirty or forty feet; has produced 40,000 lbs.

M'Clintock diggings: N. W. corner of S. E. quarter of section 19: worked on an E. and W. range, chiefly in the clay, and to the depth of twenty-five feet: a space fifty feet in width, having a general range of S. 73° E., entirely cut up with diggings; large quantities of ochre associated with the ore; has produced half a million pounds.

Dyer's diggings: S. E. quarter of section 13, T. 4, R. 4 E.; worked on several parallel E. and W. crevices, running S. 84° E. There are two openings, one above the green rock, the other in it, and fifteen feet apart, the green rock being here about four feet thick; the lower opening is the most productive, and is fifty feet below the surface. Boring was attempted here to prove the underlying strata, and was carried to the depth of 110 feet; the distance from the surface to the bottom of the glass-rock was found to be eighty feet, and the boring stopped in a "regular blue limestone," supposed to be the Buff limestone. These diggings were discovered in 1847, and worked in 1848, but chiefly in 1851 and 1852: yield estimated at one and a half million lbs.

Young's diggings: a little northwest of Dyer's, on the line between sections 13 and 14: about ten chains S. of quarter post: several E. and W. crevices, having a direction of N.

83° E.: the ore makes in crevice openings, with tumbling rock and pay-dirt; the principal and upper opening is in the green rock; depth of workings about fifty feet; discovered in 1845; working in Oct., 1859; estimated yield 200,000 to 300,000 lbs.

White's diggings: S. E. quarter of S. E. quarter of section 14: a little west of Dyer's; patch diggings on east and west crevices; worked about thirty feet deep; direction of crevices about S. 87° E.; has produced about 300,000 lbs.

Newkirk diggings: W. half of S. W. quarter of section 14: worked on a series of norths and souths, crossed by easts and wests, which run about S. 77° E.: principal body of ore at the depth of thirty or forty feet; a thin sheet followed down into the glass-rock, which is here well-characterized as a grey, brittle limestone, with few fossils; discovered in 1846; estimated yield 1,000,000 lbs.

Newkirk & Zollinger's diggings: S. E. quarter of section 15; small patch, with very shallow workings, on nearly E. and W. crevices; has produced 40,000 lbs.

Wildermuth's diggings: S. E. quarter of S. E. quarter of section 24; a crevice opening on a crevice running N. 8½° E., with an east and west meeting it on the west; water struck at twenty-five feet, and ore still going down; ore in large pieces, in clay and tumbling rock; worked in 1856–7; has yielded 70,000 lbs.

The above are the principal diggings in the Yellowstone district; a few of the less important are omitted, as no reliable information could be had concerning them.

There is a great similarity in the mode of occurrence of the ore at these different localities. The main body of the galena in this vicinity is in the lower flint beds of the Galena limestone, and much of it is found lying on the surface of the rock, mixed with ochrey clay and half decomposed dolomite, forming what are called "clay diggings." The crevices are not long and well-defined, but form as it were a net-work of intersecting norths and souths and east and wests, such as is aptly characterized by the term "patch." Considerable ore is also found as low as the brown-rock opening, but none of any consequence in the glass-rock.

These diggings appear, on the whole, to be pretty well worked out, not much over 50,000 lbs. a year being raised in this vicinity at present; nor is there much encouragement for deeper mining, although the opportunities for examination are not so good as they should be to enable me to give a positive opinion on that point.

Duke's Prairie diggings: on section 30, T. 4, R. 4 E., and section 25, T. 4, R. 3 E. Several parallel crevices, running N. 67° W., extend across the S. half of the N. W. quarter of section 30, and on to the adjoining quarter section west, for a length of over half a mile. This is called the Duke's Prairie or the Van Meter range. The *Spicer patch* is about an eighth of a mile northeast of the centre of section 30: this consists of nine crevices, seven and a half feet distant from each other, crossed by norths and souths at intervals of twelve feet. These diggings are nearly in the middle of the Galena limestone, and have been worked at intervals for the last twenty years.

Hamilton's (or Wyota) diggings. This is a well-marked and quite isolated group of diggings, about half way between Shullsburg and Monroe, and the only important mining locality in that region. The ranges are scattered over sections 18 and 19, T. 2, R. 5 E., and section 13, T. 2, R. 4 E. The *Hamilton east and west range* is the principal one worked here: it consists of three parallel crevices, about fifteen feet apart; course N. 57° W. This range crosses the S. W. corner of section 18, and runs diagonally across the S. E. quarter of section 13, to the N. and S. line dividing the section in the centre. The ore occurs in it in bunches and pocket-openings; the vertical range of the heaviest body is from the middle to the lower beds of the Galena limestone. This range has yielded heavily, having been worked at various times, latterly with the aid of a steam engine, for the last twenty-five years; it is said to have yielded over four million lbs. Towards the west end, this range is crossed by a north and south.

PLATTEVILLE DIGGINGS.

A full account of the discoveries and settlement of the vicinity of Platteville will be found in the "Grant County Herald" for September 9, 1843, drawn up by James M. Goodhue, Esq. From it we learn that the first ore was struck here by a man named Metcalf, in 1827, and soon after a considerable population of miners was collected in the vicinity.

The following very complete table of the yield, depth, &c., of the ranges worked in the vicinity of Platteville, is given by Mr. Goodhue, up to 1843:

Name of range.	Length.	Width.	Depth.	When discovered.	Whether in clay or rock.		Yield.
Rountree range	450	30	30	1827	c.	..	3,000,000
Finney patch	700	12	10	1827	c.	..	1,700,000
M'Clintock r.	150	3	20	1828	..	r.	700,000
Meeker	150	4	15	1829	c.	..	500,000
Davidson	300	13	20	1831	..	r.	700,000
Teller & Richards	330	6	12	1832	c.	..	1,000,000
Vineyard	1,320	15	17	1832	c.	..	1,600,000
Huntington	400	3	35	1834	c.	..	400,000
Flynn	450	8	20	1829	c.	..	1,000,000
Woodcock & O'Hara	200	4	25	1836	c.	..	100,000
Blundell	100	5	20	1836	c.	..	100,000
Pennington	200	5	15	1836	c.	..	100,000
Ritchie	200	6	30	1836	c.	..	120,000
Pettijohn	50	5	30	1836	c.	..	50,000
Denson	100	15	23	1833	..	r.	100,000
Holman	500	6	15	1829	c.	..	350,000
Rope	200	3	16	1827	c.	..	150,000
Goode	290	3	20	1829	c.	..	150,000
Gillis	150	6	7	1835	c.	..	150,000
Williams	300	4	10	1835	c.	..	200,000
Carrington & Co	400	6	20	1836	c.	..	690,000
O'Hara	1,300	8	15	1836	c.	..	1,100,000
Farmer	150	5	30	1837	c.	..	100,000
Robeson boys	350	5	20	1839	c.	..	150,000
Black Bill's	10	3	16	1841	c.	..	7,000

Name of range.	Length.	Width.	Depth.	When discovered.	Whether in clay or rock.		Yield.
Dorff's diggings	40	4	20	1842	..	r.	80,000
Miller & Levy	300	10	25	1840	..	r.	200,000
Dutch..................	....	..	..	1843	..	..	....
Link..................	....	..	41	1842	..	..	....
Elliott & Schwartz	200	8	20	1842	..	r.	200,000
Montplaisir.............	40	3	16	1842	c.	..	30,000
Capt. Judson	150	5	20	1842	c.	..	40,000
Orne's..................	80	6	25	1832	..	r.	100,000
							14,777,000

The following are the notes of Mr. Wilson's surveys of the crevices in the vicinity of Platteville (see diagram of the principal crevices in the vicinity of Platteville, plate X).

Commencing at quarter post on the E. side of section 14, T. 3, R. 1 W. Thence N. 60° W. 6.00 chs. to

Dry-Bone diggings: course N. 81½° W.; length 16.00 chs. Thence S. 81° E. 3.00 chs. to

Hell's Point crevice: course S. 81° E.; length 25.00 chs. 5.00 chs. S. of Hell's Point crevice is another crevice, commencing 10.00 chs. W. of quarter section line; thence runs N. 76° W.; length 66.00 chains.

Wide range is 2.20 chs. S. of the last-mentioned crevice: its W. end is 10.00 chs. W. of section line, between 14 and 15; thence it bears S. 81½° E., and is 40.00 chs. long.

Cleaveland & Robinson range: 4.00 chs. S. of the Wide range; its W. end is 10.00 chs. E. of section line; course S. 74° E.; length 15.00 chs.

Miller range commences 20.25 chs. S. of N. W. corner of section 14, T. 3, R. 1 W.: course S. 83° W.; length 20.00 chains.

Commencing at the centre of the N. E. quarter of section 15; thence S. 45° E. 4.00 chs. to

Woodcock range: course S. 89½° W.; length 12.00 chs. South of the Woodcock are two other parallel crevices.

Commencing at quarter post on E. side of section 15, thence W. 28.00 chs. and S. 1.00 ch. to

Flynn range: course S. 84° W.; length 7.00 chs. Thence S. 6.50 chs. to

Bevans range: course at W. end N. 85° E.; length 20.00 chs. Thence S. 9.50 chs. to

Roundtree level: its W. end is about 2.00 chs. W. of quarter section line; course N. 85½° E.; length 20.00 chs.

Negro crevice commences 14.00 chs. N. of quarter post on W. side of section 15: course S. 81½° E.; length 10.00 chs. From Negro range S. 5.00 chs. to

Robinson's range: course N. 88° E.; length 10.00 chs. Thence 1.75 chs. S. to

O'Hara range: course N. 83° W.; length 10.00 chs.

S. from quarter post on W. side of section 15, 3.40 chs. to

Crevice: course S. 89½° W.; length 32.00 chs. (20.00 W. and 12.00 E. of line). Thence 8.40 chs. to

Vineyard crevice: course S. 89° E.; length 20.00 chs.

Commencing at the centre of section 10, S. 5.00 chs. to

Gillis range: course N. 83° W.; length 23.00 chs.: fifty feet S. of Gillis range is a short crevice. Thence 11.50 chs. to

O'Hara range: course N. 82½° W.; length 80.00 chs. (60.00 W. and 20.00 E. of line).

There are two crevices fifty feet from the O'Hara, and parallel with it at the east end, and 20.00 chs. in length. Thence 21.50 chs. to

Dry-Bone range: course N. 80° W. for 100 yds.; then N. 78° W.; length 40.00 chs. At the point of the bend in the crevice is another one bearing S. 76° E.

South of the Dry-Bone range is another crevice, distant 4.00 chs.: course N. 83° W.; length 30.00 chs.

A crevice crosses the section line between sections 9 and 10, 1.50 chs. S. of quarter post: course N. 78° W.; length 30.00 chs. (20.00 west and 10.00 east of line). 4.00 chs. N. of Gillis range is a crevice: its W. end is 10.00 chs. E. of section line; course S. 86½° E.; length 8.00 chs.

Commencing at quarter post on line between sections 20 and 21; thence south 3.00 chs. to

Tyler's range: course N. 77° W.; length 12.00 chs. (9.00 W. and 3.00 E. of line). Thence 7.00 chs. to

Davidson range: course N. 84½° W.; length 20.00 chs. (9.00 W. and 11.00 E. of line).

Commencing at quarter post on line between sections 20 and 21, as above, thence north 4.00 chs. to

Finney patch: a space 23.00 chs. in length, entirely cut up with intersecting crevices, or patch-work.

From the above it will be seen that the crevices in the immediate vicinity of Platteville are nearly east and west; those on section 10, a mile north of the town, vary about 8° to the south of east. The same is the case with the crevices to the northeast, on section 14. The Southwest Platteville diggings, on sections 20 and 21, are chiefly in patches, but the general range of the crevices is also a few degrees to the south of east.

There are many side or subordinate crevices in each principal group of crevices, so that the whole ground is usually dug over, and it is difficult to make out their real direction. Among the heavy ranges now worked are the following:

Dry-Bone range, or diggings. An old range, with pocket openings; has produced over 1,000,000 lbs. In a new crevice, eight feet north of the Dry-Bone range, at a depth of forty-three feet, an opening, below a cap-rock, was just come upon when visited by Mr. Kimball in July, 1860. Black-jack, in a flat sheet, is found just under the cap, associated with lead ore, but no dry-bone, which was abundant in the old range of that name.

Hell's Point diggings. A series of nearly parallel crevices, with pocket openings. In the neighborhood of one leading crevice, from two to four smaller ones, not continuous, set in on either side of it, and have the same course, forming a sort of patch in one general range. This is the case with all the leading crevices. The same is true of all the heavy ranges in this vicinity, such as the Woodcock, Flynn, and Bevans.

The Rountree diggings, on section 10, N. W. of Platteville, are on open crevices, without any cap-rock; the Dry Bone, O'Hara and Gillis are each made up of several parallel crevices, forming heavy ranges, and running continuously for a long distance. They are separated by a varying thickness of rock, sometimes arranged as a key-rock, and connected occasionally by crossings carrying ore. The Dry-Bone range was the only one of this group in which that ore of zinc (the carbonate) was found.

The geological position of the Platteville diggings is about in the middle of the Galena limestone. That of the South-east Platteville is a little higher, or in the lower part of the upper beds. At the Backbone diggings, on Rountree's branch, the Blue limestone has been struck, and the level of the pipe-clay opening reached. After passing this, the ore was found extending downward in the seams. But, in general, the lowest random attained in this vicinity is the upper part of the lower or heavy-bedded flinty beds of the Galena limestone. At this level water is reached in most of the shafts near Platteville, and the workings have been carried no farther.

The characteristic features of the Platteville diggings, therefore, are their opening to the top of the rock, and their making in pocket openings, or irregular bunches, instead of regular openings with cap-rock, as is usual. The ore lies very near the surface, and the workings are consequently shallow and irregular, but in many cases of great width. Thus, in the Rountree range, when first opened and worked, a cart and oxen were driven in from the side of the bluff on the excavation, so that the ore and the accompanying dirt could be shovelled out, and loaded on the spot, as taken from the crevice.

The following estimate has been made by Major Rountree of the yield of some of the principal crevices up to the present time:

	Pounds.
O'Hara range..........	700,000
Vineyard range..................................	1,000,000
Negro range.....................................	50,000
Robinson range..................................	200,000
Woodcock range..................................	1,000,000
Flynn range.....................................	2,000,000
Bevans range....................................	1,000,000
Rountree range..................................	3,000,000

WHIG DIGGINGS.

This is a small group of ranges on the line between T. 3, R. 1 W., and the adjacent township west, on sections 1, 6, 7, and 12, but chiefly on 12 and 7. They serve, with the Brush-hill diggings, to connect the Platteville with the Potosi mining districts.

The Whig ranges are thus located by Mr. Wilson (see diagram of the principal ranges, plate X):

Commencing at a point 20.00 chs. W. of the quarter-post on line between sections 12 and 7; thence N. 32½° E. 8.00 chs.; thence N. 24½° E. 2.50 chs. to

Duncan range: course S. 80½° E.; length 24.00 chs. (20.00 chs. E. and 4.00 chs. W. of line).

From point of intersection with Duncan range, N. 33° E. 6.00 chs. to

Gillis range: course N. 86° W.; length 40.00 chs. (10.00 chs. W. of line and 30.00 chs. E.): this range is made up of five or six crevices, from two to seven feet apart.

Commencing at N. E. corner of section 12, T. 3, R. 2 W., to

Walker range: 12.00 chs. S. of the corner above-mentioned is the

Dutch range: course S. 80° E.; length 20.00 chs.

The Whig diggings are about in the same geological position as the Platteville; that is, in the middle portion of the Galena limestone.

The Gillis range is the longest, and was the first discovered, having been worked since 1840.

The following estimate was given in 1843* of the yield of the various crevices up to that time:

	Pounds.
Gillis & Carrington range	3,600,000
Duncan range	1,000,000
Dutch range	170,000
Garrison & Davidson range	100,000
Missouri range	600,000
Sub-Treasury range	100,000
Wild-Cat range	150,000
M'Kee range	80,000
Others not named	200,000
	6,000,000

It is stated, also, that the average number of miners employed in these diggings since their first opening had been about forty. This would indicate a very great productiveness of the ranges, as, at the present price of ore, it would give, if the amount raised is not over-stated, more than $1300 a year per man employed.

The Gillis range consists of six or seven parallel crevices, separated by spaces of only one or two to seven feet. Each crevice had its own series of openings, three being the usual number in this district.

But little is doing here at present, as the ranges seem to have been worked out at an early date. No new statistics can therefore be given.

POTOSI DIGGINGS.

The diggings in the vicinity of Potosi form a well-marked group, extending in a northeast and southwest direction for a distance of about six and a half miles, with occasional intervals of barren ground, by which they are broken up into several sub-districts, which are known by the following names, proceeding in the enumeration from the northeast

* Grant County Herald, October 7, 1843.

to the southwest: 1st, Red Dog; 2d, Pin Hook; 3d, Rockville; 4th, British Hollow; 5th, Potosi diggings proper. These will be taken up in the above order.

RED DOG DIGGINGS.

They were discovered in February, 1841, and were thus described by R. Carver, Esq., in 1843:*

"They were first supposed to be valuable in February, 1841, soon after which the only two very valuable lodes ever struck here were discovered, to wit: the Gilbreath and Goza, and the Druen, both of which were among the best ever struck in the Upper Mines. The two together have yielded about three million lbs. of mineral, and are now nearly worked out."

Mr. Wilson's notes of his survey of the Red Dog diggings are as follows (see diagram of the principal ranges at and near Potosi, plate IX):

Commencing at a point 20.00 chs. W. of the S. E. corner of section 7, T. 3, R. 2 W.; thence N. 20.00 chs. to

Basin range: course N. 70° W.; it intersects the Druen range at 7.00 chs. from the line; length 12.00 chs. (7.00 chs. W. and 5.00 chs. E. of line).

Druen range commences at the intersection of the Basin range: course E. and W.; length 17.00 chs.

The Red Dog diggings make in irregular crevices, open from the surface and connecting with flat openings, or in flat openings under a cap-rock. The crevices are generally short, with the exception of the above-named, and the distribution of the ore is very irregular.

PIN HOOK DIGGINGS.

Commencing at the N. W. corner of section 18, T. 3, R. 2 W.; thence S. 5.00 chs. to

* Grant County Herald, July 22, 1843.

Cornish range: course S. 70° E.; length 29.00 chs. (24.00 chs. E. and 5.00 chs. W. of line); thence 22.00 chs. to

Field range: course S. 75° E.; length 40.00 chs. (E. of line 20.00 chs. and W. 20.00 chs.); thence 23.00 chs. to

Endicott range: course S. 75° E.; length 28.00 chs. (18.00 chs. E. of line and 10.00 chs. W.); thence 24.50 chs. to

Jackson range: course S. 75° E.; length 20.00 chs. (15.00 chs. E. and 5.00 chs. W. of line); thence 42.00 chs. to

Paully range: course S. 69° W.; length 50.00 chs. (40.00 chs. W. and 10.00 chs. E. of line).

Commencing at a point 20.00 chs. N. of quarter-post on S. side of section 13, T. 3, R. 3 W.:

Warfield range: course N. 75° W.; length 25.00 chs. (20.00 chs. W. and 5.00 chs. E. of line): thence S. 7.50 chs. to

May range: course N. 76° W.; length 24.00 chs. (16.00 chs. W. and 8.00 chs. E. of line); "branches out like a tree" at W. end; thence 12.60 chs. to

Kernow range: course N. 76° W.; length 26.00 chs. (18.00 chs. W. and 8.00 chs. E. of line).

The Pin Hook diggings, as above surveyed, form two groups of crevices, connected by a quartering range, the Paully: the surface dug over is about a mile and a quarter in length northeast and southwest, and half a mile wide. The same remarks will apply to these diggings which were made above in reference to the Red Dog.

ROCKVILLE DIGGINGS, AND BRITISH HOLLOW DIGGINGS.

These are situated chiefly on the N. W. quarter of section 24 (T. 3, R. 3 W.), but also run over a little on to section 14; they occupy nearly half a square mile of area: the principal crevices are as follows:

Commencing at the corner of sections 13, 14, 23, and 24, T. 3, R. 3 W.; thence S. 2.00 chs. to

Davies & Likins's range: course N. 76° W.; length 18.00 chs. (10.00 chs. E. and 8.00 chs. W. of line); thence 15.00 chs. to

Alison range; thence 19.00 chs. to

Druen and *Seipker range;* thence 24.00 chs. to

Wooley range: course S. 80° W.; length 34.00 chs. (18.00 chs. W. and 16.00 chs. E. of line): Emery and Davies's level is at the east end of this range.

At a point 15 chs. W. of the center of section 24, T. 3, R. 3 W., is the

Seipker range: course N. 66° W.; length 23.00 chs. (5.00 chs. E. and 18.00 chs. W. of line).

Commencing at a point 20.00 chs. west of the centre of section 24, T. 3, R. 3 W.; thence N. 1.50 chs. to

Seipker range, as above; thence 7.50 chs. to

Davies's deep shaft: course of range here, N. 87° W.; thence 10.00 chs. to

Langstaff range: course N. 78° W.; length 25.00 chs. (15.00 W. and 10.00 E. of line).

Commencing at a point 21.00 chs. W. of S. E. corner of section 23, T. 3, R. 3 W.; thence north 1.50 chs. to

Hard Scrabble range: course N.; length 27.00 chs. to

Craig & Kindle range: course N. 78° W.; length 20.00 chs. (10.00 chs. E. and 10.00 chs. W. of line).

Commencing at the south end of Hard Scrabble is the west end of

Craig range: course S. 80° E.; length 41.00 chs.: from east end of Craig range starts the

Lothrop range: course N. 30° E.; length 40.00 chs.

The above are the principal ranges of the Rockville diggings, including the British Hollow, which are closely adjacent on the south, and to which the Craig & Kindle, the Hard Scrabble, the Craig, and the Lothrop ranges belong.

On the Langstaff crevice, the shafts are sunk forty feet to water, leaving ore going down: there are two openings worked, separated by a cap-rock of three to five feet in thickness. There are many north and south crevices, which carry sheet mineral, with one exception.

On the Seipker range the excavations go down from fifty

to one hundred feet before reaching water; the ore occurs in crevices, not making in regular openings; but an opening is supposed to lie beneath, under the water.

The most remarkable feature at the Rockville diggings, and one of the most interesting occurrences in the whole Lead Region is the quarry, or "level," as it is called, of Davies & Emory, which exposes seven sheets of galena horizontally interstratified with the lead-bearing limestone, as thus described by Dr. Kimball. See plate V, on which a section of the beds at this quarry is given.

"At these diggings, in following the east and west crevices to a depth, varying with the surface of the ground, from 40 to 100 feet (at which depth the shafts are commonly abandoned, on account of water), galena is found between beds of Galena limestone, thus forming horizontal sheets, uniform with the stratifications of the rock, of a thickness of from one to six inches, continuous, so far as proved, within a circuit of one-quarter of a mile. The thickness of these sheets is very irregular, the galena even in the heaviest sheet becoming attenuated to one-eighth of an inch in thickness. Fine seams of galena are disseminated through the rock in many places—especially through the beds enclosing the half inch sheet, the third from the surface.

"Seven sheets of this description have been exposed in Davies' & Emory level, as it is called, though the work here is conducted on the model of a quarry rather than a mine. An area of some 40,000 square feet has been thoroughly quarried to a depth of seventeen feet in the solid rock; while, from this depth, an open level, started from the eastern end of the quarry, is carried downwards five or six feet further. Thus a section of twenty-two and one-half feet is exposed to full view.

"The random of these beds is about the bottom of the Galena limestone, or the lower flint beds; as is indicated by the out-crop of the Trenton limestone, manifestly but a few feet lower than these, in a ravine to the east of the level."

The *Wooley* and the *Palmer* and *Lynn ranges* make regular crevices, bearing ore interruptedly; they are connected with the sheets worked at Davies & Co.'s quarry, above cited. These sheets do not appear to extend westerly to any great distance, as shafts have been sunk to the depth of eighty feet on the above crevices without meeting any flat bodies of ore; they are open to the top of the rock, and filled with clay, ochre and ore. Farther towards Rockville, a cap-rock is met with, at a depth of fifty feet, and varying from eight to twenty feet in thickness. The yield of these ranges has been large; over one and a half million pounds.

In the British Hollow diggings the following crevices were noted:

Craig crevice. In these diggings the ore occurs chiefly in flat openings, with flat and pitching sheets. Principal body of ore at a depth of sixty feet, in the water. A crevice leading from above down to the opening, and having small fragments of ore scattered through it. Yield, including the Hard Scrabble range, from one and a half to two million lbs.

In the *Hard Scrabble diggings* the ore occurs also much broken up in flats and pitches, following lines of fracture and forming floors.

Craig and *Kindle* reported as a flat sheet, making downwards into a crevice, which goes below the water-level.

POTOSI DIGGINGS.

The main group of the Potosi diggings, or those to which this name is properly applied, is situated on sections 33, 34, 35, and 36 of T. 3, R. 3 W., and the south ends of the longest crevices pass over the line into the next township south, in sections 4, 3, 2, and 1. The area occupied is between four and five square miles. The following are Mr. Wilson's notes of the survey of the principal crevices:

Commencing at the quarter-post on the E. side of section 35, T. 3, R. 3 W., thence N. 2.00 chs. to

Smith range: course N. 69° W.; length 1 mile 23.00 chs. (1 mile 7.00 chs. W. and 16.00 chs. E. of line); thence 4.00 chs. to

O'Hara range: course N. 69° W.; length 74.00 chs.; thence 8.50 chs. in line, and 4.00 chs. S. 84° E. to

Cave range: course N. 84° W.; length 36.00 chs.; thence 13.50 chs. to

Kindle range: course N. 71½° W.; length 1 mile 38.00 chs. (78.00 chs. W. and 40.00 chs. E. of line); thence 16.50 chs. to

Daniels & Burns range: course N. 71° W.; length 36.00 chs. (18.00 chs. W. and 18.00 chs. E. of line).

Commencing again at the quarter-post as above, and proceeding south 14.00 chs., to

Polkinghorn range: course N. 61° W.; length 1 mile 16.00 chs. (78.00 chs. W. and 18.00 chs. E. of line).

At a point 14.00 chs. S. of the N. W. corner of sec. 35 is the

Barbara range: course N. 63° W.; length 1 mile 10.00 chs. (48.00 chs. W. and 42.00 chs. E. of line); thence S. 14.00 chs. to

Fitch & Bell range: course N. 82° W. 8.00 chs., and S. 69¾° E. 46.00 chs.; entire length 64.00 chs.; thence 10.00 chs. to

Apple River range: course N. 60° W.; length 1 mile 45.00 chs. (25.00 chs. W. and 1 mile and 20.00 chs. E. of line).

At the above point of intersection a crevice starts and runs E.; length 45.00 chs.; 5.00 chs. from the W. end of this E. and W. crevice the

Gallagher range starts: course S. 63° E.; length 80.00 chs.

Commencing at the quarter-post on the W. side of section 35, and running S. 15.00 chs., to

Gilmore range: course N. 68° W.; length 77.00 chs. (35.00 chs. W. and 42.00 chs. E. of line); thence 17.00 chs. to

Mead & Gillet range: course N. 67° W.; length 64.00 chs. (24.00 chs. W. and 40.00 chs. E. of line); thence 34.00 chs. to

Madeira range: course N. 65° W.; length 1 mile 4.00 chs. (44.00 chs. W. and 40.00 chs. E. of line); thence 38.00 chs. to

North St. John's range: course N. 65° W.; length 50.00 chs. (44.00 chs. W. and 8.00 chs. E. of line): thence 43.00 chs. to

South St. John's range: course N. 65° W.; length 44.00 chs. (40.00 chs. W. and 4.00 chs. E. of line).

Detandabaratz range: its S. E end is near the quarter-post on S. side of section 34, T. 3, R. 3 W.: course N. 66° W.; length 20.00 chs.

Rock range: its N. W. end is near the quarter-post on S. side of section 33, T. 3, R. 3 W.; course S. 70° E.; length 20.00 chs.

Skaiff range crosses section line 16.00 chs. W. of the S. E. corner of section 33: course N. 55¾° W. 8.00 chs.; thence N. 67° W. 30.00 chs.

Hudson range: at the S. E. corner of section 33: course N. 67° W.; length 45.00 chs. (40.00 chs. N. and 5.00 chs. S. of line).

From the S. E. corner of section 33, N. 10.00 chs. to

Madeira Cave range: course N. 65° W.; length 54.00 chs. (44.00 chs. W. and 10.00 chs. E. of line).

From the above intersection, N. 20.00 chs. to

Whittaker cave: course N. 70° W.; length 40.00 chs. (15.00 chs. W. and 25.00 chs. E. of line).

The *Snake Cave* is at the east end of the *Whittaker Cave range.*

Commencing at the quarter-post between sections 33 and 34, thence north 2.00 chs. to

Wood & Dean's range: course S. 70° E.; length 33.00 chs.; on line 10.00 chs., and thence west 5.00 chs., to the E. end of *Dodson's cave,* in which sandstone was found; thence 27.00 chs. to

Wooley range: course N. 55¾° W.; length 65.00 chs. (25.00 chs. W. and 40.00 chs. E. of line); thence 31.00 chs. to

Long range: course N. 55¾° W.; length 66.00 chs. (26.00 chs. W. and 40.00 chs. E. of line).

The east end of the Potosi diggings is called Dutch Hollow. The principal diggings here are as follows:

Cave range. On this range, at a depth of forty-four feet, a large cave, fifty-five feet in width, was struck: it was partly filled with clay and masses of rock, mixed with fragments of galena.

On Preston Point, there are crevice indications; but, in addition, the lead ore is disseminated all through the adjacent rock, occupying the seams, and forming floors between the strata, together with the ores of zinc, both the carbonate and the sulphuret (black-jack and dry-bone). Excepting at the cave range, there has been no removal of rock, or formation of cavities. All is solid, and from a depth of ten feet below the surface to sixty or seventy, or as far at least as can be sunk without being troubled by water, the rock continues to be filled with seams and floors of galena. The zinc ores occupy the lowest position, and are not struck except in the deeper workings. Besides the main crevices forming openings, there are many sheets of ore closely wedged in the rock. On Preston Point this intersection of the strata with seams of ore is so general that, according to Mr. Kimball, it is difficult to find among the rubbish thrown out from the principal shafts a single mass of rock which has not more or less galena scattered through it. According to Mr. O'Hara, the Preston Point diggings have yielded not less than four million pounds of ore.

EAST POTOSI VALLEY.

Smith range. Open crevice yielding mineral, chiefly in pockets. Water reached at seventy feet on the ridge. Engine shaft 130 feet deep. Has produced 400,000 to 500,000 pounds.

O'Hara range: similar in character to the Smith range, and has yielded about the same amount.

Polkinghorn range: a long series of crevies in one range; there are three parallel continuous ones, from eight to ten feet apart. The ore gives out in these crevices at intervals, but the crevices themselves suffer no interruption. A siphon shaft has been sunk to the depth of 130 feet on this range, a little east of its centre. The crevices are all open, and carry the ore in pockets; the shafts are generally sunk from fifty to seventy feet, according to the elevation of the ground and the distance which can be sunk before water is reached.

Madeira range: shaft sunk on this range to the depth of 110 feet. It is an open crevice from the surface to the cap, which is met with at a depth of seventy-five feet, and is from four to six feet thick. The opening below the cap is ten feet wide, and has been worked out 500 feet in length; it does not, however, extend the whole length of the range. There is a pump-shaft at each end of the lower opening, and a steam engine at one of them. The material in the opening is remarkably ferruginous; large masses of pyrites occur in the crevice, and this substance, together with flints, forms two or three beds at the bottom of the opening.

WESTERN POTOSI VALLEY.

Dodson range. Three parallel crevices, open at the surface of the rock, and converging so as to meet in a common opening at the depth of fifty feet.

Madeira Cave range. An open crevice leading to a wide opening or cave, with key-rock, partly filled with ore, ochre, clay, &c.

Long range. A very long crevice, nearly a mile in extent, and open and continuous from one end to the other, not now accessible, but described as follows by an intelligent miner, who had worked in it for a long time:

The crevice carried ore near the surface, and then closed up to a seam in the cap-rock, which was eight feet thick, the bottom of the opening being 120 feet below the surface on the highest ground. The opening itself is, in some places, seventy feet wide, and averages twenty to twenty-five feet; its height was sixteen feet on the average, and in some places twenty-four feet. All through the opening was a key-rock sixteen inches wide, rising generally to within four feet of the top of the opening: this arrangement may be understood from the annexed wood-cut, which represents a cross-section of the whole as here described. The ore was found distributed in a blue and yellow ochrey clay, which filled up the opening about as high as the top of the key-rock. Above this was three or four inches of blue clay, without any galena, and from that to the cap-rock generally a vacancy of about one foot in height. The ore was disposed in the clay something in the form shown by the oblique lines in the section.

FIG. 33.—Section of Opening or Cave on Long range.

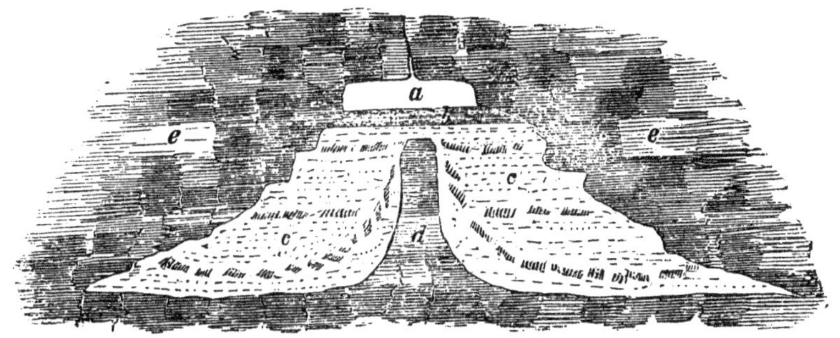

a. Vacant space.
b. Blue clay.
c. *c*. Ochrey clay and galena.
IIIII. Principal body of ore.
d. Key-rock.
e. Galena limestone.

Long range. The yield of this range is estimated at eight million pounds; five million pounds were turned out on the first working.

Wooley range. Opening below a cap-rock, as in the Long range. Towards the west end, the opening, less productive than in the opposite direction, splits into five or six open crevices, parallel with each other, and separated by partitions of solid rock. This has been a very productive range; but the entire yield could not be ascertained.

There are many north and south crevices running through the mining ground at Potosi, especially on the west side of the valley. Almost without exception, and perhaps quite so, these norths and souths are close crevices, without openings, the ore making in them in solid sheets, which are continuous and nearly vertical, and firmly attached to the rock on each side. The easts and wests, on the other hand, are mostly clay crevices, making from the surface of the rock, and carrying ore in pocket-openings. They seldom show anything like a cap-rock, but often close up to a mere seam, or become "tight." It is generally believed by the miners that the regular opening below the cap, which was come upon in the Cave, Long, Wooley, and some other smaller ranges, exists also in most of the other leading crevices, but that it cannot be reached, on account of water at this level.

The Cave range makes a large opening beneath the cap-rock; and, on its east end, terminates in a cave, known as the "Snake Cave," from which the diggings here were originally called the "Snake diggings." When this cave was first discovered, it was found to contain an incredible number of rattlesnakes—many thousands, it is said.

It is estimated that about two million lbs. of ore are raised annually, at the present time, in the Potosi diggings; but, on the whole, mining in this district is not considered as very profitable.

The geological position of the Potosi diggings is in the lower portion of the Galena limestone: no crevices have been traced down as low as the Blue limestone, so far as has been ascertained.

PIGEON DIGGINGS.

The Pigeon diggings are situated in the south half of section 17, and the north half of section 20, T. 4, R. 3 W. They form a well-marked group of nearly parallel crevices, varying in length from a quarter to a half mile. The crevices are open ones, leading to flat openings at a uniform random. The workings are mostly shallow, the shafts on the most elevated ground being down from fifty to sixty feet.

The following are the notes of Mr. Wilson's survey (see diagram on plate VIII):

Turley & Tayler range: commences 10.00 chs. S. of N. W. corner of section 20, T. 4, R. 3 W.; bears S. 85° E.; length 20.00 chs.

McDaniel & Bonham range: intersects half-section line 1.00 ch. S. of N. E. corner of N. W. quarter of section 20; bears S. 89° E.; length 30.00 chs.

Groshong range: 3.00 chs. N. of the McDaniel & Bonham range; bears S. 89° E.; length 40.00 chs.

Pullin, Cox & Turley range: E. end 3.00 chs. N. of the Groshong range; length 40.00 chs.

Old Sheet range: 17.50 chs. S. of quarter-post on line between sections 17 and 20; bears N. 57° E. 8.00 chs. S., S. 57° E.; length 28.00 chs.

The yield of the several crevices is given by Geo. Cox, Esq., of Lancaster, as follows:

	Pounds.
Old Sheet range	1,500,000
Tiff range	100,000
Water range	250,000
Pullin, Cox & Turley range	......
McDaniel & Bonham range	500,000
Turley & Tayler range	450,000
Bonham range	2,000,000

The geological position of the Pigeon diggings is low down in the Galena limestone, in the lower flint beds. Along the banks of Pigeon creek, a little way south of the diggings, the whole thickness of the Blue and Buff limestones appears, underlaid by sixty feet of the sandstone.

BEETOWN DIGGINGS.

The Beetown diggings form the most northwesterly group, or mineral district, of the Lead Region. Beyond them in that direction nothing of consequence has ever been discovered, and we soon pass on to rocks lower than those in which ore is usually found. The Beetown district is situated in T. 4, R. 4 W., and T. 4, R. 5 W., covering the larger portion of an area of about seven square miles, in sections 17, 18, 19, 20, 28, 29, and 30 of T. 4, R. 4, and sections 25 and 26 in T. 4, R. 5. These diggings are divided into several sub-groups, which are named as follows, beginning on the north-east: 1st, Hackett's diggings, in section 17; 2d, Beetown diggings proper, in sections 19, 20, 29, and 30. Adjacent to these diggings, on the east, are the Grant diggings, in sections 21 and 28. Thus far the succession of ranges has been from north to south; but, to the west of Beetown, the ranges and sub-groups extend almost exactly west, so that the whole series of the Beetown diggings are grouped together on two sides of a square.

Next west of the Beetown are the Nip-and-Tuck diggings, which are chiefly on the south half of sec. 25 (T. 4, R. 5 W). Still farther west, occupying nearly the whole of section 26, are the Muscalonge diggings. Beyond this are two small groups, not properly belonging to the Beetown diggings, called the North and the Muddy diggings. The Pigeon diggings form another small group, on the east, in the adjoining township.

The total yield of these diggings, as estimated up to August, 1843, was 2,800,000 lbs. of ore.

According to Mr. Wiltse,* these diggings were opened in 1827, deserted in 1829, and resumed again in 1835. In 1843, 140 miners were at work in that vicinity, and the following had been the yield of the principal ranges:

RATTLESNAKE DIGGINGS

	Pounds.		Pounds.
Segar & Bushnell, 1827...	250,000	Dudley, 1828............	70,000
Stewart, 1835...........	230,000	Stout & Merritt, 1843.....	20,000
Case, 1835..............	30,000	Dudley, 1843............	50,000

* Grant County Herald, August 26, 1843.

NIP-AND-TUCK.

	Pounds.		Pounds.
Stewart, 1828	80,000	Sheldon, 1835	30,000
Dudley, 1838	70,000	Brock, 1843	40,000
Cave, 1828	250,000	St. John, 1843	32,000
Price, 1843	16,000	Bunches, &c.	75,000

BEETOWN.

Bee, 1827	266,000	Doctor Snyder, 1828	175,000
M'Cartney, 1838	30,000	M'Hollister, 1838	90,000
Clues, 1829	30,000	Holliday & Co., 1828	66,000
Blessing, 1838	30,000	Doctor Griffy, 1839	30,000
Burton's, 1838	45,000	Hackett, 1828	30,000
Morey, 1828	30,000	" 1840	120,000
Morey & Woodhouse, 1839,	50,000	Bunches, &c.	60,000
Arthur, 1829	65,000		

NEW GRANT.

Day's, 1843	160,000	Hare, 1843	160,000
" 1843	55,000	Bunches, &c., 1843	75,000

HACKETT'S DIGGINGS.

The following are Mr. Wilson's notes of the position and direction of the main crevices or ranges of Hackett's diggings (see diagram of the principal crevices in the vicinity of Beetown, plate VIII):

Beginning at the S. E. corner of the N. E. quarter of the N. W. quarter of section 17, T. 4, R. 4 W., thence north 0.33 ch.; thence N. 85¾° W. 1.27 chs. to east end of

Jo Mack crevice: course N. 85¾° W.; length 5.15 chs. It is intersected by a north and south crevice at a point 3.88 chs. west of its E. end, which throws the western portion of it 0.36 ch. to the south: the north and south crevice runs S. 22¾° W. for 5.00 chs., when it intersects the

Smith & Walker crevice, which bears S. 84¾° E. to its E. end, distant 5.12 chs.; on its W. end it is thrown south at the intersection of the north and south 0.30 ch., and from here it bears N. 87½° W. for 3.00 chs.; thence N. 86¼° W. for 4.00 chs.; entire length, 12.12 chs.

Commencing at the quarter-post on line between sections 8 and 17, then running north 3.00 chs., then east 1.50 chs., to the west end of

Hackett's crevice: course E. and W.; length 6.00 chs.

Besides the above, there are a great number of short irregular crevices, so that nearly the whole ground enclosed within the dotted line on the map has been dug over. The whole diggings might properly be called a patch. The crevices make openings both above and below a cap-rock, which is about ten feet thick, and the top of it thirty feet below the surface. In some instances, shafts have been sunk below the cap for the depth of fifty feet, and productive openings struck, but in other cases a depth as great as 110 feet has been reached without coming to an opening.

BEETOWN DIGGINGS.

We resume here Mr. Wilson's surveys of the Beetown diggings, passing now to those in the immediate vicinity of the town.

Commencing at quarter-post on line between sections 19 and 20, T. 4, R. 4 W., and running north 1.00 ch. to

Brush crevice: course S. 80½° E.; length 22.00 chs. Thence 8.50 chs. to

Creger & Day's range: course S. 80½° E.; length 26.00 chs. Thence 12.62 chs. to

Gilbert range: course S. 80¾° E.; length 22.00 chs. (18.00 chs. E. and 4.00 chs. W. of line). Thence 14.28 chs. to

Turley range: course S. 80½° E.; length 32.00 chs. Thence 20.50 chs. to

Rock range: course S. 80½° E.; length 45.00 chs. (40.00 chs. E. and 5.00 chs. W. of line).

Commencing at quarter-post on line between sections 18 and 19, and running north 5.00 chs. to

Scott range: course S. 80° E.; length 45.00 chs.

Commencing again at quarter-post, on line between sections 19 and 20, and running south 7.00 chs. to

Smith & Walker range: course S. 80½° E.; length 33.00 chs. (30.00 chs. E. of line and 3.00 chs. W.)

Thence, on line of Smith & Walker range (S. 80½° E.) 21.00 chs.; then south 10.00 chs. to

Cave range: course S. 80½° E.; length 41.00 chs. (38.00 chs. E. of line and 3.00 chs. W.) Thence 15.00 chs. to

French range: course S. 80½° E.; length 21.00 chs.; then disappears for 30.00 chs. and appears again in the same direction as the

Connel & Booth range: length 8.00 chs.

Long range commences 0.20 ch. S. of S. E. corner of section 20, T. 4, R. 4 W.: course N. 80½° W.; length one mile 10.00 chs.

Commencing again at the quarter-post on line between sections 20 and 29, and running south 2.50 chs. to

Layman & Horr range: course N. 80½° W.; length 12.00 chs. (5.00 chs. W. and 7.00 chs. E. of line).

Commencing at the corner of sections 19, 20, 29, and 30, and running south 6.00 chs. to

North Nicholas Fine range: course N. 80½° W.; length 66.00 chs. (20.00 chs. W. and 46.00 chs. E. of line). Thence 9.00 chs. to

South Nicholas Fine range: parallel with and of the same length as the north range of the same name.

Commencing at the N. W. corner of the S. W. quarter of the N. E. quarter of section 29 and running east 11.00 chs. to

Bee lode, at its west end: course S. 80½° E.; length 13.00 chains.

Commencing at the centre of section 29 and running east 14.00 chs. to the west end of

Garden lode: course S. 80½° E.; length 6.00 chs.

Commencing at the S. E. corner of section 21 and running west 20.00 chs. to the east end of

Old French diggings: course N. 80½° W.; length 80.00 chs. From the east end of the Old French range, south 7.00 chs. to

Mory range: course N. 80½° W.; length 21.00 chs. (18.00 chs. W. and 3.00 chs. E. of line).

Commencing at the quarter-post on line between sections 21 and 28 and running south 15.00 chs., thence west 8.00 chs. to east end of

Grant range: course N. 80½° W.; length 23.00 chs.

Commencing at the S. E. corner of section 30 and running north 10.00 chs. to

Brown's crevice: course N. 86° W. for 25.00 chs., thence S. 86° W. for 6.00 chs. Total length 31.00 chs. Thence 17.00 chs. to the east end of

Platte & Alex range: course N. 85° W.; length 48.00 chs.

The Beetown diggings are generally characterized by the same features: they are on well-defined crevices, which are closely parallel with each other, and have a course about N. 80° W. Besides the larger and more conspicuous ones laid down on the map, there are great numbers of smaller crevices, generally having the same bearing as the larger ones, but too short to be conveniently made out and represented on so small a scale. There are generally two openings, of which the lower one is the most productive, the upper one making in pocket-openings. The thickness of the cap is about twelve feet. When the upper opening makes distinctly, water is struck on getting through the cap-rock, but, in the few instances where the rock above is firm from the surface, this is not the case. The depth to the cap varies from thirty to fifty feet, according to the variation of level of the surface. Float ore is found all over the ground, without regard to ranges, so that the whole surface is dug over, and the difficulty of making out the crevices much increased.

Among the important ranges, in regard to which some particulars were obtained, are the following:

Old Bee lode. This has been worked for more than thirty years; it had produced over a quarter of a million lbs. up to 1843. It is very difficult to make out, however, what the entire produce of any of these lodes has been up to the present time, as they have been worked by different parties, with many interruptions, and any estimates made are little better than guesses. In the Bee lode there is only one opening, which is below the cap-rock, and the top of it is reached by sinking forty-five to fifty feet on the highest ground. The cap is twelve feet thick.

Wood & Whitewood range. This consists of a large number of short parallel crevices between the Bee and Garden ranges: it has produced from 300,000 to 400,000 lbs.

Garden range. One of the first discovered in the Beetown diggings, and has been dug over at intervals for thirty years. Only the upper opening has been worked, the cap-rock being so hard as to discourage sinking beneath it.

Old French diggings. Said to have been worked by the Indians, and afterwards by the French, who had a furnace in its vicinity. This has been a very productive range, and is still worked at intervals, and a few thousand lbs. taken from it. It makes in two openings, one above and the other below the cap-rock.

Platt & Alex diggings. Worked in two openings, of which the lower is the more productive. It has produced over half a million pounds.

Creger lode. This is worked in a vertical crevice, with the usual twelve-foot cap-rock separating the lower opening from the upper crevice opening, which is open to the surface. Depth attained, from seventy to eighty feet. This has been a very productive lode, having yielded 3,000,000 lbs., it is said.

The *Gilbert* and the *Turley lodes* and the *Rock range* are worked to about the same depth as the Creger; unlike the last-named range, however, they make in a flat opening below the cap, which is of the usual thickness, namely twelve feet.

NIP-AND-TUCK DIGGINGS.

These are chiefly on the south half of section 25, running over a little on to the adjoining section south.

Some of the principal ranges have the following position and direction, as appears from Mr. Wilson's surveys.

Commencing at the S. E. corner of section 25, T. 4, R. 5 W., thence north 15.00 chs. to

Bruce range: course S. 85° W.; length 24.00 chs. (12.00 chs. E. and 12.00 chs. W. of line).

Commencing at the S. W. corner of the N. E. quarter of the S. E. quarter of section 25; thence east 4.00 chs., thence north 2.50 chs., to the west end of three or four crevices not yet worked to any extent: course S. 86° E.

Commencing at a point 23.00 chs. E. of quarter-post on the line between sections 25 and 26, thence south 2.00 chs. to the west end of

Price range: course S. 81½° E.; length 12 chs.

Commencing 23.00 chs. west of quarter-post on south side of section 25, thence north 0.50 ch. to east end of

Dudley cave: course N. 82° W.; length 18.00 chs.

The Nip-and-Tuck diggings are properly patch diggings, there being many norths and souths crossing the easts and wests.

MUSCALONGE DIGGINGS.

Situated chiefly on section 26, but occupying a small portion of the east side of 27 (T. 4, R. 5 W.). Surveyed as follows:

Commencing at the S. W. corner of section 26, T. 4, R. 5 W., thence north 5.00 chs. to

Stout range: course S. 87° E.; length 18.00 chs.

Commencing at a point 20.00 chs. E. of S. W. corner of section 25, thence north 7.00 chs. to

Le Grave range: course N. 87° W.; length 19.00 chs. (16.00 chs. W. and 3.00 chs. E. of line). Thence 16 chs., N. 87° W. 4.00 chs., to

Palmer range: course N. 87° W.; length 18.00 chs. Thence 42.00 chs., thence E. 5.00 chs., to W. end of

Barningham range: course E.; length 20.00 chs.

Commencing at a point 23.00 chs. south of quarter-post on north line of section 26, T. 4, R. 5 W., on the

Bushnell range: course S. 87° W.; length 24.00 chs. (16.00 chs. W. and 8.00 chs. E. of line).

At the center of the N. W. quarter of section 26 is a point on the

Turley & Brown range: course N. 36½° E.; length 17.00 chs. (11.00 chs. E. and 6.00 chs. W. of line). This crevice is crossed by several crevices running E. and W., and at its south end it branches out in various directions, "like the branches of a tree."

The Muscalonge diggings are on crevices with pocket openings from the surface downwards, as in the Beetown ranges; but, instead of a twelve-foot cap-rock, there is an interval of hard, unproductive rock, fifty feet in thickness, between the upper and lower openings. The deepest shafts are sunk 160 feet; this, of course, is on the highest ground. The rock through these diggings is unusually hard and heavy-bedded.

The Turley & Brown range, as noted above, is a quartering crevice, with east and west off-shoots, rich in ore, and terminating on the south in a net-work of branches.

In the Le Grave range the depth to the first opening is fifty-six feet; there are several parallel crevices forming the range, which has yielded heavily.

The Beetown & Muscalonge diggings are said to yield from one to one and a half million pounds of ore a year; within the last year or two more mining has been done here than for some time before: the number of persons thus employed, however, is always very irregular in these diggings.

In their geological position, the Beetown diggings occupy the lower beds of the Galena limestone, but we are not aware that any ore has ever been got as low down as the Blue limestone, which is well exposed in the vallies of all the streams in the vicinity.

WINGVILLE DIGGINGS.

These are situated on the extreme north of the Lead Region, in the vicinity of the village of Wingville, which is on the south half of the S. E. quarter of section 24, T. 6, R. 1 W., on the military road, and just south of the head-waters of Blue river. The lower beds of the Galena limestone occupy the surface here, having a thickness of perhaps sixty or seventy feet on the ridges. Crossing the water-shed, we descend rapidly in the vallies to the north on to lower rocks, and have only to go a mile and a half north of the village to find the Lower Magnesian rising in the bluffs, and at the junction of Dark and Badger Hollows, on the S.W. quarter of section 12, this rock is exposed with an elevation of about forty feet.

The Wingville ranges are all in the lower beds of the Galena, however, and do not seem to have penetrated to the Blue limestone. The ore makes chiefly in what are called tumbling openings, or wide, flat deposits, in which the ore is arranged in bunches and seams, in connection with partly decomposed rock.

The principal ranges worked in this vicinity are as follows:

Grasswire range. Three or four parallel crevices forming a range, running N. 74½° E., just east of the town; worked about a quarter of a mile in length. The ore occurs in a crevice opening, or tumbling opening, much mixed with ferruginous matter, among which were observed specimens of brown iron ore in pseudomorphs of sulphuret of iron (marcasite); worked nearly but not quite to the bottom of the Galena limestone.

Crooked range. Southeast of Wingville, about a quarter of a mile distant from the village; course very irregular, but general direction S. 87° E.; one-fourth of a mile in length; worked fifty to sixty feet deep. On this range, at a depth of fifty-five feet, teeth and bones of the mastodon were found with the ore, covered by clay, sand, &c., to the surface.

The *Jug range* is just north of Crooked range: it has a course nearly parallel with that range. The *Taylor range*, running N. 83° E., and the *Kirk range*, N. 53° E., are farther on in this direction, between the Crooked and Grasswire.

There are also considerable excavations, although shallow, to the northeast of the Grasswire range, in which the lead ore is said to have lain flat in the lower beds of the Galena limestone, "in masses like bricks"—evidently a horizontal sheet deposit, slightly broken up.

CENTREVILLE DIGGINGS.

These are in the vicinity of the village of Centreville, which is on the S. W. quarter of section 7, T. 6, R. 1 E. The Galena limestone here occupies only the highest portions of the elevated ground between the streams, and is quite thin, the streams cutting down to the Lower Magnesian. The diggings are principally in two groups, the *Nundorf* and *Gillam's diggings.* The former are on the N. W. quarter of section 7, T. 6, R. 1 E., and are worked in a flat sheet, which extends over a space about 300 feet square, nearly or quite continuously, and principally on the west half of the N. W. quarter of the section. The shafts sunk are on a range from northwest to southeast. Large quantities of black-jack and dry-bone, especially of the former, occur here in connection with the galena. The black-jack is chiefly in disseminated patches, or crystalline lamellar masses, scattered through a soft, shaly, argillaceous limestone. The excavations vary from a few feet to fifty, according to the level at which they start. The geological position of this sheet is in the upper part of the Blue limestone.

There are diggings on the S. W. quarter of section 8, which are said to have produced copper ore, but none could be found in the refuse thrown out, the locality not having been worked for nine years.

The Gillam diggings, west of Centreville, on the east half of the N. E. quarter of section 12, T. 6, R. 1 W., are shallow excavations, covering a large part of the quarter section. The ore occurs here in a flat sheet, much mixed with black-jack and dry-bone, in the upper part of the Blue limestone, as in the case of the Nundorf diggings. Much of the rock in the vicinity of the openings has undergone decomposition, and some of it forms a stiff blue clay, called "bull-dung" by the miners.

FRANKLIN DIGGINGS.

These are near the village of Franklin, which is on the north half of section 33, T. 7, R. 1 E. The diggings are on the S. E. quarter of section 28, running a little over on to the S. W. quarter. The main range runs diagonally through the S. E. quarter of section 28, from S. W. to N. E.; but there is another smaller range at right-angles to this, starting off south from its southern termination. The character of the diggings near Franklin is very much the same as that of the Centreville district. They are on flat sheets, in the upper portion of the Blue limestone. In the "Black-Jack diggings," on Stanley's land, shafts are sunk from eighty-five to ninety feet in depth into the glass-rock, the Galena limestone being here less than fifteen feet thick.

DIGGINGS NEAR LINDEN.

The Linden, or Pedlar's Creek diggings, are situated near the village of that name, which occupies the S. E. quarter of the S. E. quarter of section 8, T. 5, R. 2 E., and the principal diggings are on the head-waters of Pedlar's creek, in sections 5, 6, 7, and 8. There are scattered ranges of diggings also on the adjoining township west, T. 5, R. 1 E., which may be noticed in this connection.

Madden diggings. On the N. E. quarter of the S. E. quarter of section 2, T. 5, R. 1 E. They are on two crevices, having a course of S. 86° E., forming with subordinate ones a wide and long range, although worked very shallow; their length is about a quarter of a mile, and the excavations vary in depth from a few feet to fifty, according to the elevation of the ground. Their geological position is, apparently, in about the middle of the Galena limestone. These diggings were worked some fifteen years ago, and probably 1,000,000 lbs. of ore taken out: at present they are neglected. Other ranges in this township, concerning which no definite information can be given, are:

Caraco range: on the north half of the S. E. quarter of section 3; a range running a little south of east.

Patch range: crossing the line dividing the S. E. quarter of section 3 from the N. E. quarter of section 10; an east and west range.

Charles's diggings: running N. N.W. and S. S. E., and crossing the line between the N. E. and N.W. quarters of section 13.

Ludlam range: starting near the S. E. corner of section 18, and running N. N. W.; length a quarter of a mile.

These diggings are all abandoned at present, and nothing more was ascertained in regard to them.

Of the Linden diggings proper, the *Heathcock range* is by far the most important, and it is one of the most interesting ranges in the mineral district. It is situated on the south side of the S. W. quarter of section 8, T. 5, R. 2 E., a little west of the village of Linden. The range consists of three parallel crevices, running at the west end almost exactly east and west, and bending around towards the east end so as to have a course nearly southeast. The entire length worked is about 4,000 feet. The three crevices keep very nearly the same course for a distance of half a mile, and remain parallel with each other, although only a few yards apart. When first opened, they were worked in the usual manner of sand and tumbling-rock crevices, in the lower beds of the Galena limestone, and were exceedingly productive, probably as much or more so than any range in the Lead Region. Mr. Heathcock stated, in 1853, on oath, that this range had been worked for twenty years, and had produced 10,000,000 lbs. of ore, the depth to which the miners had gone up to that time having been about sixty feet, where they were stopped by the water. In 1853 or 1854, a company was chartered by the State of Wisconsin, called the "Linden Lead Company," which took a lease of this pro perty, and undertook to put up an engine and pump, and to work the mine to a greater depth, promising in their prospectus that, as soon as this was done, the mine would pay "as great dividends as any mine started in the United States, in proportion to the amount of capital employed." In accordance with this plan, and agreeably to the certificate of the State Geologist that the crevices or deposits could be worked to an unfathomable depth, a water-wheel was put on Pedlar's creek, and the power carried by flat rods to two shafts, one about in the center of the range, and the other at the east end; another one was afterwards attached still farther east, making a most cumbrous and wasteful arrangement, in the expense and loss of power occasioned thereby. With this preparation for keeping the water down, the west pump-shaft, in the center of the range, was sunk to the depth of 127 feet, which was through the Blue limestone, and two or three feet into the underlying sandstone (the Upper sandstone).

DIGGINGS NEAR THE MINERAL POINT BRANCH OF THE PECCATONICA, BETWEEN DARLINGTON AND CALAMINE.

A number of scattered groups of diggings are found along the Mineral Point branch, between Darlington and Calamine, which are little worked at present, and have never been of much consequence. The following are the principal localities, with such meagre information as could be obtained concerning them.

Forked Deer Diggings. These are divided into the following sub-groups:

Sproal's: S. W. quarter of S. W. quarter of section 7.

Miller: N. E. corner of S.W. quarter of sec. 18; a range, with several parallel north and south crevices. The Sproal and Miller diggings are in the lower beds of the Galena limestone.

Westrope: S. W. corner of S. W. quarter of S. W. quarter of section 18.

Irish: S. E. corner of N. E. quarter of N. E. quarter of section 18.

Cap's: N. E. corner of N. E. quarter of N. E. quarter of section 19.

Jayhawk: N. E. corner of section 24. These are in T. 5, R. 2; all the others above mentioned are in T. 5, R. 3.

The *South Forked Deer diggings* are chiefly in the Blue lime stone, in the glass-rock opening.

Pillings diggings: N. W. quarter of N. E. quarter of N. E. quarter of section 17, T. 5, R. 3 E. No regular crevice here: the ore is disseminated through the lower beds of the Galena limestone, which has been quarried out over a considerable area to a depth of thirty feet.

King's diggings: S. W. quarter of S. W. quarter of section 29, T. 5, R. 3 E. Several east and west crevices, crossed by smaller norths and souths, forming a patch, having a general east and west direction.

French diggings: N. E. corner of S. W. quarter of section 33, T. 5, R. 3 E.

MINERAL POINT DIGGINGS.

This is one of the most extensive and productive groups of diggings in the Lead Region, which, although not as important as it once was, is still yielding a considerable amount of lead.

Mineral Point is situated on section 31, T. 5, R. 3 E., and the diggings which may properly be considered as belonging to this district are comprised within a circle of about eight miles in diameter, having that town as its centre. The name Mineral Point was given in allusion to the long narrow point of ground between the two smaller streams which here unite to form the Mineral Point branch of the Peccatonica. In this vicinity all the smaller streams even have cut their beds deep down into the sandstone, which forms the bluffs along the Mineral Point, Rock, and Legate branches, rising on the latter to the height of nearly a hundred feet, and consequently displaying its whole thickness, where crossed by the road to Linden, about a mile west of Mineral Point. About one and a half miles farther down the stream, the Lower Magnesian limestone is exposed in a low arch for a short distance. Particulars of the thickness and lithological character of the rocks exposed in this vicinity will be found in a preceding part of this Report; it needs only here to be recalled to mind that the lower beds of the Galena limestone occupy the higher levels, while the Blue limestone forms the slopes of the hills above the bluffs of sandstone: the Blue being exposed along the sides of the streams, even up almost to their very sources. The thickness of the different members of the series is about as follows: Galena limestone, forty to eighty feet; Blue limestone, twenty to thirty feet; Buff limestone, or quarry rock, twenty to twenty-five feet; sandstone, one hundred feet.

Throughout the Mineral Point diggings the larger portion of the lead is raised from flat openings in the Blue limestone, which are connected with crevices coming down from the

Galena limestone above, where this rock has not been denuded. The particulars of this mode of occurrence will be given under the head of the different diggings, which, although in the main resembling each other, are yet distinguished by many peculiarities of detail.

Beginning on the northwest, the diggings in the southeast corner of T. 5, R. 2 E., may first be noticed; these are the Lost Grove and Diamond Grove.

Lost Grove diggings: on section 33, T. 5, R. 2 E., and also crossing over on to section 4 of the next township south. The principal ranges are the Goldthorpe (there are two of that name), the Dyer and the Jim Brown. The *Goldthorpe range* is somewhat irregular in its course, bearing about S. 58° E.: it is worked in the lower beds of the Galena. The *Jim Brown range* is worked in the glass-rock opening. Nothing doing at these diggings when visited; they seem never to have been of any great importance.

Diamond Grove diggings: on the N. W. quarter of section 26, and N. half of section 27: principal ranges, Ross range, McKnight & Evans, Kimball, and Blackhawk.

The *Ross range* is a series of north and south crevices, pitching westerly in the lower beds of the Galena limestone; they also carry some dry-bone.

McKnight & Evans: a flat opening above the glass rock (the pipe-clay opening), ranging N. 82° E. The Ross range intersects this opening at its east end.

Blackhawk: vertical crevice in the Galena limestone, running N. 64° E.

We come now to diggings a little farther east, and one to two miles north of Mineral Point, which have been, and still are, very productive. For want of any distinctive name, they may be designated as the North Mineral Point diggings. They are on the N. E. quarter of section 25, T. 5, R. 2 E., the N. half of section 30, the S. half of section 19, and the S. E. quarter of section 20, T. 5, R. 3 E.

On the north half of section 30 the principal ranges are

the Scantling, Redman, Hoard, Sublette and Ash Bank ranges. These are all on the ridge running E. N. E. between two branches coming in from the east on section 30. They are all chiefly worked in the pipe-clay opening, and have produced heavily. The *Scantling range*, near the south line of the N. W. quarter of section 30, runs N. 84½° E.: it was worked fifteen years since by James Scantling, and over a million lbs. taken out at that time; has since been worked at intervals, and perhaps 2,000,000 lbs. taken out in all; workings chiefly within a length of seventy or eighty yards.

Ash Bank range: course just east and west; in the pipe-clay opening, which is here four to five feet thick; worked fifty feet wide, and about two hundred feet long.

Hoard range: a very long and heavy range, also chiefly in the pipe-clay opening; course of range a few degrees south of east and north of west; worked nearly half a mile in length. This range is estimated to have produced several million lbs.

Sublette range: S. 84° E.; worked wide and shallow, in the brown-rock opening.

Redman range: course of range S. 67° E.; worked about two hundred and fifty yards in length, and twenty to twenty-five yards in width; chiefly in the brown-rock opening.

Short's diggings: three parallel crevices running S. 52° E.; not worked down to the pipe-clay.

Bird lot: extensive workings, of which no particulars can be given. A side range from this lot was worked by Thomas Short, seven years since, and a shaft sunk 125 feet to the pipe-clay opening; direction of the range S. 49° E.; this range produced largely.

Bennett range: a very long and heavy range; direction S. 87½° E.

Martin (or *Trebilcock & Chenoweth's*) *range*: has also produced heavily in former days—1,700,000 pounds, it is said, course, S. 75½° E.; a level was started on the pipe-clay opening, which would drain this range to the depth of 95 to 100 feet on the high ground, by an association of miners and others at Mineral Point. At the last accounts this work was still being pushed forward.

Hederick, or *Dreadnaught range:* 787 feet north of the Martin range; very heavy workings formerly carried on here, on a range running S. 67° E. The ore was found in heavy sheets in clay and ochre, and several millions of pounds were taken out in a space not over 300 feet in length. There appeared to be two deposits of ore, pitching towards each other, according to Rev. J. Murrish; but it is not possible to make out the arrangement at present, as the place has been abandoned for some years. The "Mississippi Mining and Manufacturing Company" erected a steam engine at this place, and endeavored to sink to the point where the two lodes would come together. After foolishly spending a good deal of money, they still more foolishly stopped the work just before the shaft arrived at the point where, if there had been anything to find, they might have expected to find it—at the depth of seventy feet, and within a foot or two of the probable position of the lode. None of the excavations on the Dreadnaught ridge are down to the Blue limestone, except the level above mentioned as going in to strike the Martin lode. There must be a thickness here, therefore, of between eighty and ninety feet of the Galena limestone.

DIGGINGS IN THE IMMEDIATE VICINITY OF MINERAL POINT.

The city of Mineral Point is entirely surrounded by diggings, all of which have been of importance, while a large portion of them are pretty much worked out. The amount of information which can be collected in regard to them is, in many localities, but scanty.

On the Point, between Vivian's and the Mineral Point branches, the whole ground is cut up with diggings, several heavy ranges crossing it in an E. S. E. and W. N. W. direction. These are chiefly worked in the brown-rock opening:

none of them have gone down to any depth in the Blue limestone, apparently. Nothing is raising here now.

Porter & Terrill range: half a mile north of the Court House; course S. 54° E.; traced over one-fourth of a mile in length. This was worked down to the pipe-clay opening. Some preparations were making last year to drain this range by a level, and work it again.

M'Knight range: about an eighth of a mile north of the last mentioned one; range about S. 54° E.; worked formerly to a depth of 130 feet, it is said, in the pipe-clay opening. The rock taken out is full of pyrites, and soon crumbles on exposure.

Sinapee diggings: these are a little north of the last-named, near the old furnace, and on the N. E. quarter of the S. E. quarter of section 30. There has always been some ore raising in this vicinity when I have visited the place. A section obtained here gives:

Variable thickness of Galena limestone, brown-rock, green-rock, &c.

"Dice-mineral opening" (pipe-clay opening), with ten to fifty pounds of ore to the load, two inches to six feet.

Glass-rock, ten to twelve feet.

"Dry-bone opening" (glass-rock opening), one to one and a half feet.

No ore found below this.

South of the town there are very numerous and still somewhat productive diggings. These are worked in the green-rock, brown-rock, pipe-clay and glass-rock openings, and in one or two instances have gone down as low as the second pipe-clay opening. The ore frequently goes down from one opening to the other in flat and pitching sheets, and the rock in many places is so thoroughly mineralized in the spaces between the different productive beds, that it is hard to distinguish the usual lithological characters of the rocks.

An extensive series of ranges goes off to the southwest of the town, beginning with the Barber and the Harrison ranges, near the town corner, between towns 4 and 5, R. 2 E, and R. 3 E. The *Irish diggings* extend over part of the N. E. and N.W. quarters of section 1. They are worked chiefly in the glass-rock opening, and have yielded about two and a half million pounds of ore. A large amount of black-jack and dry-bone accompanies the galena.

There are several long and important ranges near the line between the southeast quarter of section 1 and the southwest quarter of section 6, to the east of the road from Galena to Platteville. They are laid down on the map from information given by Mr. John Hoar. I have found but little doing here when I have examined these diggings, and cannot, therefore, speak of them from a personal acquaintance.

The *Lenahan diggings*, near the south line of section 7, have been formerly extensively worked, but are now abandoned. The green-rock opening was productive at this point, and the deposit of ore went down as low as the lower pipe-clay opening.

These mineral ranges have a course nearly east and west, but they are worked over a very considerable width in proportion to their length, so that no exact direction can be given.

On the east side of the Mineral Point branch there are also a number of heavy ranges; but the ore raised there, at present, is small in quantity. At the Lampshier range, three crevices making flat openings, worked seventy to eighty feet wide in the green-rock, and found productive, have also been traced down to the pipe-clay opening. The section here gives, below the usual Galena limestone:

Green rock	4 feet.
Green-rock opening, in which the ore makes in flats and pitches	10–12 inches.
Crystalline dolomite, called "rough sand rock" by the miners	10 feet.
Brown rock	18 inches.
Pipe-clay opening (probably)	3 feet.

The "rough sand rock" in the section above is properly part of the "brown rock;" its coarse crystalline texture and peculiar aspect cause it to be considered a sandstone by the miners, as is very often the case with some varieties of the lead-bearing dolomite, their peculiar harshness and grittiness of feel often leading even the practiced geologist into error.

There are a great number of ranges and tracts formerly worked as patches in this vicinity; but there has never been any great activity here at any time when I have visited it.

The amount of lead shipped over the Mineral Point railroad to Warren, in 1858, was 48,596 pigs, or about 1500 tons. This would, therefore, be about the produce of the Mineral Point, Dodgeville, and Linden diggings, with the other smaller ones scattered between and near them.

BLACK-JACK, OR MIFFLIN DIGGINGS.

The village of Mifflin is in the northeast corner of section 34, T. 5, R. 1 E., and on the west branch of the Peccatonica. At the level of this stream, near the town and above it, the Buff limestone is exposed, overlaid by the other members of the Blue, and on the higher ground there is perhaps a hundred feet in thickness of the Galena limestone. The upper surface of the underlying sandstone passes beneath the river at a point about half a mile below the town.

The diggings are on the N. E. quarter of section 34, and are chiefly on two distinct groups of ranges, of which the eastern one is called the Black-Jack, and the other the Penitentiary range. The workings on these are wide and shallow, and have a general course of N. 35° W. The principal body of ore is in the position of the pipe-clay opening, and occurs very much mixed with sulphuret of zinc, or black-jack. A large amount of the mineralized portion of the opening now lies on the surface, and shows itself as a rather disintegrated mass of somewhat magnesian limestone, containing a large percentage of sulphuret of zinc, in small tetrahedral crystals, but not well formed or regular. Some portions of the sulphuret are yellow and transparent; others are dark colored, or black, like the usual black-jack of the region. These crystals are about one-tenth of an inch in diameter, and they form from ten to twenty percent of the mass. Associated with the zinc is a smaller portion of galena, in crystals from one tenth to one quarter of an inch in diameter, constituting perhaps three to five percent of the whole. There is little doing at present at the Mifflin diggings, and their former yield could not be ascertained.

CROW BRANCH DIGGINGS.

These very interesting diggings, remarkable as being lower in their geological position than any others in the Lead Region, are situated in Clifton township (T. 5, R. 1 W.), on the head-waters of Crow branch, a tributary of Platte river; the principal diggings are near the S. W. corner of section 23, on both sides of the branch, but chiefly to the south of it. In the stream, at this point, the Upper sandstone is exposed, forming low ledges, rising from ten to twenty feet above the water.

The range as worked runs nearly N. W. and S. E., and has been worked for a length of about one third of a mile, and in some places to a width of from 200 to 300 feet. Shafts have been sunk from the surface downwards along the line of the range, to the depth of about 100 feet on the highest ground, and meeting an adit-level driven in for about one fourth of a mile from the edge of the branch. This adit starts on the sandstone, and was, when examined, with difficulty accessible, and so much filled with mud and water that the relations of the rocks it passes through could not be well made out. As it rises, however, it passes into the Buff limestone, and from that—owing, as it would appear, to a basin-shaped depression or rapid undulation of the strata—into the glass-rock, in which it continues most of the way. This rock is of the character of an opening, being filled with pyrites and galena, and rapidly decomposing to a blue clay. So extensive has been this mineralization of the rock, and subsequent decomposition, that it is difficult to say how many openings there are, and what is their exact relation to each other. It would appear, however, that the mineralization has affected the strata nearly down to the bottom of the Buff limestone, or as low as the second pipe-clay opening, and from this random up to the top of the Blue limestone. The vertical thickness of the mineralized layers is perhaps twenty to twenty-five feet. Everywhere in this space the material, when excavated, is observed to be made up to a large extent of pyrites, with an immense number of the usual fossils of the shell-beds of the Blue limestone, many of which are converted into pyrites. Almost as soon as raised to the surface, this mass begins to decompose, and in a few months becomes a heap of ferruginous and sulphurous clay. Through this material of the opening the galena is disseminated, frequently in large masses or sheets, and also in small cubic crystals, with the corners truncated. At one of the shafts the annexed section (fig. 37) was made, which

Fig. 37.—Section at the Crow Branch Diggings.

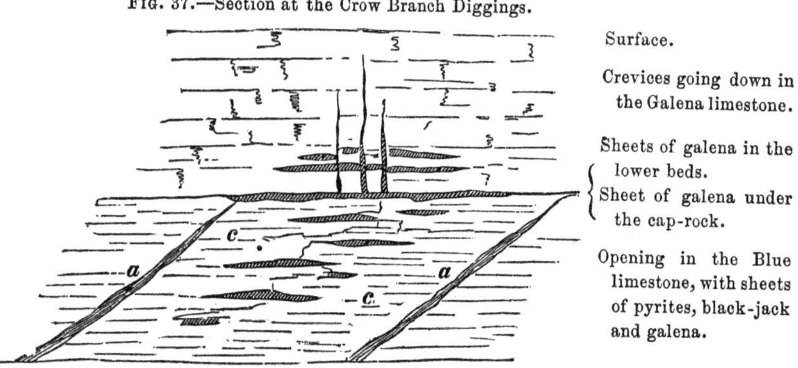

will serve to convey an idea of the distribution of the ore at this locality.

In the Galena limestone the usual crevices are seen going down to the cap-rock, here some sixty feet from the surface; in the lower beds of this rock the lead ore also makes to some extent, in flat sheets, in connection with the crevices. Directly under the cap is usually a heavy sheet of ore, and this is the position where the largest body of it is found. Below this, the opening or mineralized mass in the Blue limestone was observed passing obliquely downwards, as represented in the section, and taking on in some respects the character of a vein, especially in having on both sides a layer, or selvage, of flucan, some four inches thick. In the lower portion of the Galena limestone the ore is associated with calcareous spar, as is so frequently the case at other diggings in this geological position.

The limits of this remarkable deposit in length and width are not known. When last visited, in the autumn of 1859, it was still producing largely, having already yielded, it is said, between four and five million pounds of ore.

Up to that time, no ores had been observed in the sandstone, although the mineralized deposit was thus brought down nearly into contact with that rock. I have recently (August, 1860) learned, from A. K. Johnston, Esq., that in a visit made to these diggings, in July preceding, he ascertained that "two distinct veins of galena had recently been discovered running through the sand-rock." Of the size of the veins, or depth to which traced, no information was given. At all events, the fact is an interesting one, as it is the first authentic occurrence of lead ore in this rock, so far as I have been able to ascertain. It is not probable that these veins will be found penetrating to any considerable depth; but, of all the localities in the Lead Region, this was the one where it might be most naturally expected that, if anywhere, the ore would be found making in the sandstone.

Other diggings on Kirkpatrick's land, a quarter of a mile from the Crow Branch, are very similar to those just described: the material thrown out has become entirely decomposed, and is filled with immense numbers of fossil shells, of which *Leptæna sericea* is the most abundant. These fossiliferous beds rest on the glass-rock. These diggings have produced, it is said, about 50,000 lbs. of ore.

There are other localities in this vicinity where some mining has been done, but no very productive diggings; although it would appear, from all that can be seen on the surface, that there is an excellent chance for farther discoveries in the same position in which the Crow Branch diggings are situated. The facility with which levels can be driven through the soft decomposing opening ought to lead to a thorough exploration of it at other points not yet proved.

NOTICE OF VARIOUS COPPER DIGGINGS.

Under the head of Mineralogy, the different ores of copper observed in the Lead Region have been noticed, and the principal localities specified. It remains, in this connection, to add some further remarks as to their geological mode of occurrence and economical importance.

The copper ores of Wisconsin have repeatedly been the object of exploitation, and it has been a favorite idea with many that copper mining would become an important branch of the business of the Lead Region. Dr. D. D. Owen, in his Report of 1839, says: "the copper ore of the Wisconsin territory forms an item in its mineral wealth which would be considered of great importance, and would attract much attention, but for the superior richness and value of the lead, the great staple of the territory." Assays are given by this gentleman of "three average specimens of the solid copper ore from Wisconsin," which yielded 23., 24.32, and 35.7 per-cent of copper. It is farther stated that there had been raised at the Mineral Point mines "upwards of a million and a half pounds of copper" (qu., copper ore).

Mr. J. T. Hodge visited these copper diggings, either at the time they were working or soon after, and gave the following account of the locality: "There is a large fissure, in places fourteen feet wide, that has been traced about a quarter of a mile. It is on the old Ansley tract, and extends in a westerly direction towards Mineral Point. For about the depth of fifteen feet, the fissure was found to be filled with "gossan," and lumps of sulphuret and carbonate of copper mixed in it. Below this depth is clay, with a little ore scattered through it. The lumps above were of all sizes, up to two hundred pounds weight. No shafts were ever sunk to prove this fissure at greater depths; but there is every reason to suppose that it will be found productive in other parts besides the strip near the surface." Farther on he gives some account of the smelting operations, as follows:

"It is said that 1,640,000 lbs. of ore (probably including unwashed and gossan) have been raised from this fissure: 50,000 pounds were sent to England, and 100,000 lbs. are now on the banks of the river at Sinapee; 620,000 lbs. have been taken to the old furnace and the little one at New Baltimore, and between 500,000 and 600,000 lbs. remain now on the surface at the mines. This is evidently a very rude estimate. It is also said that the ore sent to England yielded twenty percent of copper; at any rate, however, it brought in a bill of expense."

When I first visited these copper mines, in 1852, I could see but little, as they had been abandoned for some years, having never been a source of profit to any one. There seemed to be good and sufficient reasons, however, for considering the prospects of mining copper successfully in the Lead Region as in no way encouraging, as I have stated in the "Metallic Wealth of the United States."*

Within the last two years, I have had an opportunity of seeing practical copper mining in the Lead Region, and am

* Published in 1854. See pages 308–310

fully satisfied that my previously expressed opinion of the worthlessness of these copper mines was well founded.

The old copper diggings referred to above by Messrs. Owen and Hodge were situated on the Mills & Ansley tract, forming the S. E. quarter of section 32 (T. 5, R. 3 E.), one mile E. N. E. of Mineral Point Court House. The crevice had a course of about S. 85° E., and had been traced for over one-third of a mile. This locality does not seem to have been worked since Mr. Hodge's visit, and the old copper furnaces near Mineral Point and New Baltimore have long since gone to ruin.

The new copper mining enterprise is on a crevice running nearly east and west, in the N. E. corner of section 5, T. 4, R. 3 E., a mile and a quarter east by south from the town. A small steam engine was erected, and a shaft had been sunk to a depth of 106 feet, last spring (1860), and below this a boring of four feet had been made. The general features of the crevice with its openings are the same as those of the lead-bearing crevices in the vicinity, the only difference being the substitution of copper for lead ore. There are five openings, of which the bottom of the first is thirty-nine feet, of the second, fifty-two feet, and of the third, sixty-eight feet below the surface. The third opening is seven or eight feet high, and six to seven feet wide, and it is from this that most of the copper ore was obtained. On this opening they had driven 400 feet east and 280 feet west from the engine shaft. The third and fourth openings, the latter of which had then been bored into, and has since been sunk to, while the boring has been continued twelve feet deeper, represent the pipe-clay opening, which is not unfrequently thus divided into two parts. It carried some copper pyrites, black-jack, and galena; but not enough of either to be of any value.

In the third opening, the copper ore occurred chiefly in connection with a dark-grey, hard, crystalline dolomite; interspersed through which in every direction, so as to give the mass almost a brecciated appearance, is the yellow copper ore, forming the exterior coating of the cavities in the dolomite, or that nearest to the rock, while the interior of each seam, nodule, and bunch of ore is filled with white iron pyrites, which material unfortunately forms the larger portion of the metalliferous mass. The annexed figure (38) will

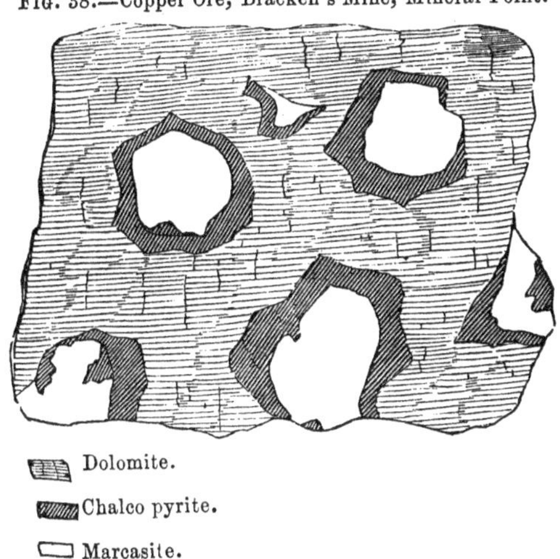

FIG. 38.—Copper Ore, Bracken's Mine, Mineral Point.

illustrate this, the part shaded with oblique lines representing the copper pyrites, that by horizontal ones the dolomite, and the unshaded portion the pyrites. In some places in the opening the pyrites occurs in this way, unaccompanied by any copper at all. As will be seen, this ore is a difficult one to wash and dress, even where the rock is decomposed and disintegrated in the usual manner of the opening material, as is the case here in a part of the mine.

About $18,000 had been expended at this place in mining up to the time of my last visit, in the spring of 1860, and, as the net result, there was on the surface about five tons of ore, dressed up to perhaps eighteen or twenty percent, and a small lot, worth about ten percent; the remainder, perhaps fifty tons or so in all, would hardly go over two percent, certainly not over five. Indeed, only the best sample would pay the expenses of shipping, or approximate even to that point.

The Plum Creek copper diggings, near Wauzeka, on the north side of the Wisconsin, are in the Lower Magnesian, and near the top of it. It appears, from the descriptions which have been given me by Rev. Mr. Murrish and others, to have formed a flat seam or bed in the rock, not over two inches in thickness, in which the copper ore is in fragments mixed with clay. The ore was too lean to be of any value, even if abundant in quantity, to judge from the specimens which have been shown me; but there was nothing in the mode of occurrence to justify any expenditure at this place, or search for farther light on the subject.

The deposit of copper ore at Mt. Sterling I have not visited; but the specimens I have received from that place are precisely similar to those of the Plum Creek diggings, and the character of the deposit is described as being very much the same as that of this locality.

There are many places in the Lead Region where copper ore, usually copper pyrites, occurs in small quantity, but in no case have I seen anything whatever to lead to the idea that this metal can ever be profitably mined in this part of the State.

REMARKS ON THE ZINC ORES OF THE LEAD REGION.

The question of the value of the zinc ores so widely distributed through the Lead Region, and the probability of their being profitably smelted in this district, or exported to other parts of the country for that purpose, is one which comes up for consideration in this connection, and to which I have given all the attention possible. It is a point much more difficult to settle than that which relates to the value of the copper ores of the district, and one in regard to which all the facts must be carefully weighed before pronouncing a definite opinion in the matter. Before writing on this subject, therefore, I have visited all the localities in the country where either metallic zinc or its oxide are now being manufactured; and, having previously examined the most important establishments in Belgium where this metal is smelted, I feel able to throw some light on the subject.

The only ores of zinc occurring in any considerable quantity in the Lead Region, as before noticed in the chapter on mineralogy, are the sulphuret, blende, or "black-jack," and the carbonate (Smithsonite or calamine), called "dry-bone" by the miners. As has been already described, these ores occur together, in connection with galena and pyrites, in various parts of the Lead Region, and with the same general mode of occurrence. As a general rule, however, the zinc ores are more abundant low down in the geological series, and especially in the Blue limestone, in the flat openings by which that group of strata is characterized. Nothing farther need be said here in reference to the mode of occurrence of the zinc ores, as that subject has been necessarily treated in discussing the character of the lead deposits. Something may, however, be added in regard to their distribution and abundance, as compared with other zinc producing districts.

The ores of zinc in the Lead Region resemble those of lead in this respect, that they are scattered over a large area, and occur in very many localities, without forming in any one place a deposit which could compare with those of Belgium, of Silesia, or of New Jersey and Pennsylvania. There is no one range or crevice where more than a few hundred tons of ore could be obtained, although there is no doubt that, taking the whole Lead Region through, a vast amount of zinc really does exist, either on the surface or under ground: of course, when not necessary for convenient working, heretofore, the dry-bone and black-jack have not been raised to the surface, having had no pecuniary value: but they have been used to support the roofs, &c., just as the ordinary rock is. The scattered nature of the deposits makes it very difficult to say how much of these ores really exists in the region, and quite impossible to estimate the cost of raising it and sending it to market in case there was a demand for it. For the present the miners are willing to furnish the dry-bone at a very moderate price, because they hope thus to aid in the establishment of smelting-works: this state of things would naturally cease to exist as soon as the works became profitable. It is the general opinion of the miners that there is a very large quantity of zinc ores in the region; but I have not yet been able to satisfy myself that the amount required to keep an extensive smelting establishment in operation would be forthcoming for any great length of time, without having to pay a pretty high price for it.

The districts where the ores of zinc are most abundant are the Mineral Point diggings, the Holyhead diggings near Messersmith's, the Dry-bone diggings near Shullsburg, the Black-Jack diggings at Mifflin, and the diggings near Franklin and Centreville. The Holyhead diggings seem rather more productive in zinc than any others, in proportion to the ground opened.

In Illinois, but little dry-bone occurs in the crevices, as they are too high in the series to be productive in zinc; in Iowa, the same remarks hold good, except at Ewing's diggings on the Makoqueta, a few miles northwest of Dubuque, where a large amount of dry-bone is to be seen on the surface, although the interior of the workings was not accessible when I last visited them. The range is a very extensive one, and, according to the testimony of those who worked in it, contains a large amount of zinc ores. The analyses of some of these, as given in the Iowa Report, showed the ore to be very pure, containing about fifty percent of metallic zinc, and only a small amount of impurities.

It has been again and again recommended by geologists and others, since the date of Dr. Owen's first Report, that the zinc deposits of the Northwest should be worked, and the ore smelted on the spot, but it is not until quite recently that any attempt has been made in this direction.

In 1859, Mr. Robert George, in connection with some capitalists of Pennsylvania, erected a small furnace for smelting zinc about half a mile south of the town of Mineral Point, on the railroad; it appears, however, to have continued in operation but a short time, as nothing was doing there in June of that year, or of the following one. The furnace was constructed after the Belgian model: there were twenty-three cylindrical retorts, each five feet long, eight inches in interior diameter, and ten inches in exterior. The retorts were arranged in four rows of five in each row, and three above, and set in a cast-iron framework; it was the estimate of the superintendent that sixty or seventy retorts would be required to make one ton of zinc per day, each retort averaging thirty-three lbs.; but the amount actually made would appear to have been considerably less than this. It was said that 200 lbs. had been produced in a day by the twenty-three retorts when going on best, and the whole quantity of metal made appears not to have exceeded two or three tons. The ore used was the dry-bone from the adjacent diggings, picked up from the surface, and for which a nominal sum only was paid. It was roasted in an old furnace chimney, stamped by hand, and smelted with La Salle coal. The ore was estimated to contain thirty-three percent of zinc; but what the actual yield was, we have no means of knowing. It is said that the consumption of coal was about two tons per day. At any rate, it is evident that the experiment was not a successful one, either as regards the quantity made or the cost of production. Great difficulty was experienced in getting any clay suitable for the retorts. The fire clay of La Salle, which accompanies the coal, was found to be filled with nodules of pyrites, and could not be made serviceable; the Missouri clay was also found to answer little purpose. The first cost of the furnace was stated at $2,000.

Up to the present time it is believed that no further progress has been made in this experiment.

Another attempt has also been made to smelt the zinc ore by carrying it to the coal, namely at La Salle, Ill., where a furnace was erecting last year by Messrs. Matthiessen & Hegeler; but of its ever having gone into successful operation I am not informed. They were expecting to procure ore from the vicinity of Shullsburg.

A furnace is said to have been erected at a place called Calamine, in Lawrence Co., Arkansas, for smelting zinc; but it appears from Dr. Owen's Report not to have gone into successful operation up to as late as 1858. These are all the attempts, of which any accounts have reached me, to make zinc at the West.

Taking all the circumstances into consideration, and comparing the facility of procuring ore, the cost and quality of coal, the facilities of transportation, the cost of labor, and the value of capital at the West, I am of the opinion that, at present at least, zinc cannot be profitably smelted in the Lead Region.

For convenience of reference, the following facts are added in regard to one of the zinc-smelting establishments of the Atlantic States.

At the New Jersey Zinc Works the annexed statement was obtained from the officers of the company.

The ore yields, in the furnace, about thirty-three percent of oxide of zinc, and two and a third tons of coal are required to make one ton of the oxide; or 175 tons of coal will make 75 tons of oxide. Of this coal, 100 tons of slack is used, and 75 tons of pea coal: the one costing at the works $1.50 per ton, the other $2.00; the coal is of course anthracite.

There are now thirty-two furnaces in operation, and eight more are in process of construction (April 1860). With thirty-two furnaces, the amount of oxide of zinc made is about ten tons per day, or 3,000 tons a year. The price of the oxide at this time is four and a half cents per pound. But a small portion of it is ground in oil by the company, although it would appear to be for their interest to have the control of this part of the business, for the purpose of preventing fraud, and ensuring their customers a uniformity of quality.

The very peculiar character of the ore used by this company enables them to utilize the material left in the furnaces, after the zinc has been driven off, for the manufacture of iron. The ore is, as before remarked, a mixture of Franklinite and red zinc, the residuum left containing about forty percent of iron and about twelve percent of manganese, as well as a small amount of zinc. It is therefore a highly manganesian iron ore, and is capable of furnishing a quality of pig iron well suited for conversion into a very tough wrought iron. For this purpose a blast furnace has been erected, and has been some time in use, and in April, 1860, a puddling furnace and train of rolls for merchant bar was erecting. When these arrangements are completed, 5,000 tons a year of bar iron can be puddled and rolled from the residuum of the zinc furnaces, and there is no doubt that the business will be a very profitable one. The pig iron smelted hitherto, of which 1800 tons were on hand last April, has been sold at from $30 to $32.50 per ton.

There has been no attempt made at this establishment to manufacture metallic zinc.

IV. *Theoretical Considerations.*

Having, in the preceding sections, given a résumé of the mining operations which have been carried on in Wisconsin, and described the peculiar forms under which the ores of the Lead Region occur, it will be proper to enter into some theoretical considerations with regard to the manner in which the crevices have been formed, and filled with the earthy and metalliferous substances which they are now found to contain. This is the more important, as it is believed that no other mining region has ever been described by geologists, in which the same phenomena are displayed as have been described in the preceding pages. The great deposits of the metals and their ores, throughout the world, are almost invariably found connected with rocks of an igneous or eruptive origin, or with those which have undergone metamorphism since their original deposition, in which process every theory recognizes heat as one, at least, of the principal agents. The instances in which ores are worked in any considerable quantity in any other rocks than those of igneous or metamorphic origin are comparatively few, the metals occurring in the unaltered strata in sufficient abundance to be extensively mined being lead and zinc, as also iron; which latter, being a metal of universal diffusion, may be considered as not coming under any rule: indeed, the ores of iron are only worked in veins exceptionally, it being more convenient to attack the large masses of it which occur in the stratified or massive form, and which are not analogous to the vein-form of deposit.

More is understood in regard to the formation of what are called "true veins" than of the other and less regular modes of occurrence of the useful ores, and consequently there is more uncertainty in working mines on the latter class than on the former. Perhaps the irregular deposits, and especially those which are found in the unaltered limestone and dolomitic rocks, have been less studied than the other forms: it is certain that there is still much to be learned concerning them. The interesting mining districts of the North of England would furnish a fine field for research in this direction. They have never been carefully studied or clearly described, from the point of view of the occurrence of the ores. No doubt there are many analogies between the deposits of the Upper Mississippi and those of Derbyshire and the other lead-producing counties of England. Probably farther investigations in the Spanish lead-mining regions will also develop more points of resemblance there with what has been observed in the district to which this Report is devoted. It is with the hope of setting forth some points in a clearer light than has yet been done, that the following generalizations are offered with regard to the theory of the mode of occurrence of the lead ores of Wisconsin. We shall first consider the surface arrangement of the crevices, or their position and grouping with reference to each other, as exhibited on the surface, and the way in which they have been formed and brought into their present shape: we shall then proceed to discuss the probable way in which they have been filled with ore, and the changes which have taken place in the crevices and the surrounding rock since this was accomplished.

SURFACE ARRANGEMENT OF THE LEAD-BEARING CREVICES.

In the surveys made for the crevice map which accompanies this Report, the direction of the lines representing the mineral-bearing ranges, lodes, or crevices, is only to be taken as indicating approximately their course, since it would have been rarely possible to locate the crevice by underground surveys, so few of them being accessible at any one time; and even had each been carefully surveyed out, with all its deflections from an exact straight line, it would have been difficult to represent the facts except on a map on a very large scale. The average direction of the crevices, as near as it could be ascertained from the position of the shafts opened on them, is all that the crevice map can claim to exhibit.

The term "surface arrangement" was applied by Dr. Percival to express the relations or grouping of the ranges, as thus referred to the surface of the ground, and it was a happily selected one; while the map on which the geologist endeavored to represent this surface-grouping was on so small a scale (one fourth of an inch to the mile), and so defective from not having been laid down from accurate measurements or surveys, but only from estimation of distances, that it is of little or no value in enabling one to form even an approximate idea of the real position of the crevices

Where these are numerous and well-defined—as for instance in the vicinity of Galena, Dubuque, Shullsburg, Hazle Green, &c.—a scale of two inches to the mile is hardly sufficient to show the principal facts; and for especially complicated regions, like that about Hazle Green, we should need a special map on a scale not smaller than a foot to the mile for this purpose. The reasons which have guided me in the arrangement and scale of the maps for the different crevice-districts have been already given in the introductory chapter. It is from the study of these that we shall best be able to come to any general conclusions as to the connection of the lead-bearing crevices, in their origin, with any of those great general, or deep-seated, causes to which similar phenomena are usually referred in other parts of the world.

The first fact which is apparent in regard to the lead-bearing crevices of the Upper Mississippi region is their arrangement, or concentration, in districts of limited extent; so that numerous sub-districts or mining centres are formed within the area of the Lead Region, each in a measure isolated from the others, and frequently separated from them by wide intervals of almost or quite barren ground. Thus, beginning on the northwest, we have:

1st. The Beetown Diggings, divided into the following sub-groups: *Muddy*, *North*, *Muscalonge*, *Nip-and-Tuck*, *Beetown*, and *Hackett's* diggings, and extended to the east by the *Pigeon* diggings, a group of crevices covering about half a square mile, and about five miles east of Hackett's diggings.

2d. The Potosi Diggings: these are subdivided into the following groups: *Potosi*, comprising the main body of the crevices of that district, and extending over nearly four square miles of ground, and connected to the northeast with the *British Hollow diggings*, then in the same direction, successively, with the *Rockville*, *Pin Hook*, and *Red Dog* diggings. These connect on the northeast again with the *Platteville* diggings, by the *Brushhill* and *Whig* diggings.

3d. Platteville Diggings, divided into three sub-groups,

the *Platteville*, surrounding the town of Platteville; the *Southwest* and the *Southeast Platteville diggings.* These connect again, to the east, with the *Elk Grove* and *Strawberry diggings.*

4th. *Big Patch diggings:* a small group intermediate between the Platteville and the Upper Menomonee.

5th. *Upper Menomonee diggings:* a well-marked group, occupying nearly two square miles of area, connected by the Lower Menomonee diggings with the Fairplay.

6th. *Lower Menomonee diggings:* a small group occupying less than half a square mile. There are a few unimportant patches of diggings connecting the Upper and Lower Menomonee.

7th. *Fairplay diggings:* a well marked group surrounding the village of Fairplay, with minor outlying groups on the northeast, of which the *Hunsacker*, and *Carnes & Van Vleck's* are the most important.

8th. *Dubuque diggings:* the very extensive diggings in the vicinity of Dubuque, occupying nearly twenty square miles of area, and closely assimilated with each other in geological position and character, form a conspicuous group on the west side of the Mississippi.

9th. *Galena diggings:* a very extensive assemblage of diggings, occupying about eleven square miles in the immediate vicinity of Galena, to the north, east and west of the city. They are distinctly separated from the Vinegar Hill diggings and Council Hill diggings, on the north and northeast, by a barren space of ground about three miles across.

10th. *Elizabeth diggings:* these are a prominent group of diggings, occupying an area of six square miles around Elizabeth. They are chiefly remarkable as forming the southern limit of the Upper Mississippi Lead Region.

11th. *Hazle diggings:* a small group lying two miles to the southwest of Warren, marking the eastern limit of the mining ground in Illinois.

12th. *Apple River diggings:* a small group covering about a section in all, to the southwest of Apple River Station on the Illinois Central R. R.

13th. *Vinegar Hill* and *Council Hill diggings:* these two sets of diggings form a pretty continuous group, intermediate between the Galena district on the south, and the extensive mining ground about New Diggings, Benton, and Hazle Green on the north. They include an area of some twelve square miles, of a somewhat semi-circular shape.

14th. *Hazle Green diggings; Benton diggings; New Diggings:* the diggings surrounding Hazle Green, Benton, and New Diggings form geographically one group, occupying an area of nearly fifty square miles. The Hazle Green district and the Benton district, it may be said, are separated by the dividing ridge between Bull Branch and Coon Branch, whilst Fever river may serve equally well to distinguish between the Benton and New Diggings districts. The diggings about *White Oak Springs* form a small group, outlying New Diggings on the southwest.

15th. *Shullsburg diggings:* a scattering group of diggings, lying east of, and nearly continuous with, the extensive groups of diggings in the Benton, Hazle Green, and New Diggings region. *Stump Grove diggings* lie to the northeast of Shullsburg, a mile distant from its most northerly diggings.

16th. *Hamilton,* or *Wyota diggings:* passing northeast from Shullsburg, these diggings occur next in order. They form an isolated group, and, though of considerable importance, occupy an area of not more than two square miles.

17th. *Skinner's diggings:* a small group, four miles north of Monroe.

18th. *Sugar river diggings:* these diggings determine the eastern boundary of the Lead Region. They are distributed over two sections, in the most southerly of which the town of Exeter is situated, in its southeast quarter.

19th. *Blue Mound* or *Brigham's diggings:* intervening

between these and Sugar river diggings to the southeast at the distance of eighteen miles, the ground is wholly barren of mineral. They are scattered over an area of about six square miles, longitudinally one mile south of the Blue Mounds.

20th. *Porter's Grove diggings:* lying seven miles west of the Blue Mound diggings, forming a small group by themselves.

21st. *Dodgeville diggings:* these are a pretty distinctly marked group to the north of Dodgeville, and partly in the town itself. Outlying them, southeast and east, are two or three inferior groups, the *Garrison diggings*, and *Norway diggings;* while midway of the main Dodgeville diggings and Porter's Grove diggings are *Messersmith's diggings*, sparsely scattered over two sections.

22d. *Franklin diggings:* a small but well-defined group situated the farthest north of any in the Lead Region. They cover about a section, partly in, and adjoining on the north, the town of Franklin.

23d. *Centreville diggings:* a small group lying four miles southwest of Franklin, and three miles north of the *Wingville diggings*, which are also a small group extending something less than a mile north and west of the town of that name.

24th. *Crow Branch diggings:* passing from the Wingville diggings south, and thence in order to the extensive mining region about the head-waters of the Peccatonica, the Crow Branch diggings are next indicated. They are a marked, isolated group of diggings, situated at the head of the branch of Platte river of that name, and two miles to the northeast of the town of New California.

25th. *Mifflin diggings:* a small group, situated in the same section with the town of Mifflin. Thinly distributed over the Mifflin township are a few other diggings, among which, as worthy of mention, the *Madden* and *Hall ranges* in section first, and the *Ludlam range* in section eighteen, may be denoted.

26th. *Linden diggings:* a scattered group west and northwest of Linden. They are within an area of about four square miles.

27th. *Mineral Point diggings:* the diggings at Mineral Point and vicinity form an extensive and highly important group, including an area of about fifty square miles. The Mineral Point diggings proper entirely surround the city, while to the northeast and northwest extend several subordinate groups. Intervening between Mineral Point on the northwest, and Linden on the southeast, and nearly midway of the two places, are the two noteworthy groups of diggings, *Lost Grove* and *Diamond Grove.* To the north, the diggings along *Van Meter's survey*, in the same township with Mineral Point, form a sort of connecting group between the Mineral Point diggings on the south, and the Dodgeville diggings on the north.

28th. *Forked Deer diggings:* a small though clearly marked group, lying opposite Calamine, about the confluence of the Forked Deer creek and the Peccatonica. They occupy an area of nearly two square miles. On the western bank of the Peccatonica, near the village of Calamine, *Pillings' diggings* form a separate, inferior group.

29th. *Duke's Prairie diggings:* a small, isolated group, six miles southeast of Mineral Point, situated near the southern limit of the extensive prairie region, which in the direction of Mineral Point is continuous nearly to that city.

30th. *Yellowstone diggings:* these are a prominent group, scattered over an area of about six square miles at the headwaters of the Yellowstone river, a branch of the East fork of the Peccatonica. Three miles southeast of these are the *Fretwell diggings*, a small group on the East fork of the Peccatonica.

In regard to the division into districts of the mining region, it may be remarked, as bearing on the question whether the areas between the different groups of crevices are really destitute of ore, or whether it may yet be found in those regions where up to this time no mining has been carried on, that substantially the same groups of crevices or mining centres were recognized more than twenty years ago, as are now known. On examining Dr. Owen's map, which accompanies the Report of his survey made in 1839, and on which the quarter-sections containing lead mines are designated, we find every one of the principal districts referred to above represented by the mark for lead on one or more quarter-sections, and we are unable to find a single instance of any important mining district which was not known at that time. All the discoveries which have been made since that early period are of new crevices in old districts, and such are of constant occurrence. This agrees with the concurrent testimony of several of the best informed miners, who have assured me that, with a few unimportant exceptions, all the diggings of the Lead Region were discovered in the course of the two or three years after the active explorations were commenced, namely about 1828. This fact, taken in connection with another—namely that the rocks are not unfrequently well exposed over considerable areas, where no mining has ever been done or important discoveries made—seems to indicate that a considerable portion of the Lead Region is quite destitute of valuable deposits of ore.

Secondly, these groups of diggings are, in general, characterized by the main lead-bearing crevices in each district being nearly parallel with each other. This is not mathematically true, but still the parallelism of each group or subgroup of crevices is on the whole one of the most striking features of the Lead Region.

The following are the bearings of some of the heavy mineral ranges in each of the principal districts :*

Beetown diggings	S. 80° E.	Lower Menomonee	N. 83° W.
Potosi	N. 60° W.	Fairplay	S. 85° E. to N. 85° E.
Platteville	N. 85° W.	Dubuque	E. and W.
Upper Menomonee	N. 50° to 60° W.	Vinegar Hill	N. 80° W.

* Bearings are always given, in this Report, from the true meridian.

Galena......N. 85° E. to S. 85° E.	Shullsburg..............S. 68° E.
Hazle Green............N. 85° E.	Dodgeville ......N. 10° to 17° W.
Benton.................S. 75° E.	Mineral Point...........S. 50° E.
New Diggings....N. 84° to 88° E.	

However, an inspection of the various crevice maps will sufficiently satisfy every one that there is, on the whole, a marked parallelism in the different sets of productive crevices forming each sub-district or district. As it was not in our power to obtain materials or space for delineating the unproductive crevices, or the seams which carry no mineral or only a trace of it, the remarks in regard to these cannot be illustrated by reference to the map; but must be taken as the results of observation in the field, and as embodying the experience and practical knowledge of the miners.

We proceed, then, to remark, that *thirdly*, there is everywhere a tendency to the formation of two sets of crevices, nearly at right-angles to each other, but of which only one set is productive in ore, the other set being mere seams or cracks in the strata, which are of no practical importance except when followed for the purpose of facilitating the mining operations necessary for reaching the productive crevices. In those districts where the crevices are less perfectly developed, as in the southeastern part of the Lead Region, east of the West Peccatonica river and south of the Yellowstone, there is less system in this respect, and the mining operations are chiefly carried on as "patch-work," as it is significantly called: a "patch" meaning a limited area where the crevices are numerous and ill-defined, and where the ore is near the surface. Yet, even in these patches, there will usually be a predominant set of fissures, which will give a general character to the diggings, and carry a large part of the ore, while the other set will be in a measure subordinate.

The existence of two sets of fissures, and their approximate direction at right-angles to each other, are facts well understood by the miner, who is accustomed to drive on one of the unproductive set in order to cross and prove those of the productive series, the existence of a fissure facilitating, of course, the miner's progress. Quartering crevices (swithers or counters) are not entirely wanting, but by no means common; they sometimes form a connection between two different sets of crevices, having the appearance of producing a lateral shifting of the body of ore.

Fourthly, there is a close approximation, throughout a large portion of the Lead Region, to an east and west and north and south direction in the two principal sets of crevices; and, farther, the easts and wests are the main productive or lead-bearing crevices.

An inspection of the crevice map will show more clearly than can be described in words how far these statements are based on truth, and what and how numerous the exceptions to the general rule above enunciated. At the same time, reference may be made to the table of the bearings of the crevices in the principal districts, given on a preceding page (page 381). The Dubuque and Galena districts, and the Fairplay, show in the direction of their principal productive crevices and openings a very close agreement with an east and west line; a variation from it of more than two or three degrees is not at all common in either of those districts. So, too, throughout all the eastern portion of the Lead Region, where the crevices are not very extensive or well-defined, there is almost everywhere a close approximation in their general direction to east and west or north and south.

The districts which show the most marked deflection in their main crevices from an east and west line are the Upper Menomonee, the Potosi, and the Beetown, and that in the north part of Benton township. In the Beetown diggings the deflection averages about ten degrees, in the Potosi nearly twenty-five degrees, in the Upper Menomonee about thirty degrees. In the district between Quimby's mill and Buzzard's Roost, north of Benton, the deflection from an east and west line is irregular; some of the crevices belong to the north and south system, others to the east and west, and the latter vary about twenty degrees from that direction.

To give a more precise limit to the statement in regard to the east and west crevices being in the main the productive ones, it may be said without hesitation, we think, that at least four-fifths of the ore raised in the Upper Mississippi mining region is obtained from crevices varying not more than ten degrees from a true east and west course.

The norths and souths play a much less conspicuous part as mineral-bearing ranges. In the Dubuque district, there does not seem to be a single one of any importance; in the Galena and Vinegar Hill, there are a few productive crevices varying only a few degrees from a north and south course, and from the Wisconsin State line, near Fever river, along the eastern limits of the great central productive area from New diggings to White Oak Springs and by Shullsburg to Irish diggings and Stump Grove, there are numerous sets of crevices with an average direction of about five degrees to the east of north, some of them carrying heavy bodies of ore, principally in sheets: these norths and souths seem to have cut off the ore in this direction, as there are no farther diggings to the east for many miles; and few, indeed, anywhere east of the line of these crevices extended northwards, which are of any value whatever.

Having thus given a general idea of the surface arrangement and vertical distribution of the crevices, it remains to be enquired—how have these fissures originated, and in what way have their mineral contents been introduced into them?

And first, with regard to the general cause or causes by which the different sets of fissures have been produced.

The origin of the cracks or fissures in the crust of the earth, which by subsequent filling from below with mineral and metalliferous substances have become converted into mineral veins, is not a question of much doubt, when these belong to what are called *true veins*. These we suppose, coinciding in opinion with the large majority of geologists, to have been formed by the filling up of pre-existing fissures, which have been produced by deep-seated movements of the earth's crust, and which consequently have affected the whole mass of strata down to an indefinite depth. Hence the leading characteristic of a *true vein*, namely that it shall be continuous in depth. Any fissure, on the other hand, even if filled with mineral matter, which is confined to a particular bed or set of beds, and which does not extend upwards or downwards into groups or subdivisions of a different lithological character, cannot be considered as coming under the head of a true vein. But we have already shown that the lead-bearing fissures of the Northwest are absolutely limited to one set of strata, and frequently to one subdivision of that set, or, in many cases, to a single bed; furthermore, we have noted the fact that evidences of dislocations of the strata, or faults, are exceedingly rare in the whole Lead Region, and that in no instance has any proof been obtained, in connection with any crevice, of motion or upheaval, such as would be given by displacement of the beds on either side of the fissure in relation to each other, or rubbing of the walls of the fissures against each other, and the consequent formation of slicken sides and striated walls. The exceptions to this rule are so unfrequent and insignificant that they amount to nothing as proving any analogy with true veins. Where proofs of subsidence of masses of rock in connection with the crevices can be obtained, the movement may usually be seen at once to have originated in some cause entirely local, and confined to a very limited thickness of strata; as, for instance, at Stewart and Bartlett's lode, near Dubuque, where we have shown that the sinking of a large mass of rock, and consequent formation of a saddle-shaped crevice, took place as the result of the washing out of the softer strata below.

Hence, we are forced to the conclusion that the crevices originated through the action of some local cause, or of forces limited in their field of action to a comparatively narrow vertical range, and to rocks of similar lithological character. In short, we conceive the lead-bearing fissures to have been originally closely allied to what are called "joints," and formed in the same manner as those planes of division, which we know to be of common occurrence in almost every possible variety of rock formation. Observation teaches us that all sedimentary deposits—and, in a less conspicuous degree, even those of eruptive or igneous origin—have a tendency to a division by at least two sets of planes, and that, when there are two sets, they are frequently pretty nearly at right-angles with each other. We can also refer to numerous records of geological investigation which show that, as a general thing, the more homogeneous and crystalline the texture of the mass of rock, the more regular and extensive will be the systems of joints traversing it.* The general fact insisted on by all these observers is, that the limestone beds are frequently traversed by nearly vertical joints, arranged in two sets, which cross each other nearly at right-angles, and thus divide up the mass of rock into rudely cuboidal blocks. The dolomitic limestones are particularly liable to be thus traversed by divisional planes.

As has been shown in the preceding pages, the well marked lead-bearing crevices are limited to the Galena limestone, a remarkably pure and crystalline dolomite, containing sometimes as little as one percent of foreign substances, and generally not over three or four. Those beds in which the fissures are best developed are the purest and most homogeneous in their texture. In the extreme upper

* See the following authorities on the nature of joints: HARKNESS, "On the Jointings in the Carboniferous and Devonian rocks near Cork" (Quart. Jour. of Geol. Soc., vol. xv, p. 93). "The two analyses show the important bearing which chemical composition has on jointing; justifying the conclusion, so far as the limestone of this neighborhood is concerned, that the perfection of the jointings is in proportion to the purity of the limestone."

Also PHILLIPS'S "Manual of Geology," p. 41, where the joints of the Mountain limestone are described.

Farther, JUKES'S "Manual of Geology," p. 193, &c.; and DE LA BECHE'S "Geological Observer," p. 723.

and lower portions of the Galena, where shaly layers and impure argillaceous materials predominate, the crevices are quite indistinct, if not wholly wanting. Nor do they extend up into the Hudson-river shales above, or downwards into the thin-bedded argillaceous limestones and magnesian limestones of the Blue below. We conceive, therefore, that the fissures were determined in their origin by the lithological character of the rock, and the changes which took place in it as it became consolidated, and acquired a crystalline structure. Exactly how far shrinkage may have been concerned in the matter, and how crystalline action may have co-operated, we are unable to say; the subject is one of difficulty; but it will be sufficient at this time to recognize the fact that either or both these causes united would have produced a tension in the mass of rock which would lead to the production of fissures in two different directions.

We farther consider that the direction of the fissures may have been influenced, if not absolutely determined, by an elevatory movement of the region in which the fissures are developed.

Considerations connected with the phenomena of denudation and the surface geology of the lead district show that it once was elevated far above its present level, and we are disposed to consider the direction of the axis of upheaval as having been instrumental in determining the direction of the principal system of fissures. Thus, then, we should have two concurrent causes acting to produce the crevices and give them direction. Chemical composition, and texture, the result of that composition, act to predispose the crystalline mass to a division into cuboidal blocks, and the mechanical tension or stretching force, which is the necessary result of upheaval, determines the direction in which the separation of continuity shall take place; which, in the case in question, was in a general east and west direction. As a proof, or, at least, a strong indication that the axis of elevation was an east and west one, the fact may be here again alluded to which was stated in a preceding chapter, in regard to the water-shed of the district being an exact east and west line, through the whole extent of the Lead Region, as will be seen by referring to the map. That no well-marked sets of fissures were produced in the Upper sandstone or in the Blue limestone is explicable on the ground of the soft and yielding character of the one, and the thin-bedded, shaly, and non-homogeneous character of the other. Everything in the geology of the region shows that the elevation in question, as well as the subsequent subsidence, was regular and gradual, and not attended by any dislocations or deep seated disturbances.

Having thus briefly explained how the crevices themselves may have been formed, we proceed to another branch of the enquiry, which is, in what manner they were filled with the various materials which we now find in them.

The first thing we have to notice in regard to the introduction of the metalliferous materials into the crevices is, that the causes by which this was accomplished must have been limited, in point of time, within the period which elapsed between the deposition of the Upper sandstone and that of the Hudson-river shales, since the intermediate groups of strata are the only ones which contain any noticeable amount of ore.

As no lead has ever been found in the shales of the Hudson-river group, it follows, as a matter of course, that whatever influences, *coming from above*, were concerned in the formation of the metalliferous deposits of the Lead Region, they must have ceased to act after this group of strata began to be deposited; at least, it is hardly conceivable that a lead solution should have been filtered through it so completely, as to leave no traces of its presence behind. Indeed, everything connected with the lithological character of the Hudson-river shales, as developed in and near the Lead Region, seems to indicate that very different conditions prevailed during their deposition from those which were predominant during the accumulation of the great mass of dolomite below.

That the metalliferous solutions from which the sulphurets of lead, zinc, and iron, found so abundantly in the lead-bearing groups, did not come *from below*, seems evident from the following considerations:

1st. There is no evidence of fractures, fissures, or faults, running down into the subjacent rocks: no crevice, carrying ore, has ever been traced more than a few inches, and this only in one or two instances, if at all, so far as can be ascertained, into the sandstone underlying the Blue limestone. Although this sandstone is almost everywhere in the Lead Region well exposed in its whole, or the greater part of its thickness, yet we can nowhere find in it anything like a system of fissures or veins, or any metalliferous substances other than a few nodules and stains of brown oxide of iron. No trace of either lead or zinc has ever come under my notice as occurring in this rock.

This being the case, it appears almost incredible that the metalliferous solutions, or gases, should have passed through this sandstone, without leaving a trace of their presence behind, and only have given rise to a deposition of zinc and lead after having got entirely above the silicious rock, and into the calcareous and dolomitic beds. Indeed, the deposits of lead ore are very rarely found even in the limestone above the sandstone, until we have passed through the whole thickness of the "buff beds," or the dolomitic strata which lie between the sandstone and the calcareous, highly fossiliferous and metalliferous beds above, of the Blue limestone proper.

Again, after passing through the sandstone, we find below a series of beds of dolomite, very similar in character to those above it, and also containing lead ore, although in small quantity. This lead is confined, in the lower dolomitic formation—the "Lower Magnesian limestone," as it is usually called—to the upper beds only, and no case is known where the crevices have been found going down in this rock to any considerable depth. Now if it be maintained that the sandstone was not lithologically, or chemically, or mechanically favorable to the retention of the metalliferous solutions or gases passing through it, on the theory of the origin from *below* of the material conveying the metallic matter, and that this was the reason why no trace of lead or zinc is found in this rock, we should, at least, expect to find the evidence of the origin from below in the continuity in depth of the lead-bearing crevices through the Lower Magnesian limestone, which is certainly as favorably constituted for this purpose as the Galena limestone above. If it be urged, in reply to this, that the Lower Magnesian has not been sufficiently explored or mined to ascertain the fact stated above, it may be replied, that the very circumstance that mining operations in it have always been suspended at a short distance from the surface shows pretty conclusively that the crevices or metalliferous deposits have not been followed down, because there was nothing to follow. We have failed to find, in a single instance, where mining has been carried on in the Lower Magnesian, any evidence of there being crevices going downwards in this rock, and the unbiased statements of many miners who have worked in it are all to this effect. All the assertions with reference to the existence of fissures or crevices going down in the Lower Magnesian have come from those having property in this geological position which they were anxious to dispose of. This subject will be more fully discussed farther on, and the occurrence of galena in this rock noticed at length.

If, then, the closing up of the fissures in going downwards; the gradual disappearance of all signs of metalliferous matter before reaching the sandstone; the absolute non-existence of any traces, even, of ore in that rock; the superficial character of the lead deposits in the Lower Magnesian, and the entire absence of the ores of the metals in question in all the lower portions of this thick body of strata, as well as in the still heavier deposit of sandstone, the lower or Potsdam beneath, so far as can be made out—if all these facts be taken into due consideration, it will, we apprehend, be difficult to give assent to any theory of the deposition of these ores requiring action from below.

But, secondly, there are numerous facts connected with the deposits of the lead and zinc, as well as iron, in reference to their mode of occurrence or position in the rocks, which seem to militate strongly against the theory of an origin from below. Some of the more striking instances of evident deposition from above may here be instanced.

In the very remarkable cave opening discovered by Mr. T. Levens near Dubuque in 1850, the following appearances were observed, according to Mr. Whittlesey's description, who visited it a day or two after it was first opened. He thus represents the position of the ore in the crevice, as it appeared before it had been touched by the miner. After speaking of the difficulty of squeezing between the walls of the narrow and winding crevice, he goes on as follows: "We had not gone far in this uncomfortable manner, when a handsome cave appeared before us, illuminated by the lights in front. It was a square room, with a mud floor and a rock ceiling, along the middle of which was a seam or vertical crevice, containing galena. This crevice was about two feet broad, the sides covered with mineral six to eight inches thick, leaving a space between the inner faces of the mineral, up which we could see several feet. There was about this crevice an entirely new feature, so far as I know. The solid mineral projected from this crevice downward, a foot to a foot and a half, in a "sheet," as they call it, eight to ten inches thick, and twenty-five to thirty feet long, spreading, fan-like, as it descended." The annexed woodcut (fig. 39), (borrowed from the Iowa Report), will convey an idea of this peculiar and interesting feature: it represents a section across the cave at the point where the depending sheet of ore was observed, as described above. "A part of the way there were three sheets, two thick and heavy

FIG. 39.—Section of Cave Opening at Leven's Lode, near Dubuque.

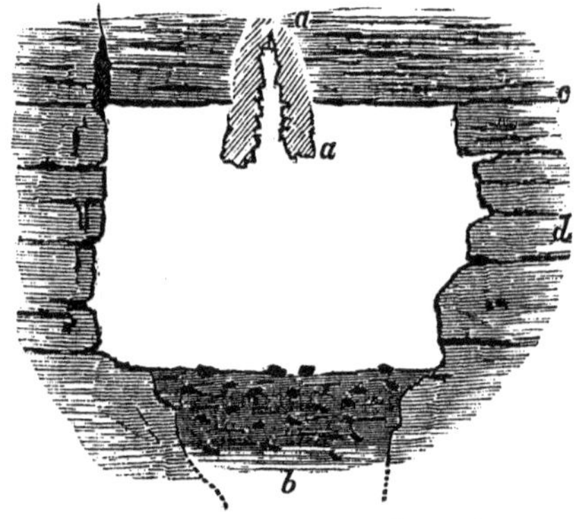

a. Galena. *c.* Cap-rock.
b. Galena in detritus. *d.* Galena limestone.

ones with coarse irregular surfaces, composed of aggregated cubes, from two to ten inches on a side, and one thin or light sheet, the whole covered with carbonate of lead, and having, in consequence, a pure white color. This depending mass was wholly clear, except where it was attached to the rock above, and projected downwards into space, the most rich and beautiful object I ever saw of a mineral kind."

I have myself observed several cases of this kind, but none on so large a scale as that described above by Mr. Whittlesey. Is it possible, in this and other similar instances, to conceive of any other mode of formation than that by the percolation through the crevice, from above downwards, of a solution, which allowed the galena to crystallize out where sufficient room was afforded, just as we see so often, in every-day operations of the chemical laboratory, a solution oozing through a crack in the side of a vessel and crystallizing on the outside?

Some of the heaviest deposits of ore ever found in the Lead Region have had a sort of saddle shape, as represented in figures 26 and 30, previously given (see pages 245 and 286), the upper or flat portion of the mass being by far the heaviest and purest body of ore, which, when followed down on either side, by a series of "flats and pitches," as they are called, had gradually given out, or become much less valuable than it was above. The fine discovery at Mills's lode, near Hazle Green, was of this character, and all the flat and pitching sheets which I have examined, where the mass of ore has had this saddle shape, have been richer above than below. These facts would also indicate very clearly that the metalliferous solution was introduced from above rather than from below.

In some instances, the openings have been found entirely lined by a solid shell of ore, of considerable thickness. A very remarkable one is noticed by Dr. Owen, in his first Report, as having been discovered on Vinegar Hill, near Galena, some years since: this was described to him as having been large enough to afford a dining room for a large party, for which purpose it was used on the fourth of July. I have never met with so extraordinary a display of ore as this must have been; but have observed large cavities in the Galena limestone, like immense geodes, six or eight feet in diameter, which had been entirely closed on every side before being broken into by the miner, and on the walls of which large crystals of galena were attached, although not forming a complete incrustation or shell around the whole cavity. In such cases as these, we are almost driven to the conclusion that the crevice or cavity must have remained for a long time filled with the plumbiferous solution, which was gradually supplied with material, as that which it had previously contained crystallized out.

Again, there is no evidence in the Lead Region of the deposits of ore, or the crevices, being situated over or near faults or dislocations of the surface, or of their being in any way connected with subterranean or deep-seated movements of the crust of the earth, such as would allow of the metalliferous solutions having access from below. In most mining districts, at least in such as are situated in the igneous and metamorphic rocks, the character of the vein fissures, or the cracks which are filled with ore and its accompanying gangue, is such as to show conclusively that their formation was due to causes acting through a very great vertical range, and producing extensive displacement of the rocks, thus permitting the rise of metalliferous vapors or fluids from the heated regions below, which we are accustomed to look upon as the great source from which such materials are supplied. Thus we know that thermal springs are almost or quite exclusively confined to disturbed regions, or those which have been broken up by extensive faults, giving rise to fissures, which have thus formed the chimneys or conduits through which the water finds its way to the surface, from the region where it had become impregnated with saline or mineral substances, under the combined influences of heat and pressure. And intimately connected as the phenomena of thermal springs and mineral veins are known to be, we have this connection in no way more strongly indicated than it is by the evident dependence of both on deep-seated disturbances for their existence.

Not only do the deposits of the metallic ores in the form of true veins show themselves as originating from below, and connected with the heated interior, as above suggested; but even many of the irregular deposits—namely, such as come very near, in many points, to those of the regions we are now describing—show by their position and mode of occurrence that access has been allowed to the metalliferous matters of which they are composed from below. Thus the remarkable accumulation of zinc and lead ores, calamine and galena chiefly, accompanied by brown iron ore, which occur in Upper Silesia, have been proved by the workings on them to extend down to a depth which has never been reached, and thus to communicate with the region below, through tunnel shaped masses of ore, which have all the appearance of having once been the channel or pipe through which the metalliferous solutions reached the place in which they were deposited, and which, after flowing over at the surface and producing the flat and irregular masses of ore which are so extensively worked, became at last filled up with the same materials—exactly as a pipe, through which a saturated saline solution flows for a long time, may become lined with a crystalline deposit, and finally entirely choked up.

In a similar manner, the investigations of geologists on the extensive workings near Aix la Chapelle, where some of the most extensive zinc deposits known in the world are situated, especially those of the Vieille Montagne (German, Altenberg), have shown that the heaviest accumulations of ore are at the intersections of the crevices or fissures with the planes of contact of two different geological formations, where access could be most readily afforded to metalliferous solutions rising from below.

Farther, the great lead-producing districts of the north of England, where galena is found so abundantly distributed through the calcareous rocks, are intersected by numerous faults; and, in some cases, they have been subjected to the influence of igneous masses, which have intruded themselves between the strata, or which traverse them in the form of dykes.

Impressed with the fact that, almost everywhere, heavy accumulations of metalliferous substances are connected in their origin with disturbances of the strata, contact of dissimilar formations, or the presence of igneous or eruptive rocks, proofs of some one of these mineralizing conditions have been carefully sought for in the Lead Region of the Upper Mississippi.

And first, in regard to the presence of masses of rock of igneous origin, or the relative distance of the crystalline formations from the productive lead-bearing strata. Geologists who have examined the mining district of Wisconsin have been so much impressed by the necessary connection between a metamorphic condition or eruptive origin of the associated rocks and metalliferous veins capable of being wrought persistently, that, in their anxiety to prove the lead deposits of the Northwest to be of this class, they have ascribed their existence to the influence of the underlying azoic rocks, and have thence argued that the deeper the mines were carried the more profitable they were likely to be. Thus Dr. Owen, in his Report of 1852 (page 62), says: "There can now be little doubt that the whole mining region of the Mineral Point and Dubuque districts of Wisconsin and Iowa is based upon a syenitic and granitic platform, which would, in all probability, be reached by penetrating to the depth of from two thousand to four thousand feet." This fact Dr. Owen considers "favorable to the metalliferous character of F. 2" (the Lower Magnesian limestone). Dr. Percival says, in his first Report (1855, page 100): "The probabilities are thus strongly in favor of a continued descent of the mineral to a lower depth in the strata than is yet ascertained. The appearances seem no less to indicate the origin of the mineral and the accompanying ores from beneath, probably from the primary rocks underlying the lowest secondary; and that they rose in such a condition that they were diffused through a certain definite extent of the materials of the rocks, and then segregated in their present form, and this along certain lines which have determined their arrangement * * * But even now, I have a strong impression that the mineral has been derived from beneath, and that the prospects of deep and continued mining are here as favorable as in other more established mining districts."

The practical importance of this matter to the mining interests of the Lead Region must be an apology for considering the subject at more length than would be proper or necessary were it one of scientific interest merely.

On Lake Superior we have, thanks to the denuding action of its waters, an opportunity of examining the junction of the azoic rocks with the Lower Sandstone, the formation next beneath the Lower Magnesian, so confidently referred to by Messrs Owen and Percival as being a metalliferous one.

We find here—and the same thing is shown all through the region of northern Wisconsin—that the azoic rocks, which are made up of slates and quartz rock, with intercalated masses of trap, granite, and similar rocks, had their present position and form of surface before the deposition of the unaltered sedimentary rocks began to take place. There have been no disturbances worthy of notice in the underlying rocks since the Lower Sandstone began to be accumulated upon them. The only exception to this is along a line of igneous action parallel with the south shore of Lake Superior, where great changes have taken place in the sandstone, as regards its thickness, stratigraphical position, and metallic associations. These changes, however, are strictly confined to the immediate vicinity of the trappean ranges, and at only a few miles distance from these we find the sandstone with its normal condition, which is that of a nearly horizontally stratified mass, absolutely destitute of metalliferous ores, and, to all appearance, hardly disturbed at all since its deposition. Nowhere in northern and central Wisconsin, where this rock is the highest one exposed, over an area of several thousand square miles, do we find any evidence of its having been mineralized by the underlying azoic rocks; a few faint traces of copper, and infiltrations of brown iron ore, make up the sum total of its metallic contents, so far as is yet known.

Now, as this sandstone comes to the surface, and is admirably exposed, in the valley of the Wisconsin, in close proximity to the Lead Region, it would seem, to say the least, highly probable that, were it a metalliferous formation underneath the present lead-bearing strata, it would not be entirely wanting in proof of this fact, at so short a distance from the mineralized area. That the Lower sandstone is everywhere recognized as an absolutely barren formation seems strong presumptive evidence that it would be found so, were it to be penetrated anywhere within the limits of the productive mining district. Where it has been mineralized by the intrusion or contemporaneous formation of igneous rocks, it has developed itself as a cupriferous formation, and not as one containing lead ores.

Taking these circumstances into consideration, in connection with the facts already advanced in relation to the non-metalliferous character of the Upper sandstone, and the absence of well-defined crevices and consequent poverty in ore of the Lower Magnesian, both of which groups are well exposed in the very heart of the mining region, we feel justified in asserting that the metalliferous character of the lead-bearing strata is in no way connected with, or dependent on, the existence of the azoic rocks beneath, and that it is entirely unphilosophical to suppose that their influence could be felt through 2000, or even 200 feet of intervening strata, without some evidence of that fact being found in those strata.

Again, with regard to the contact of dissimilar formations, or the occurrence of the ores of the Lead Region as "contact deposits," it may be remarked that this mode of occurrence has hardly an existence except in stratigraphically disturbed regions, since it is only in such districts that the mechanical and chemical conditions necessary for the formation of these deposits can co-exist. But, at all events, as the heaviest deposits of ore in the Lead Region are included within a series of strata of the same character, and extend neither to the top nor the bottom of the formation, there can be no question here of any relationship between them and contact deposits. Where ore is now found accumulated between two beds of rock, taking into view the stratigraphical position of the formations in the district in question, it must be considered to have been deposited on one stratum before the next succeeding one above was laid down upon it.

In view of all these facts, we consider it as a matter settled beyond all possibility of doubt that the lead deposits of the Northwest must have been introduced into the fissures from above, and by precipitation from a solution. In reference to this last clause, we have not thought it necessary to adduce any evidence to disprove the theory of the igneous origin of the ore, or of its having been brought up from below, either by sublimation, or by actual injection. Since, however, both of these ideas have been maintained by different persons writing on the region, although every fact seems to be entirely opposed to any hypothesis of igneous action, it may be proper to sum up as concisely as possible the evidence in favor of aqueous deposition.

1st. The generally recognized aqueous origin of the sulphurets: deposits of sulphurets of iron and other metals are frequently produced accidentally or intentionally in the chemist's laboratory, by the decomposition of solutions containing the metals by sulphuretted hydrogen.

2d. The occurrence of the sulphurets of lead and iron in the Lead Region, in forms which they could not have assumed, except as deposited from a solution—as in the form of casts of fossils, and in connection with stalactites and stalagmitic masses of calcite. An instance of this kind is to be seen in the Wheatley collection at Union College, and is shown in the annexed wood-cut (fig. 40), which represents a large stalagmite, with a small mass of galena on the end of it, in a position which it would be difficult to imagine it to have reached, except in solution, dropping from above, exactly as the rest of the stalagmite was formed. Instances have been mentioned to me by the miners (I have not met with such myself) of stalagmites made up of alternating layers of galena and calc. spar. The replacement of organic forms by galena is not infrequent, and that by pyrites is very common; blende has never been met with in this relation, so far as is known.

FIG. 40.—Stalagmite with Galena.

3d. The impossibility, absolute and entire, of the introduction of the ore into the crevices from below, either as a molten mass or in the form of a sublimate: this point has been already sufficiently insisted on. It is inconceivable that any one at all familiar with chemistry, or mining geology, should have ever imagined the possibility of the igneous origin of these ores.

If, then, we enquire by what agent the sulphuretted combinations of the metals now found so abundantly disseminated through the Lead Region could have been deposited in their present position, we need not look far for an answer, since there is but one agent capable of affecting it, namely sulphuretted hydrogen gas. This decomposes nearly all metallic solutions, and precipitates the metals in the form of sulphurets, provided the resulting sulphuret is one insoluble in the medium in which the decomposition takes place. If, then, the metals zinc, lead, and iron were present, in solution, in the oceanic waters, at the time of the deposition of the lead-bearing strata, or if the strata became impregnated with these metallic substances, by the infiltration of waters charged with their salts through them, then all that would be needed to produce a deposition of the sulphurets would be a source of sulphuretted hydrogen gas, slowly disengaged in or beneath the rocks permeated by the metalliferous solutions.

That the oceanic waters were highly impregnated with metalliferous salts during the early geological periods seems not improbable, from the fact that the lower formations are those which contain the largest deposits of ores: these are found both in the unaltered sedimentary rocks, and in those which have undergone metamorphism. The palæozoic strata, and especially the Lower Silurian groups, all over the world, are emphatically the great store-houses of the metals. The azoic rocks, on the contrary, are poor in ores, with the exception of such as have been introduced into them by direct igneous or intrusive action. Thus, in this country, for instance, the lowest series of strata, or those deposited, so far as the evidence goes, before the appearance of organic life on the globe, are but scantily supplied with any of the metals except iron, which occurs in this geological position in the oxidised form, and in mountain masses. The Lower Silurian rocks, on the other hand, either in their unaltered state, as at the West, or as metamorphosed in the Atlantic States, are the seat of active mining operations for a variety of metals.

It will be argued, of course, that, the crust of the earth being thinner during the earliest geological periods, thermal springs conveying metalliferous solutions could more easily have found their way to the surface in regions broken up by faults and dykes, so that the abundance of ore deposits would be due rather to the facility of access from below, than to the pre-existing condition of the oceanic waters above. But in regions like those of the Mississippi valley, where there are no dykes or intrusive masses of igneous matter, and where the formations have been so slightly disturbed, since their deposition, as to make it exceedingly improbable that the ores they contain could have been introduced from below, we are driven to the necessity of presupposing their existence in the oceanic waters, either during the deposition of the metalliferous formation, or after it had taken place.

That the appearance of the first considerable deposits of metalliferous ores in the Northwest should be closely connected with the introduction of animal life in profusion in that region, seems an important fact, which should be carefully considered in this connection. In all the thick mass of the Potsdam sandstone, from 300 to 500 feet in vertical development, there are nothing more than the merest traces of ores, and none of lead or zinc, so far as known. The insignificant deposits of iron and copper in this sandstone are exclusively in the oxidised form. In the Lower Magnesian limestone, which is next above, and whose lithological character is in every respect as favorable for the deposition and retention of metalliferous substances as is that of the lead-bearing rock above, we have only a few irregular deposits of galena, in the upper part of the formation, so that there is a thickness of 600 to 800 feet of stratified rocks above the azoic which is almost absolutely barren of metallic ores. It is not until we rise into the Blue limestone that noteworthy quantities of any of the metals are found, and it is pecisely here that the evidences of organic life begin to be abundant; portions of this group of strata are almost exclusively made up of the remains of animals, and these are nowhere more abundant than in the immediate vicinity of some of the heaviest deposits of the ores of lead and zinc. In the Lower Magnesian, the only traces of fossils yet discovered are in the upper portion of this rock, while the Potsdam sandstone is, except in a few extremely circumscribed localities, completely destitute of animal or vegetable remains. The same is true of the Upper sandstone, which is alike characterized by the entire absence of any traces of organic life or of metalliferous ores.

It is hardly possible, in view of these facts, not to recognize a general law connecting the absence of the mineral deposits in the non-fossiliferous portions of the stratified groups with their abundance in those which contain organic remains. Whether we suppose the metalliferous solutions to have originated below, and to have been conveyed upwards by thermal springs, or whether we suppose them to have been contained in the waters of the ocean, we are, in either case, equally dependent on some conditions connected with the rocks themselves to account for the deposition or non-deposition of the metalliferous ores in the rocks in question. In the first named case, we should have to account for the zinc and lead solutions having been conveyed through rocks of precisely the same lithological character as those above in which deposition really did take place, without leaving a trace of their presence; in the other view, we should be called on to give a reason why no precipitation from the oceanic waters took place, while either the silicious or dolomitic strata were depositing, with a thickness of several hundred feet. To suppose that the ore-depositing springs could have passed through so great a vertical range of rock without a portion, at least, of the metallic substances having been left behind, we must assume that there was some cause to favor deposition present in the upper strata which was absent in the lower.

The agent, then, which we conceive to have been efficient in producing the deposits of the metals which are found in the region in question, was the organic matter of the Blue limestone and the lower beds of the Galena; which, either by its reducing action, while undergoing decomposition, acted on the sulphates of the metals held in solution in the surrounding waters, and converted them into sulphurets; or, still more directly, generating sulphuretted hydrogen from the sulphur which they themselves contained, furnished the necessary material for the precipitation of the metals as sulphurets.

It has been demonstrated by repeated experiments, as well as by observation of natural phenomena, that organic substances undergoing decomposition in solutions impregnated with the sulphates of the metals cause a precipitation of the metal in the form of a sulphuret. The immense quantity of pyrites found in connection with all the coal beds of the West may be here referred to as evidence of this kind of chemical action. No other combination of iron than the sulphuret is found in the coal beds, and it is hardly possible to find a fragment of coal, however small, which has not some of this substance attached to it, or intersecting it in thin plates and veins. As we have in the strata of the Blue limestone the most fossiliferous portion of the whole series of rocks, many beds of it being made up almost exclusively of fragments of shells, we are not at a loss for organic matter, and it is especially in the neighborhood of the productive openings, in those districts where the mining is done in the Blue limestone, that the fossils are most abundant. Thus, at the Crow Branch diggings, the stuff thrown out from the pipe-clay opening is a mass of shells, many of which have been themselves converted into pyrites. The same is true of the openings in this geological position near Mineral Point.

The immense number of remains of marine plants, which we have spoken of in a previous chapter as occurring in the lower and upper beds of the Galena limestone, may here be adverted to, in connection with the investigations of Forchhammer,* who has shown that many sea weeds contain a large amount of sulphuric acid, the quantity in one instance being equal to 8.5 per cent of the weight of the dried plant. He mentions that, in the vicinity of Copenhagen, the disengagement of sulphuretted hydrogen from the decomposing sea weeds on the coast is often so great as to blacken the silver in the houses, at a considerable distance. Here, then, we have an ample source of sulphur to enter into combination with the iron and other metals contained in the sea water in which the Galena limestone was deposited, which rock we conceive to have been made up in no small degree of the remains of this class of plants. No one can deny that we have, in the conditions set forth above, a *possible* means for the production of the deposits of the metals which have been described in the preceding pages. And as we conceive it to have been clearly shown that all other modes of deposition were impossible—that is to say, requiring conditions which have not existed in the Lead Region—we are forced to accept the theory advanced above, which is essentially that advocated by the author of this Report six years ago, in the "Metallic Wealth of the United States."

There are many points requiring farther elucidation, in connection with the formation of the lead-bearing crevices and openings; but it will be necessary to defer the consideration of them to another occasion, as this Report has already swollen to an unexpected size.

One or two conditions we may touch briefly upon before closing this section. The first is, the probable reason why the east and west crevices are so much more open, through a large part of the Lead Region, while the norths and souths

* See Bischof's Lehrbüch der Chemischen und Physikalischen Geologie, i, 925; and Report of the British Association for 1844.

are, to a considerable extent, filled with sheet ore, as has been previously set forth. We explain this by referring to the gradual opening of the east and west crevices by an uplift of the region along an east and west axis: one or more undulatory movements of the strata, if effected in this direction, would necessarily tend to open the fissures running in the same direction as the axis of upheaval. The fissures being thus expanded, so as to give a passage to the system of under-ground drainage, they would become worn out into such shapes as we find them to have at present, while the norths and souths, remaining much more tightly closed, would show this effect in a less marked degree, as is the case in the Lead Region generally.

Another question which will naturally be asked in reference to the views advanced above, is this: why, if the metalliferous solutions from which the ore deposits of the Lead Region were thrown down were diffused through the oceanic waters, there was not a precipitation of the metallic sulphurets over every part of the valley of the Upper Mississippi? or why is the productive mining ground confined to a limited area, while over a vast extent of country, for all that can be seen on the surface, there is no reason why equally important deposits should not exist.

To this we reply, that we believe it would be found that, were the earliest highly fossiliferous formations everywhere exposed, they would be found to a considerable extent impregnated with the sulphurets of lead, zinc, iron, &c.; and in proof of this we refer to the fact that the Silurian, and especially the Lower Silurian rocks, are much more metalliferous than any other series of strata occupying the same area and with the same thickness. But these are not commonly exposed, being almost everywhere covered by other groups. Where metalliferous ores do exist in the upper strata, nothing forbids the belief that they may have been derived from previously deposited masses below, carried up in solution by thermal springs or otherwise. If the original conditions under which the ores were deposited in the lower rocks were not favorable to their segregation in large masses—as was the case in the Lead Region, where the rock was intersected by numerous fissures—then the deposition would take place in a more diffused manner, and we might have a mass of strata impregnated with ore, in small particles, which would thus be liable to oxydation, and would easily be dissolved out and transferred to the upper strata by thermal springs rising through them from beneath.

To recapitulate as briefly as possible. The oceanic waters, during the earliest geological epochs, may have been, and very probably were, impregnated with metallic salts, although not to such an extent as to prevent the development of organic life. When this development took place, if the circumstances were otherwise favorable, by the reducing action of the decaying organic matter entombed in the strata, or by that of plants containing sulphuric acid, the metalliferous combinations in the surrounding waters were decomposed, and the metals precipitated as sulphurets. These were collected by segregation in masses of considerable size, when the rocks had the necessary lithological character, and when crevices, fissures or cavities existed, in which these masses could find room for their formation. When this was not the case, the strata were impregnated with metalliferous substances, which were diffused through the mass of rock, and which may afterwards have afforded an almost inexhaustible magazine of material to be drawn upon for the formation of mineral veins and other deposits in the overlying rocks.

It is believed that with the adoption of these views some facts may be explained, with regard to the occurrence of ores in mineral veins and other forms of deposit, which have not hitherto been well understood: the subject will be farther discussed, however, in another place, as a sufficient space in this Report has already been occupied with theoretical views.

V. *Practical Considerations.*

From what has been already said in the preceding pages of this Report, it will be evident that we do not intend to come forward in this closing section of the chapter as the advocates of deep mining in the Lead Region, although most of those who have published on this subject have strongly insisted on an entire change in the system pursued, and maintained that all which was necessary to make persistent and paying mines on the lead crevices was the want of capital and energy among those who have hitherto worked in that district. It is not a little singular that, in spite of the repeated recommendations of geologists—not, however, of those familiar with mining—no attempt has ever yet been made to sink through the Upper sandstone; or, if any such thing has been attempted, it has been abandoned before that rock had been penetrated to the depth of five feet. When one considers how trifling a thing it would be to sink to the bottom of a mass of sandstone only 80 to 100 feet thick, if there were really any assurance of finding anything of value beneath it, it seems hardly credible that there can be any real faith in deep mining among the miners themselves. We doubt, indeed, whether any considerable changes will ever be made in the present system of mining, and feel confident that the miners themselves would never invest any large amount of money in any undertaking having for its object the proving of the rocks below the Upper sandstone, although some might be disposed to advocate its being attempted by others, with a view to advantages to be indirectly derived from the expenditure of large sums of money in this way. As, however, it has been more than once seriously proposed that the State should undertake the work of proving the metalliferous character of the lower rocks, by sinking $50,000 or more and a shaft, for the supposed benefit of the Lead Region, and as the matter may come up again for discussion, we are disposed, at the risk of some repetition, to recapitulate and resume the arguments for and against a project of this kind.

We believe that no one is disposed to consider the Upper sandstone a metalliferous formation, or to advocate sinking in that rock in the expectation of finding anything of value in it. This sandstone is so well exposed in the Lead Region, and has been so uniformly found destitute of all metalliferous ores, that no one could be found to advocate the possibility, even, of its being worked in with profit.

Neither have we met with any person who believed that the Lower sandstone, or the azoic rocks beneath, would be found to contain workable deposits of ore, or that such would be reached and profitably mined in the Lead Region. At any rate, we presume that all would admit that whether the Lower sandstone and azoic were or were not metalliferous formations, there would be no possibility of sinking into them with profit, unless the intermediate 250 to 300 feet of Lower Magnesian limestone were found to contain sufficient ore to pay the expenses of mining, as the work was carried through it. The question of deep mining, then, for all practical purposes, turns on whether the Lower Magnesian contains deposits of lead of sufficient magnitude to be worked with profit; and, if so, whether these can be hit upon by sinking through the sandstone above, without so great an expense as to render the undertaking a hopeless one.

Let us first, then, examine the arguments in favor of the metalliferous character of the Lower Magnesian, and then endeavor to ascertain whether it could by any possibility be proved or worked in the Lead Region.

The advocates of deep mining bring forward several instances of the occurrence of lead ore in the Lower Magnesian, where this rock is exposed on the surface to the north of the Lead Region, from which they infer that it can be profitably mined in, by continuing the workings in the regular lead-bearing rock of the district down into the underlying formations. Now it might be that the Lower

Magnesian could be profitably worked in when it lies next to the surface, and yet that it would not pay to sink to it through a thickness of one hundred feet or more of unproductive strata, when necessarily expensive machinery would be required to keep the mines free from water, in addition to the increased expenditure for the machinery required for hoisting from a considerable depth. We will go farther, and make the assertion, based on pretty extensive observation in the region, that if the present lead-bearing formation, the Galena limestone, were covered by one hundred feet of unproductive rock, as difficult to sink through as the Upper sandstone, the deposits of lead which it contains could only in very exceptional cases be worked with profit; and, as these cases could not be known beforehand, the result, on the whole, would be unsatisfactory. Therefore, even if it be admitted that the Lower Magnesian does contain, beneath the Lead Region, as large and valuable deposits of ore as the Galena limestone, it could not be mined with profit except where it crops out in the vallies, or is overlaid by only a thin stratum of other rocks. This statement is made, of course, with reference to the present condition of prices, wages, &c., in the Lead Region.

But, on the other hand, we are not prepared to admit that the Lower Magnesian ever has been, or is likely to be, profitably mined in for lead, either when it comes to the surface, or when it is overlaid by other rocks. For the purpose of determining this point, we have examined all the localities where galena has been reported as having been found in any noticeable quantity, and are able to affirm that, at the present time, no profitable mining is carried on in the Lower Magnesian, and that none ever has been for any length of time; and, farther, that no well-developed crevices, or such as could be followed to any distance, have ever been found in it.

The principal localities which have been quoted and relied on as affording evidence of the productiveness of the Lower

Magnesian are the Kickapoo, and Oleking's or Moosan's diggings, near Franklin, although neither of these has yielded as much ore, or been as worthy of notice, as those at New Galena, on the Upper Iowa river, in Iowa. The last named diggings are thus described by me in the Iowa Report:

"Along the face of the bluff, in which a thickness of 120 to 150 feet of the Lower Magnesian limestone is exposed, a number of drifts have been extended into the rock, a little below its junction with the sandstone, and considerable galena has been taken out. The limestone at this point is brecciated in its structure, appearing as if it had been partially broken up after its deposition, and then re-cemented; portions of the rock have also a concretionary structure, and its whole appearance is that of a material which has been subjected to both mechanical and chemical disturbances. The ore appears to be associated with irregular strings and bunches of calcareous spar, ramifying through the rock, but nowhere assuming a regular form, like that of a vein, or appearing to occupy a well-developed fissure. Sometimes a little decomposition of the rock has taken place, which has given rise to a sort of opening; but none were observed which were more than a few inches wide and a few feet long. It is said that between fifty and one hundred thousand pounds of ore had been obtained from these diggings; but it seems hardly possible that the operation should have been, on the whole, a profitable one; and, taking into consideration the hardness of the limestone, and the very limited extent to which it has undergone decomposition in the vicinity of the mineral deposits, we see little to encourage farther expenditures at this point."

Since the above was written, we have had no farther news from that quarter; but consider ourselves safe in presuming that all thoughts of doing a profitable mining business in the vicinity have been abandoned. Probably over five dollars were expended there for every dollar's worth of ore taken out.

The Little Kickapoo diggings were visited by Dr. Kimball in the spring of 1860, and from his notes I learn that they are occasionally worked by one person, but with no favorable results. A great number of shafts have been sunk for the purpose of proving the ground, some of them to the depth of forty or fifty feet, and, as there is no trouble from water, there is no difficulty in the way of following down the ore, if there were any to follow. There are fissures in the rock without a uniform direction, which lead down to a sort of opening, in which the ore is found disseminated in large masses of flint. The material of the opening is ferruginous, and sometimes soft, the whole appearance resembling that of the openings in the Galena limestone. The quantity of ore, however, which is found here, is too small to repay the labor required to get it out; only about 20,000 lbs. have been taken out, in ten years that the locality has been worked over—or about $60 worth a year. It appears, also, from descriptions given me by intelligent miners who had worked at these diggings, that the opening-like character of the rock only extended for a short distance into the bluff, and that, on following the deposits beyond the point to which atmospheric agencies have had an opportunity of reaching, the strata became hard beyond all hope of profitable working. There can be no doubt that the locality in question is not one which can be adduced in favor of profitable mining in the Lower Magnesian.

More recently, the occurrence of lead ore in this rock, near Franklin, has been made the subject of much comment, and given rise to unbounded hopes of profitable deep mining. These diggings, which are known as Oleking's or Moosan's old diggings, are situated about two miles southwest of Franklin, on a branch of Blue river; the valley is narrow and enclosed by bluffs, which rise with a steep but grassed slope to the height of 230 to 250 feet, of which the lower seventy belong to the Lower Magnesian, and the next eighty to the Upper sandstone, which is overlaid by seventy to eighty feet of the Blue, with thin outliers of the Galena limestone on the summit. Dr. Percival says that three successive openings here occur; one eight to ten feet below the sandstone, another just above the harder middle bed, and the third below the bottom of the ravine, in that bed, and at the depth of about seventy feet in the Lower Magnesian. He farther adds: "The openings appeared partly narrow and vertical, partly wide and flat, with appearances of decomposition and stain in the rock, deposits of clay and ochre, and arrangement of the mineral, similar to those in the Upper Magnesian (Galena limestone). The mineral in these openings generally appeared in more or less detached masses (chunk mineral), often very large, weighing more than 100 lbs., a few even more than 500 lbs. After examining this locality, I could not doubt that the Lower Magnesian is a good mineral-bearing rock."

On visiting this locality in 1859, I found only one person at work there, from whom a very dismal account of the prospect of mining in the Lower Magnesian was obtained. He had sunk a shaft twenty-five feet deep, from which he had raised about ten lbs. of ore; but I was unable to detect any sign of crevice or opening in the excavation; and, as no other was accessible, my impressions were necessarily very unfavorable in regard to the prospects of mining in this formation, especially after listening to the vehement objurgations of this solitary miner against his own stupidity in continuing to "prospect" in so barren a rock. According to this individual, the ore obtained here was all taken out "in the grass-roots"—i. e., close to the surface—and no crevices had ever been found leading down to anything workable, a statement which agrees with all I have myself observed in the Lower Magnesian.

On the whole, it will be safe to say that no profitable mining has ever been carried on in this rock, and that it is entirely wanting in well-developed crevices, or openings promising enough to justify expenditure in proving them. Of course, it is not impossible that some locality may hereafter be discovered which shall be worked for a time with profit: but that the Lower Magnesian can be called, on the whole, a "good metalliferous rock," is what we are not, in view of the above facts, disposed to admit.

But it will be urged that, although the Lower Magnesian may not contain any large deposits of ore without the limits of the productive Lead Region, yet it may be found rich in this metal underneath the productive portion of the Galena limestone; or, for instance, in the vicinity of Galena, Dubuque, Hazle Green, &c. That this is *possible* is not to be denied, but that it is in any degree *probable* seems to us unsupported by satisfactory evidence. All the facts collected during the progress of the survey indicate a limited vertical range of the ore deposits; and, although the geological horizon of the lead-bearing beds sinks lower as we go towards the north, we have ample proof, as above, that the productive crevices or openings are limited to the rocks above the sandstone. According to the analogy of position, we should expect to find the Lower Magnesian productive along the northern edge of the Lead Region, and as this rock is well exposed on all the streams which descend from the water-shed to the Wisconsin, we are fully justified in believing that, had this been the case, it would have been discovered before this. If we take the mining district of Dubuque as an illustration, we find that on one side, and in the very heart of the diggings, the rocks are very thoroughly exposed down to the top of the Blue limestone, which just comes to the level of the Mississippi river at that place. Had any of the crevices, which are here worked right in the river bluffs, extended down as low as the Blue limestone, it could not fail to have been observed, and there could be no possible reason why they should not have been followed. But, in point of fact, there is not a single locality along this part of the district where the workings have ever reached, certainly within fifty feet, and probably not within a hundred, of the bottom of the Galena limestone. And yet it will be allowed by all, that the crevices near Dubuque are longer, better defined, and as productive as anywhere in the Lead Region. If, then, all the evidence presented here, where the exposures of the rock are so good, goes to show that the crevices actually terminate before reaching the top of the Blue limestone, with what possible chance of success could one sink still farther, into the sandstone and below it? The same may be said of the diggings near Galena and Fair-play, none of which are down as far as the Blue limestone. As we proceed north from this central point of the Lead Region, we come into a district where the lead deposits extend into that rock, but only in one or two exceptional cases has any considerable amount of ore been obtained as low down as the Buff limestone. Unless it be at Crow Branch diggings, I do not know of a single locality where ore is now being raised from as low a position as that rock.

All the testimony collected in the Lead Region goes to show that no ore worthy of notice has ever been traced into the Upper sandstone, and nothing like an independent mineral-bearing fissure has ever been found extending into it more than a few inches at most; and, as before noticed, the formation is so thoroughly exposed all through the mineral region, that there is not the slightest reason to suppose that there could be any system of mineral veins intersecting it of which some evidence would not have been already discovered.

It has been argued by some that, even if the crevices entirely disappeared on entering the sandstone, they might be resumed in the Lower Magnesian, so that, on sinking through the former rock, the fissure would be found again in the same line of working; and that thus nothing further would be required than to follow it down until new openings were met with in the favorable strata. The analogy of the North of England mines has been invoked, as a reason for expecting success in deep mining in the Upper Mississippi region. We have seen, in the preceding pages, that in the Alston Moor district there are some irregularities in the vein-fissures; but that they can be followed down through different strata, uninterruptedly, although narrower and much less rich in ore. The limestone is here the productive rock, while the sandstones and shales are almost barren of ore; but, as the vein-fissure continues down through the unproductive masses of rock, there is little analogy here with what has been shown above to be true of the Lead Region of the Upper Mississippi. If ever a well-marked continuation of a lead-bearing crevice should be capable of being followed uninterruptedly through the Upper sandstone, it might perhaps be advisable to sink upon it; but as no approach to anything of that kind has been yet observed, we must take the facts as we find them. And let it not be supposed that a mere crack in the sandstone, somewhere in the line of the crevice worked above, can be assumed, as a matter of course, to be continuous with, and necessarily dependent on, the mineral-bearing fissure. The sandstone is, like every other mass of rock, not destitute of joints and cracks, but there is not the slightest evidence that they did not originate independently of those in the groups of strata above and below, or that they are at all connected with any deposits of minerals or ores. Although the deposition of galena had commenced on a small scale in the upper beds of the Lower Magnesian, the process must have been completely interrupted during the accumulation of the sandstone, when it is evident that very different physical and chemical conditions prevailed from those which existed while the dolomitic strata above and below were formed.

Time and space will not allow us to go into an elaborate discussion of the mode of occurrence of the galena in the Derbyshire mines; but, from a careful study of the phenomena, as described by the most reliable geologists, we have been unable to gather any encouragement for deep mining projects in the Wisconsin Lead Region. If, as is asserted by some, the veins are entirely interrupted in the "toad-stone," a fact which is not yet satisfactorily ascertained, then we regard the metalliferous fissures of each set of limestone strata as independent of the others, and as originating in causes confined to that set; in short, as what we have denominated "gash-veins." In such cases, each metalliferous stratum or series of strata is to be judged by itself as to its profitable working, the barren rock between being regarded as an obstacle just in proportion to its thickness, hardness, &c. That the fissures in one set of calcareous beds are to be considered as continuous with those in the other, if separated by a stratum through which they do not pass, is not to be admitted: in certain localities, however, they may be so numerous in either series as to make the striking of one a matter of probability, without any considerable divergence from the line of working in the ore-bearing strata above.

To put the best possible aspect on the matter, the miner sinking through the sandstone into the Lower Magnesian would be in no better position than he would be in if he were to commence sinking a shaft in the Galena limestone anywhere at random, in the expectation of striking a valuable deposit of ore. It may be alleged that it is not beyond the bounds of possibility that his undertaking should be crowned with success, but let the practical miner decide what the chances in his favor would be.

To resume what has been said on the subject of deep mining:

1st. Each mining district in the Lead Region has its metalliferous deposits, confined to a certain vertical range, which does not in any one locality, or group of diggings, extend through the whole series of lead-bearing strata.

2d. The mineral deposits do not extend into the Upper sandstone, and the cracks or joints in that rock are not continuous with or dependent on those in the groups above or below.

3d. The Lower Magnesian limestone has nowhere been proved to be a rock which can be mined in profitably for lead for any length of time.

4th. If the Lower Magnesian were as rich in ores as the Galena limestone within the boundaries of the present productive Lead Region, the chances are greatly against the possibility of its being worked with profit, under the present condition of things.

In answer to the questions: what can geology do towards developing the resources of the Lead Region? and what practical conclusions can be drawn from the work thus far accomplished, which will be of benefit to the miner? we would offer the following considerations:

So far as the mode of operations pursued by individual miners, or by companies of two or three, united in partnership, as has usually been the system followed in this region, is concerned, we anticipate but little change. No amount of science or practice will ever enable any one to say beforehand just where a productive crevice may be found: the causes on which the formation of the fissures, and their subsequent filling with ore, depend, are too complicated and uncertain in their nature to allow of the result being predicted with certainty from an examination of the surface. In all mining districts, the principal result of scientific observation is to limit the area over which explorations or actual mining operations may be carried on with a chance of success, and to put a stop to wild schemes of speculation, engendered by a want of knowledge of general laws, as applicable to the particular district in hand.

If, for instance, this Report should be the means of preventing the State of Wisconsin from embarking in the utterly useless expenditure of say $50,000 or $100,000, in carrying out a project often advocated in the Lead Region, of sinking a deep shaft to prove the Lower Magnesian, then from ten to twenty times the cost of this work would have been saved. If private companies should be deterred from undertakings of this kind, those who otherwise would have furnished the capital will be benefited to the exact amount thus saved. Undoubtedly a work of this kind might be for the benefit of a few persons, on whose land, or through whose hands, the expenditure was made; but the people in general would gain no more than they would if the same amount were applied to carrying the water of Lake Superior across by land in barrels, and emptying it into Lake Michigan. In this case the contractors for the barrels, teams, &c., would probably make a good thing of it; but would not the neighboring States look on with astonishment at so ingenious a method of getting rid of the public funds?

But to pass to the positive result of the survey, we have endeavored to show in the preceding pages that there was a certain vertical range of the metalliferous deposits for each district, beyond which nothing worth working was likely to be found. If this view be the correct one, and the future experience of the miners should be carefully gathered up with a view to a more precise limitation of the vertical range of the lead deposits, then much labor and expense will be saved by seeking for ore where it actually exists. and not beyond its limits; and especially ought these considerations to be allowed due weight in any new combinations of capital or labor to more thoroughly prove districts which have already been partly worked out and then abandoned. Undertakings got up on the plan of the chartered stock companies which are so frequently organized in our cities for working mines, or rather for creating mining stock, have invariably proved entirely unsuccessful in the Lead Region: among a considerable number of them, with whose operations we have become acquainted, we cannot recall one in which the amount invested has not proved almost or quite a total loss: certain it is, that in no case has anything approaching a dividend been reached. The customary machinery of mining organization, which, as arranged in this country, is bad enough even for the most persistent mines, is utterly ruinous for the kind of deposits to be worked in the Lead Region. There has never been, and there never will be, a crevice discovered which can be worked on an extensive scale, and make a great permanent mine, like those opened on true veins, and thus justify an extensive plan, and all the still more costly machinery of directors, superintendents, clerks, and city offices. Any association to work the lead mines of Wisconsin must be economically organized and managed, and must be directed by some person having local experience and a thorough knowledge of the ground. It is one thing to lay out a great mine on a regular vein, with its levels and shafts symmetrically arranged for a permanent work, to go on for centuries perhaps, and quite another to have to change from day to day to meet the varying conditions of an irregular deposit, and to know at what point to discontinue sinking or driving, where to open new ground, and how, in general, to lay out the work so as to suit best the character of the deposit to be mined.

In the Iowa Geological Report, I insisted strongly on the importance of horizontal excavations or drifts, in preference to shafts, as a means of exploring and opening new ground, and I especially recommended the driving of levels for draining such ranges as could be unwatered by this simple method, where work was to be resumed on ground previously abandoned on account of water. There is reason to believe that, in several instances, where this means of working has been resorted to in preference to sinking shafts and draining off the water by horse or steam power, good results have been obtained. As an instance of how a level judiciously carried in on the random of the productive ground may give a new impulse to mining at a locality where, previous to this, everything was languishing, Shullsburg may be specified; although here the work has only been partially completed, as the level brings the water to what is called a "bull-pump" to be raised. Comparison between the two plans of driving and sinking may be made, at this place, by referring to the shafts and works of the Mississippi Mining and Manufacturing Company, not far distant.

In the region of flat openings, where there is almost always a soft stratum, if not a productive metalliferous one, at a certain geological horizon—as the pipe-clay opening, for instance—advantage may be taken of this circumstance to drive in and prove a large amount of ground at a very small cost. If the opening should not prove metalliferous under the crevices coming down from above, then the ground can at least be unwatered through the level, with little expense, by boring down to it from the upper workings. This idea has been taken up in several localities, and bids fair to meet with general acceptance throughout the mining region. If close attention be paid to the real position of the productive strata, and it be not attempted to carry in the level at a much greater depth than that at which the ore really occurs, there is reason to believe that this system of proving, and at the same time draining the ground, will prove the means of infusing new life into the mining business of many localities now almost deserted.

We fully believe that the time will come when those interested in the mining region will see the propriety of making a thorough topographical survey of the district, and of having a series of levels run, so that the amount of denudation, and the exact position of the mining ground, at each locality, will be as accurately known as the formation of the surface will admit. If this Report should be the means of hastening the commencement of such a work, and if, in the meantime, it should prevent any wild expenditures on the part of the State, such as have been suggested by some, we shall feel that our labor has not been in vain.

CHAPTER VII.

OBSERVATIONS UPON THE REMAINS OF EXTINCT AND EXISTING SPECIES OF MAMMALIA FOUND IN THE CREVICES OF THE LEAD-BEARING ROCKS, AND IN THE SUPERFICIAL ACCUMULATIONS WITHIN THE LEAD REGION OF WISCONSIN, IOWA AND ILLINOIS :

The remains found in the lead-crevices, and in the superficial accumulations of the Lead region of Wisconsin and Iowa, belong to the following genera :

I. Genus Bos : 1° Upper portion of a right femur, the head and trochanter of which are broken off; 2° A right metatarsal bone ; 3° An os calcis ; 4° A first phalanx from the foot. These are all of the size, and closely resemble the same parts from a Buffalo:

Prof. WHITNEY'S Collection : Blue Mounds.

II. Genus CERVUS : 1° An imperfect humerus, closely resembling that of the Red Deer, and of intermediate size between this and the humerus of a Caribou ; 2° Left metatarsal bone of the same ; 3° An imperfect humerus of a much smaller animal than the preceding, but closely resembling it ; 4° A piece of the radius of the same.

From Prof. WHITNEY'S Collection.

In Prof. HALL'S Collection is a series of several molars, which, in form and size, correspond exactly with those of the Red Deer (*Cervus virginianus*). They are nearly all from a young animal.

III. Genus MASTODON : 1° Fragments of the cranium, including the occiput, from a very young Mastodon. The bones are mostly about a half an inch in thickness, some of the pieces having serrated edges, showing that the sutures were still open. In one of them, the two fossæ for the attachment of the ligamentum nuchæ to the occiput are well preserved. The air-spaces, or sinuses between the two tables of the skull, which are so large in the adult, had not begun to be developed. 2° Three small molars, M. I, M. II, M. III, of a very young animal, probably from the same as the preceding. 3° M. IV & M. VI, from an adult Mastodon. 4° Portions of right and left femora of a very young animal. The shaft of the right femur, from which the articulating ends are broken off, is about one foot in length : they are probably from the same individual as the cranial bones. 5° Left scaphoid bone of an adult. Prof. WHITNEY's Collection.

IV. Genus MEGALONYX : 1° In Prof. HALL's Collection are large numbers of fragments of bones, consisting of pieces of ribs and vertebræ ; also several teeth : these last belong to *M. jeffersonii*, and are from two individuals of different ages. Those from the adult consist of the three hinder molars of the lower jaw on each side, and are attached to the outer alveolar portion of it : the first molar is missing, but one of the canines is preserved. Besides there are three molars from a smaller and younger individual ; also the two canines, both of which are but slightly worn, and their shape is such as to show that they ended in sharp points. A canine from an adult animal also exists in Prof. WHITNEY's Collection. 2° A metacarpal bone from Prof. HALL's Collection.

V. Genus DICOTYLES : Three molar teeth of a dicotyline animal. They differ very much from either of the fossil species, but agree with *Dicotyles torquatus* in having the points on the crowns quite short.

VI. Genus CANIS : The remains of this genus belong to two species, of quite different sizes. The remains belonging to the larger species are of the size of those of the Gray Wolf, *Canis occidentalis* (DEKAY), *C. griseus* (SABINE), and could not be distinguished from them. They consist, 1° of the left half of a lower jaw, containing all the teeth behind the first molar (this, with the canines and incisors, is missing); 2° of a second specimen of the same, but without teeth ; 3° of a fragment of the right upper jaw, containing M. I ; 4° a right humerus ; 5° a right femur (both of the preceding broken); 6° right and left tibia, the last entire; 7° metatarsal bone of the same.

From Prof. WHITNEY's Collection : Locality Blue Mounds.

The remains of the smaller species belong to an animal of the size of the Prairie Wolf (*Canis latrans*, SAY), and could not be distinguished from the corresponding parts of it. They consist of a portion of the skull, containing nearly the whole series of the upper teeth, excepting the incisors, the first premolar on both sides, and the last molar on the right.

From Prof. HALL's Collection.

It will be seen from the above catalogue, that the remains of animals enumerated belong to the Genera BOS, CERVUS, MASTODON, MEGALONYX, DICOTYLES and LUPUS. The two species of Wolf appear to be identical with the existing Gray and Prairie wolves; and the teeth of the deer in Prof. HALL's Collection, with those of the common Red deer. The remains of Mastodon and Megalonyx are the only ones which may be said with certainty to belong to extinct animals.

CHAPTER VIII.

OBSERVATIONS UPON THE MAMMALIAN REMAINS FOUND IN THE CREVICES OF THE LEAD-BEARING ROCKS AT GALENA, ILLINOIS :

The fossil bones discovered in the crevices of the lead-bearing rocks of Galena, Illinois, which have been submitted to my inspection, have been referred to the following list of animals :

1. DICOTYLES COMPRESSUS. An extinct species of Peccary, the bones of which constitute the greater part of the fossils from the crevices of rocks of Galena. Similar remains have also been found in Kentucky, Iowa and Virginia. From some variation in anatomical characters, the specimens were referred to several distinct species under the names of *Platygonus compressus*, *Hyops depressifrons*, *Protochœrus prismaticus*, and *Euchœrus macrops*. Later investigations lead to the conclusion that all belong to a single species, bearing the name at the commencement of this paragraph.

2. PROCYON PRISCUS, Leconte. A species of Raccoon, apparently different from the recent one, indicated by several fragments of jaws with teeth, and several phalanges.

3. ANOMODON SNYDERI, Leconte. Apparently a carnivorous animal, indicated by a single tooth.

4. ARCTOMYS MONAX.

5. PSEUDOSTOMA BURSARIUS.

6. LEPUS SYLVATICUS.

7. ARVICOLA ——? These four rodents are indicated by a number of teeth, chiefly incisors, not differing from the corresponding ones in the recent species.

INDEX.

www.ingramcontent.com/pod-product-compliance
Lightning Source LLC
LaVergne TN
LVHW010141110826
845151LV00002B/390

* 9 7 8 1 4 2 5 5 3 9 2 7 6 *